Innovations in Youth Research

Also by Sue Heath

RETHINKING WIDENING PARTICIPATION IN HIGHER EDUCATION: The Role of Social Networks
(*co-edited with A. Fuller and B. Johnston*)

RESEARCHING YOUNG PEOPLE'S LIVES
(*co-authored with R. Brooks, E. Cleaver and E. Ireland*)

DOING SOCIAL SCIENCE: Evidence and Methods in Empirical Research
(*co-edited with F. Devine*)

YOUNG, FREE AND SINGLE: Twenty-Somethings and Household Change
(*co-authored with E. Cleaver*)

SOCIAL CONCEPTIONS OF TIME: Structure and Process in Work and Everyday Life
(*co-edited with G. Crow*)

SOCIOLOGICAL RESEARCH METHODS IN CONTEXT
(*co-authored with F. Devine*)

PREPARATION FOR LIFE? VOCATIONALISM AND THE EQUAL OPPORTUNITIES CHALLENGE

ACTIVE CITIZENSHIP AND THE GOVERNING OF SCHOOLS
(*co-authored with R. Deem and K. Brehony*)

Also by Charlie Walker

LEARNING TO LABOUR IN POST-SOVIET RUSSIA: Vocational Youth in Transition

YOUTH AND SOCIAL CHANGE IN EASTERN EUROPE AND THE FORMER SOVIET UNION
(*co-edited with S. Stephenson*)

Innovations in Youth Research

Edited by

Sue Heath
University of Manchester, UK

and

Charlie Walker
University of Southampton, UK

First published 2012 by
PALGRAVE MACMILLAN

Palgrave Macmillan in the UK is an imprint of Macmillan Publishers Limited,
registered in England, company number 785998, of Houndmills, Basingstoke,
Hampshire RG21 6XS.

Palgrave Macmillan in the US is a division of St Martin's Press LLC,
175 Fifth Avenue, New York, NY 10010.

Palgrave Macmillan is the global academic imprint of the above companies
and has companies and representatives throughout the world.

Palgrave® and Macmillan® are registered trademarks in the United States,
the United Kingdom, Europe and other countries.

ISBN 978–0–230–27849–3

This book is printed on paper suitable for recycling and made from fully
managed and sustained forest sources. Logging, pulping and manufacturing
processes are expected to conform to the environmental regulations of the
country of origin.

A catalogue record for this book is available from the British Library.

A catalog record for this book is available from the Library of Congress.

10   9   8   7   6   5   4   3   2   1
21   20   19   18   17   16   15   14   13   12

Printed and bound in Great Britain by
CPI Antony Rowe, Chippenham and Eastbourne

Contents

List of Figures

Acknowledgements

This book has its origins in a seminar organised back in 2009 under the auspices of the Youth Study Group of the British Sociological Association. The seminar, jointly sponsored by the BSA and Sage, focused on the theme of 'new methodological challenges for youth research'. Many (but not all) of the contributors to this book presented at this event, and we are delighted that this book has been one of its outcomes. We are extremely indebted to each author for their hard work in response to our task as editors. We have both learnt a great deal from our contributors and it has been a pleasure to work with them.

We would also like to thank Anna Marie Reeve, Philippa Grand, Olivia Middleton and Andrew James at Palgrave for their helpful assistance at the various stages of production, and our partners Jayne Williams and Olia Walker for their patience in the final stages of production.

Sue Heath, University of Manchester, UK
Charlie Walker, University of Southampton, UK

Notes on Contributors

Nicola Allett is a Research Associate at the Department of Social Science, Loughborough University. She is currently working on the Leverhulme Trust funded project 'Media of Remembering: Photography and Phonography in Everyday Remembering', which investigates how photography and music act as vehicles of memory in everyday contexts. Nicola's Ph.D. explored the nature of attachments, investments and commitments to Extreme Metal music and subculture. Her research interests are in music cultures, collective identifications and kinship, music in everyday life, and qualitative methodologies.

Anna Bagnoli is Research Associate at the University of Cambridge, based at the Cambridge Intellectual and Developmental Disabilities Research Group of the Department of Psychiatry. She carried out her Ph.D. at the Centre for Family Research of the University of Cambridge and has had previous research posts at the Universities of Cambridge and Leeds. She has a keen methodological interest, particularly in qualitative and mixed methods, and the use of visual and arts-based approaches. Her research interests include young people and gender and she has investigated science interest among girls and boys, the process of identity construction, and the identities of young migrants. Her publications have appeared in *European Societies*, the *Journal of Youth Studies*, *Qualitative Research* and *Sociological Research Online*.

Andrew Bengry-Howell is a Research Fellow at the Hub of the ESRC National Centre for Research Methods, based at the University of Southampton, where he is researching methodological innovation in the social sciences. He is interested in qualitative methodology and research ethics in relation to youth research, and has conducted research on youth and identity. He was primary investigator on the ESRC project 'Negotiating managed consumption: Young people, branding and social identification processes', which investigated young people's consumption of music festivals and free parties. Prior to that he was a named Research Officer on the ESRC grant 'Branded consumption and social identification: Young people and alcohol'. He has published in the *Journal of Youth Studies*, *Sociology*, *European Journal of Marketing*, and, *Drugs: Education, Prevention and Policy* among other journals.

Shane Blackman is Reader in Cultural Studies at Canterbury Christ Church University, UK. His publications include *Youth: Positions and Oppositions, Style, Sexuality and Schooling* (1995); *Drugs Education and the National Curriculum* (1996) and *Chilling Out: the Cultural Politics of Substance Consumption, Youth and Drug Policy* (2004). He is on the editorial board of the *Journal of Youth Studies* and *Sociology* and is a member of the ESRC Peer Review College.

Amanda Brown is a postgraduate research student at Northumbria University, Newcastle upon Tyne. She has recently submitted her Ph.D. entitled *'McGeneration'? An examination of the continuing importance of place in cultural regeneration.* Her thesis investigates urban regeneration to uncover a narrative of two particular and related concerns within cultural urban regeneration: on the one hand, the risks of homogenisation as standardised practices are transferred globally; on the other, the demand for distinctiveness, and for regenerated areas to demonstrate unique and appealing characteristics to mediate global processes. Amanda is also currently working at City University London and her research interests include geography, urban policy and strategy.

Gemma Commane completed her Ph.D. at Canterbury Christ Church University in 2011. Her doctorate examines the construction of female sexuality and femininity through the use of the body in burlesque striptease and BDSM/fetish club-scapes. Her main research interests include emotions and ethnography, subculture, striptease, objectification and the pornography debates, body cultures and social control. Her paper 'Bad girls and dirty bodies: performative histories and transformative styles,' was published in *Queering Paradigms* (Scherer (ed.) 2010). She is currently writing a journal article on ethnography and ethics.

Anne E. Green is a Professorial Fellow at the Institute for Employment Research, University of Warwick. Her research interests include local and regional labour markets; spatial aspects of economic, social and demographic change; trends in employment and non-unemployment; policies to address worklessness; demand for and supply of skills; labour market information and other local indicators; migration and commuting; urban, rural and regional development; and evaluation studies – welfare-to-work and area regeneration initiatives. She has published widely on these subjects. She has undertaken research projects funded by a wide range of sponsors, including the Joseph Rowntree Foundation, the ESRC, Department for Work and Pensions, UK Commission for Employment and Skills, and the OECD.

Christine Griffin is Professor of Social Psychology at the University of Bath. Her work explores the relationship between identities and consumption for young people, and representations of youth, femininity and young women's lives. Recent projects include a study of young people's negotiation of branded leisure spaces at music festivals and free parties with Andrew Bengry-Howell; a project on clubbing and dance cultures as forms of social and political participation with Sarah Riley; and a major study on the role of branding and marketing of drinks in relation to young adults' everyday drinking practices. She has published widely in *Feminism and Psychology, Discourse Studies, British Journal of Social Psychology, Sociology* and *Journal of Youth Studies* among other journals.

Sue Heath is a Professor of Sociology at the University of Manchester and a Co-Director of the Morgan Centre for the Study of Relationships and Personal Life. Her main research interests focus on young people's domestic and housing transitions. She also has longstanding interests in research ethics and the methodological challenges of researching youth, and in the sociology of education. Recent publications include *Researching Young People's Lives* (Sage, 2009, co-authored with Rachel Brooks, Elizabeth Cleaver and Eleanor Ireland), and *Rethinking Widening Participation in Higher Education: The Role of Social Networks* (Routledge, 2011, co-edited with Alison Fuller and Brenda Johnston).

Alex Hillman is a research fellow at Cardiff University. Initially based within the QUALITI node of the National Centre for Research Methods, she worked as part of a team on the '(Extra)ordinary Lives' project: a participatory study exploring the lives of children and young people who are 'looked after'. Currently she holds a Wellcome Trust fellowship award to explore the social and ethical implications of early detection and diagnosis of dementia in memory clinics. Her research interests are in medical sociology and anthropology, ageing and identity and the organisation and delivery of health care.

Sally Holland is a Senior Lecturer in Social Work at Cardiff University. She was previously a social worker with children and families. She is currently researching child risk and safety in neighbourhoods and life history research with care leavers. Her book *Child and Family Assessment in Social Work Practice* (2004) is published by Sage.

Yvette Morey is a Research Fellow at the Bristol Social Marketing Centre at the University of the West of England. Her primary research interests are youth, identity and practices of consumption. She has conducted research on a range of youth(ful) cultures, including recent research into the underground free party scene in the South West, and music festival culture in the UK. Her research has contributed to current understandings about the recreational use of the drug ketamine in the free party scene and more broadly. She is particularly interested in the use of social media and Web 2.0 platforms in digital ethnography and online research. She has published in *Sociology*, *Young*, and *Addiction, Research and Theory*.

Suzanne Powell is a Senior Research Assistant at Northumbria University. She is currently working in the field of undergraduate health education, undertaking evaluative studies as part of the CETL4HealthNE in partnership with universities and NHS partners in the North East of England. Her research interests include youth aspirations for education and employment, inter-professional education in health and social care curricula, and participatory research methods.

Nicola Ross is a researcher affiliated to the Glasgow School of Social Work at the University of Strathclyde. She has worked in the academic and voluntary sectors for a number of years, conducting research with children, young people and families. She specialises in the use of visual and mobile research methods, while her doctoral research on children's geographies explored children's experiences of space and place in their everyday negotiations of their localities. She has published on these subjects in *Children's Geographies* and *Qualitative Research*.

Emma Renold is a Reader at the Cardiff School of Social Sciences, Cardiff University. She is the author of *Girls, Boys and Junior Sexualities* (2005 Routledge). Working at the intersection of queer and feminist poststructuralist theory her research has explored the gendering and sexualisation of UK childhoods across diverse institutional sites and public spaces. Her current research project foregrounds place, identity and gender in a participative multi-media ethnography of girls' and boys' negotiations of private and public places in rural and urban communities.

Nadine Schäfer is Lecturer in the Sociology of Youth at the Graduate School of Education at the University of Exeter. She has a particular interest in participatory approaches which aim to include young people actively in the research process. She has published, for example, on the implications of training young people as co-researchers, and the meaning of space and local contexts for young people's understanding of risk. Her main research interests are: marginalised young people; equal opportunities; careers education and guidance; young people's everyday lives in international contexts; young people as (co-)researchers; and youth participation.

Darren Sharpe is a Postdoctoral Research Fellow in the Childhood and Youth Research Institute at Anglia Ruskin University. He is a sociologist and specialises in the involvement of children, young people and vulnerable adults in research, theoretical developments and practice of participation in connection with youth citizenship, and innovations in qualitative research methods and methodologies. Prior to his appointment at Anglia Ruskin University Darren was the Young People's Participation Development Officer at the National Youth Agency and coordinated the Young Researcher Network. Darren also lectured in social sciences at Nottingham Trent University and Loughborough University, teaching subjects such as Qualitative Research Methods and Criminal Justice Research. At Loughborough University he was a Research Associate in the Young Carers Research Group.

Dirk Schubotz is Research Fellow with ARK, a joint initiative between the University of Ulster and Queen's University Belfast, where he is based in the School of Sociology, Social Policy and Social Work. Since 2003 Dirk has been directing *Young Life and Times*, an annual study of 16-year olds in Northern Ireland (www.ark.ac.uk/ylt). Dirk's main research interests lie in the development and application of participatory research methods, in particular work with peer researchers, in biographical methods, sexual health, community relations, as well as more generically in young people. In 2008 Dirk edited *Young people in Post-Conflict Northern Ireland*, published by Russell House.

Helene Snee is a Temporary Lecturer in Sociology at the University of Manchester. Her research interests include: cultural practices and social divisions; young people and consumption; Web 2.0 and new social media; online research methodologies and ethics; and narrative and representation. Her Ph.D. thesis examined the practice of gap year travel with reference to ideas about place, taste and self-development, and utilised weblogs as primary data. She is currently writing up her findings for publication, including papers on the implications of her research for debates surrounding cosmopolitanism and cultural capital; using blogs in social research; and self-representation.

Charlie Walker is Lecturer in Sociology at the University of Southampton and Honorary Research Associate at the School of Slavonic and Eastern European Studies, University College London. His main research interests lie in transformations of class, gender and place-based identities and inequalities amongst young people in Russia, Eastern Europe and the former Soviet Union, particularly in relation to emergent forms of work and education. He is author of *Learning to Labour in post-Soviet Russia: Vocational Youth in Transition* (Routledge 2011) and co-editor (with Svetlana Stephenson) of *Youth and Social Change in Eastern Europe and the former Soviet Union* (Routledge, forthcoming).

Richard J. White is a Senior Lecturer in Economic Geography at the Faculty of Development and Society, Sheffield Hallam University. Richard's main body of research has broadly explored the geographies of the informal economy in order to (1) better map the limits of capitalism in contemporary society and (2) advocate new ways to imagine and develop alternative economic futures. This research has been particularly intent on better understanding the daily coping practices of lower-income neighbourhoods and the life choices that individuals make in relation to education, work and formal employment. He has published and lectured widely on these subjects both in the UK and abroad.

1
Innovations in Youth Research: An Introduction

Sue Heath and Charlie Walker

This book celebrates imaginative and creative approaches to conducting youth research. Over the course of the last decade, it has been hard to ignore the repeated rallying cries for methodological innovation in the social sciences. One would be forgiven for thinking that we should all be innovators now; all of us expected to develop new and original ways of researching the social world. As Coffey (2011) argues, the current emphasis on innovation partly arises from a 'business case', as a response to the perceived need for improved quality and impact in social research. But importantly, it has also arisen from what she describes as 'the ongoing creative process of methodological development' within the social sciences (Coffey, 2011: 1). So while there have undoubtedly been external pressures to reconsider the scope of our methodological repertoires, there have also been internal, intellectually driven reasons for the recent surge in claims to methodological innovation, driven by academic curiosity and by the demands of new research questions, new sources of data and new areas of enquiry.

The field of youth studies has not been exempt from these twin drivers. In relation to the business case, many new opportunities arose under the previous Labour government for youth researchers to engage in evidence-based dialogue with policymakers and other key stakeholders, with many of these opportunities driven by the emergent participatory research agenda, which we discuss later in this chapter. It has made good sense for researchers to engage in certain forms of methodological development in order to argue for the enhanced authenticity and credibility of their research, especially but not exclusively within policy circles. More generally, however, we seem to be witnessing a wave of methodological creativity, linked to a degree of discontent with long-favoured methods for youth research, such as more traditional approaches to ethnography,

1

qualitative interviewing and the survey method. These are methods that have been dominant for many years now. There has been willingness – especially on the part of newer generations of youth researchers – to shake up this orthodoxy and to engage in what are often represented as more creative approaches to researching young people's lives. This has been prompted to some extent by continuing advances in communication technologies, which have opened up both new sources of data and new ways of generating them, as well as by the growing appeal of experimenting with 'youth-friendly' approaches to the design, conduct and analysis of youth research. Equally critical to these developments, however, have been intellectual concerns relating to a desire to capture better the complexities of young people's lives, both the mundane aspects of everyday life as well as the more extraordinary aspects of 'youth' as a life stage, and underpinned by an interest in developing methods which are capable of accessing the multifaceted nature of young people's lives. These concerns have, then, been as much about epistemology (the study of what counts as valid knowledge, in this case valid knowledge of young people's lives) as they have been about methodology (the study of methods and their philosophical underpinnings), ultimately driven by the question: how can we *better know* young people's lives?

In his influential 2004 book *After Method*, the sociologist John Law questioned the capacity of what he called 'standard' research methods to handle the complexities of the world around us. Law's position is not that we *cannot* know about the complex realities of life as it is lived, but that so many existing methods are 'badly adapted' to its study. He is particularly critical of methods which, he argues, operate on the basis of 'methodological rule following' and of the 'normativities' that are attached to such rule following. These normativities, he asserts, tend to produce the realities which followers of particular methods set out to explore. So, for example, if we ask young people to provide us with narrative accounts which by definition place them at the heart of their own stories, we should not be surprised if our research then generates accounts which seem to chime with, say, theories of individualisation. This is an argument rooted in Law's background in the sociology of scientific knowledge, a field of study which seeks to unpack scientific and technological knowledge claims and to demonstrate how certain practices actually produce the objects that they describe – no less within the social sciences, through our particular choice of research methods, than in the physical sciences.

In contextualising his central argument, Law paints a picture of contemporary social research practice, which portrays researchers as being engaged rather unreflexively in slavish methodological rule following. This is not a picture that we readily recognise, not least because of the current burst of methodological creativity within the social sciences, but also because social research rarely proceeds on such a basis. In fact, it is probably impossible for it to do so, as the practice of social research – in common with the real world practices which social researchers seek to explore – is itself a complex, uncertain, and invariably messy process, which rarely goes according to our initial plans. In other words, real-life social research is predicated on the need for constant reflexivity and pragmatic creativity. This may be particularly emphasised within the field of youth research, with young people perhaps more willing than participants of other ages to challenge the assumptions underpinning our research practices. Law, then, establishes his case for the need for a new approach to the practice of social research on shaky ground: in our own view, slavish methodological rule following is not the major threat.

Law's general prognosis, though, is one that we find more recognisable. Law is concerned that certain aspects of the social world are 'hardly caught by social science methods'. His list of examples includes 'pains and pleasures, hopes and horrors, intuitions and apprehensions, that slip and slide, or appear and disappear, change shape or don't have much form at all' (2004: 2). These are aspects of the social world which may be particularly salient to the experiences of young people in transition from childhood to adulthood, especially under the conditions of extreme uncertainty which so many young people face today, yet they are indeed much more difficult to capture through conventional methods. Law continues:

> It may be of course that [these examples] don't belong to social science at all. But perhaps they do, or partly do, or should do ... if much of the world is vague, diffuse or unspecific, slippery, emotional, ephemeral, elusive or indistinct, changes like a kaleidoscope or doesn't really have much of a pattern at all, then where does this leave social science?
>
> (2004: 2)

Law's call, then, is for methods which allow us to tap into these uncertainties, including through 'techniques of deliberate imprecision', and he makes a plea for 'quiet methods, slow methods, or modest methods', and in particular for methods that do not come with 'accompanying imperialisms'.

The essence of Law's plea – as opposed to the specific solutions he proposes – is less controversial than he perhaps anticipated, as a willingness to experiment, to take risks, and even to make mistakes in pursuit of better ways of capturing the complexity of the social world is, we would argue, very much a hallmark of much recent methodological innovation, especially among qualitative researchers. His plea, then, appears to chime with the concerns of many empirically engaged researchers in the UK over recent years. Not least, it chimes with the views of many, including those involved in qualitative research, that reliance on a standard repertoire of research methods does not always allow them to get at the facets of social life that may be of most interest. Mason (2008) and Mason and Davies (2009), for example, advocate the engagement of social researchers not just with the tangible but also with the intangible and sensory aspects of the social world. They propose the use of a wide range of creative sensory methods, including but not limited to the use of various kinds of visual methods and imaginative elicitation techniques, albeit usually as a complement to, rather than a replacement for, the in-depth interview. Similarly, Back (2007) has sought to explore the intangible without feeling the need to argue – as Law does – for the fundamental 'unknowability' of the social world. In *The Art of Listening*, Back writes of the ephemeral nature of social life and how our research can only ever capture fleeting moments. He states that

> The fact that those traces of life are opaque and that the person who made them is always to an extent unknowable doesn't mean that all is lost. In fact, I have become tired of reading elegant pronouncements on the unknowability of culture and social life; there is no compensation in these bold statements of defeat for me any more.
>
> (2007: 153)

Law's own elegant pronouncements have undoubtedly been important ones, and have presented a provocative challenge to social scientists. Nonetheless, his proposed solution, with its language of 'methods assemblages', 'performative allegory' and 'non-coherent representation', has not been taken up widely outside of the intersecting worlds of actor network theory and the sociology of scientific knowledge. Other, more empirically grounded responses have, though, emerged, including – as this book demonstrates – within the field of youth research.

A rather different form of intervention in the debate on methodological creativity, but one which has had a similarly powerful impact, at least in the United Kingdom, has been Savage and Burrows' (2007) account of what they have described as 'the coming crisis of empirical sociology'. Their argument is that, far from having a monopoly on methodological innovation, academic social researchers have in fact been left behind by developments occurring outside of academia, especially within the commercial sector. Much of their argument is concerned with innovations relating to large scale sources of quantitative data, such as commercial panel surveys with sample sizes which eclipse those of many well-established social surveys traditionally used by researchers. Similarly, they cite the collection of transactional data by, for example, telecommunications companies, online companies such as Amazon, and large supermarket chains operating loyalty card schemes, resulting in new data sets consisting of millions of records.

Although their argument focuses largely on developments in relation to quantitative research, qualitative researchers are not let off the hook by Savage and Burrows. The dominance of the in-depth interview within British social research comes in for particular criticism, with Savage and Burrows invoking the concerns of writers such as John Urry (2003) that interviews are ill-suited for researching 'the kinds of myriad mobilities, switches, transactions, and fluidities that are claimed to make up contemporary social life' (Savage and Burrows, 2007: 894). In their view, the qualitative interview is just not up to the job of developing sophisticated understandings of the social world, as the data it generates are limited in their scope: useful for exploring 'practices, histories and identities' (2007: 893), but not much else. Their criticisms with respect to qualitative methodological innovation are, then, very much directed at a particular method, rather than at qualitative methods in their totality, and many exponents of qualitative interviewing would probably want to challenge their claims. More importantly, though, Savage and Burrows seem to have ignored the plethora of imaginative and creative approaches to interviewing which have been emerging within the qualitative research community over the last decade *precisely in response to* some of the recognised limitations of the conventional in-depth interview. Many of these approaches are exemplified in this book.

Nonetheless, Savage and Burrows' wider call to pay attention to what is happening in the world of commercial research is a valid one. A glance at the contents pages of a journal such as *Qualitative Market Research* suggests that methodological reflexivity and innovation are not unique to academia, even if we may be uncomfortable with the consumerist focus of much of the work of researchers in this field. Methodological innovation is particularly evident within youth-orientated market research. Take, for example, the following description of the work of a US-based organisation, *Girls Intelligence Agency*, who conduct market research on the 'opinions, ideas, motivations and goals' of girls and young women aged under 30 via a network of 40,000 'Secret Agents' with whom they are in daily contact:

> Girls Intelligence Agency stays totally up-to-the-minute by running ongoing shopping trips, hosting slumber parties and off-sites [sic] and doing in-room hang-outs. GIA provides the girls a place to voice their opinion, make a statement or simply to text and IM [instant message] with other like-minded agents. During these sessions, analysts listen to their music, watch their body language, and hear how they relate and communicate with friends. GIA has become a recognised voice of authority for the young female market. We connect with girls on a deep and continuous level, forging a working relationship with the target audience from the very beginning.
> (http://www.girlsintelligenceagency.com, accessed March 2011)

As this example suggests, then, commercial researchers are indeed developing some interesting and imaginative approaches to research: but so are academic researchers! There have in fact been many claims to methodological innovation over the last decade (see Xenitidou and Gilbert, 2009). Wiles et al. (2010b) attempted to assess the extent to which such claims for originality could actually be substantiated. Through analysing a sample of journal articles published in the 2000s, they concluded that 'there was limited evidence of *wholly new* methodologies or designs' (2010: 2, emphasis added). Rather, they found that claimed innovations related either to 'adaptations to existing methods or innovations, or to innovations involving the transfer and adaptation of methods from other disciplines, primarily from arts and humanities' (ibid.). This could be seen as confirmation of the old adage that there is nothing new under the sun; for example, it could be argued that most online research methods are essentially adaptations of offline methods. Nonetheless, applying established methods in new substantive areas of enquiry or in new disciplinary contexts can undoubtedly represent a powerful challenge to methodological orthodoxies in specific fields. Xenitidou and Gilbert's (2009) definition of innovation in research methods is helpful in this regard, as they refer to innovation in terms of research practices that have not yet filtered through to the mainstream.

It is in this spirit that we frame the contributions to this book. As many of the contributors themselves acknowledge, few of the methods described in this volume are totally new to the social science community, yet they represent a wave of creative adaptation that has been sweeping through the field of youth studies as in many other areas of social science research. For the most part, the approaches which our contributors describe are not yet 'mainstream' methods, if by mainstream we mean *a dominant tendency*, yet they are becoming increasingly popular and much less open to question, particularly among younger generations of researchers. That is not to say that their use does not still need to be justified, as any methodological innovation is only as good as its fitness for purpose. In this sense, innovation should not be about gimmickry or innovation for its own sake (Wiles et al., 2010b), but should be about its usefulness in helping researchers to explore aspects of the social world which might otherwise be unknowable or less readily accessible. These sorts of concerns are reflected in each of the following chapters, with the methods adopted in each case primarily being determined by the nature of the research questions that were under investigation. In some cases this was accompanied by an explicit desire to experiment with imaginative methods of data generation, but this desire was always grounded in the substantive concerns of the respective research teams or individual researchers.

This book, then, focuses on specific examples of methodological creativity grounded in recent research by UK-based researchers (although the geographical focus of the various projects extends well beyond the UK). Each chapter focuses on a particular innovative approach, and the specific contribution of each chapter is outlined in the final section of this introductory chapter. Nonetheless, a number of shared themes can be traced throughout the book, and we wish to highlight four of these here. The first relates to the rise of participatory approaches to youth research. As we shall see, this is a justification for innovation explicitly drawn upon in many of the chapters, and is implicit in all of them. The second cross-cutting theme relates to the importance of ethical concerns linked to the methodological challenges of youth research, and how these play out in innovative contexts. The use of mixed methods approaches almost as a default option in contemporary youth research is a third theme evident across the collection, while the importance of reflexivity in relation to the social relations of fieldwork emerges as a fourth theme. In the following sections we briefly consider each of these in turn.

Participatory approaches to youth research

An important element of the push for creative methods in the context of youth research, particularly but by no means exclusively in the UK context, has been the rise of the participatory research ethos. This was initially driven by concerns arising out of the new sociology of childhood, which sought to place the agency of children and young people firmly on the research agenda. It was, however, given further impetus in a global context by the United Nations Convention on the Rights of the Child (1989), and in the UK context by legislation such as the UK Children's Act 1989 and, more recently, the *Every Child Matters* and *Youth Matters* agendas of the New Labour government (see e.g. HM Government, 2004; Department of Education and Skills, 2005; Department for Children, Schools and Families, 2007). All of these initiatives placed the rights of children and young people centre stage (Heath et al., 2009: 59–62). In the UK context, local government stakeholders have been expected to consult with young people in matters affecting them, and were given 'participatory budgets' in order to do so. Out of these various interventions has emerged an emphasis on the right of young people to be *properly researched* (Beazley et al., 2009), which has included an emphasis not just on listening to young people's concerns through their involvement as research participants, but an emphasis, too, on finding ways of facilitating young people's active involvement as young researchers.

Participatory approaches to youth research are, as Darren Sharpe points out in Chapter 9, sometimes thought of in 'all or nothing' terms – young people participating as *either* active researchers *or* passive research objects – yet in practice there are many possible positions to adopt, with young people capable of being involved to a lesser or greater extent at all stages of the research process. In some cases, their involvement may be fairly limited: for example having some input into the topics to be researched. In other cases, they may be centrally involved in all stages, including in the conduct of fieldwork, in analysis and in dissemination. Both Dirk Schubotz (Chapter 6) and Darren Sharpe (Chapter 9) demonstrate the differing degrees of involvement which can come under the umbrella of participatory research. In Schubotz's case, this was under the auspices of a variety of projects linked to the ARK research centre in Northern Ireland, while in Sharpe's case it was in his role as a development officer with the Young Researcher Network of England's National Youth Agency. Both highlight some of the practical and methodological challenges that can arise from working directly with young people in this way, yet also demonstrate the potential effectiveness of involving young people as co-researchers. Some of these challenges cohere around concerns relating to the quality of research conducted with input from young researchers. Both Schubotz and Sharpe argue that, far from having a detrimental effect on the quality of research outputs, involving young people at key stages of the research process has the potential, if managed well, to increase the validity of youth research. Key to that potential, though, is the quality of research training that is available to young researchers, a point which is explored by both Schubotz and Sharpe, as well as by Nadine Schäfer (Chapter 8).

Schäfer notes that a particularly common way of encouraging a participatory ethos is to present young people with a palette of 'youth-friendly' methods, as was the case in her research on young people's everyday lives in East Germany. The young people involved in Schäfer research received training in, and were subsequently able to choose from, a range of visual methods, including photography and videoing, alongside more conventional methods such as interviews and focus groups. Rather than imposing a pre-selected set of methods, her research participants were able to decide for themselves which methods were best able to represent their lives. Nicola Ross and colleagues (Chapter 3) and Anna Bagnoli (Chapter 5) similarly describe how, in their respective research, they gave their participants a choice of different methods. In Bagnoli's research on young migrants, these varied methods 'were designed to offer young people the possibility to express themselves in their own ways, and were intended as a supporting frame that could be elastic enough to adapt to their needs without being too rigid or constraining'. In their account of their research with young people in public care, Ross et al. also write of the importance of allowing young people to exercise control over the use of different research outputs, both during analysis and dissemination. These are sentiments shared by Amanda Brown and Suzanne Powell (Chapter 7) in their account of experimenting with 'Photovoice', a method that has been specifically developed as a tool to encourage participation. In describing their collaborative research on space, place and identity among university students in South India, they highlight how participants' initial unease about being encouraged to voice their own opinions was transformed into enthusiasm for a method that gave the young people the chance to express themselves through visual means. Their chapter demonstrates how effective a method this was in accessing students' aspirations and sense of place-based identity.

The examples of participatory research included in this book accentuate the advantages of approaches that promote young people's active participation in research, while also acknowledging some of the potential pitfalls. One of our own concerns relates to France's (2004) assessment that participatory youth research has become 'a new orthodoxy'.

This mainstreaming of participatory research not only has the potential to create a situation where those who do not adopt participatory frameworks are put on the defensive (even though there may be sound reasons for not going down the participatory route), but also creates the potential conditions for tokenistic deployment of this approach in a way that might in fact be detrimental to young people's interests. One of us has previously noted the link between participatory approaches and critiques of new forms of self-governance by young people (Heath et al., 2009: 15). This highlights the way in which social science is often complicit in creating the conditions of its own knowledge production. As Savage (2010: 68) has argued, 'the social sciences ... do not merely respond to a changing external environment but are themselves implicated in new forms of governmentality, regulation and social imaginary'. This, then, is 'the youth researcher's dilemma' (Heath et al., 2009: 13): through seeking to give voice to young people's experiences via participatory approaches, we may in fact find ourselves contributing not just to the governance, but also the *self*-governance, of young people's lives. This raises important ethical issues in relation to youth research, a further cross-cutting theme within this book to which we now turn.

Ethical concerns in youth research

In recent years, ethical concerns in social research – not least, social research involving young people – have been in danger of becoming overshadowed by, and at times subsumed within, bureaucratic procedures of ethical review and research governance. Back (2007) cites Rabinow's assertion that 'the main mode of regulation now is ethical' (Rabinow, 2003: 115), a view with which many youth researchers might well concur, especially those who have experienced formal ethical review processes in recent years. Yet ethical review procedures constitute only one small aspect of ethical research practice, while some commentators (e.g. Atkinson, 2009; Dingwall, 2008) have argued that they have very little, if anything, to do with ethical research practice. Certainly, the main challenges of ethical research practice occur in researchers' everyday interactions and research encounters in the field as well as in the processes of analysis, interpretation and dissemination, and these are the sorts of ethical concerns that are addressed in many of the chapters in this book.

A commitment to participatory approaches represents a very specific ethical stance in relation to youth research, and we have already introduced some of the key issues raised by our contributors in this regard.

As we have seen, 'youth-friendly' methods are frequently deployed within participatory research, yet their very 'friendliness' can sometimes be a source of ethical concern. Nicola Ross and her colleagues (Chapter 3) highlight, for example, how using seemingly quite informal and non-threatening methods of data generation, such as walking interviews or car journey interactions, carries the potential for inadvertently encouraging young people to be less guarded about their personal lives than they might be in the context of more formal research encounters. One young woman, for example, 'sometimes appeared somewhat blasé about the sharing of information about her life and this was at times a concern for the researcher who had formed the closest bond in the project with her'. This highlights how 'too much information' may sometimes be as problematic, albeit for different reasons, than too little. A related concern potentially arises from the involvement of young people as peer researchers. Dirk Schubotz (Chapter 6) notes that some of the commonly claimed advantages of using young researchers as field-workers include their ability 'to access the real life world of their peers more accurately' than adult researchers as a consequence of shared experience and shared language; the likelihood that young people will 'feel comfortable enough to say what they really think' in interactions with their peers, especially in relation to sensitive topics; and the ability of young researchers to access hard-to-reach groups of young people. There is an interesting parallel here with Finch's (1984) argument in her classic paper on the ethics and politics of interviewing women (which Schubotz in fact cites), in which she notes her concerns about the readiness with which female research participants divulged very personal information about their lives. She describes this in terms of 'the exploitative potential' of 'the easily established trust between women' (1984: 81). There is arguably an even greater exploitative potential in using young researchers to gain data from their peers which otherwise may be off-limits to older researchers, yet which are then analysed and interpreted by those same older researchers. The apparent youth-friendliness of certain approaches is not necessarily, then, an unqualified good when considered in ethical terms.

The availability of online data and the development of online research methods have likewise presented researchers with many ethical challenges in recent years, although whether these are genuinely new challenges or merely old ones in new contexts is open to debate. Many of the challenges of online research coalesce around familiar ethical concerns relating to informed consent and anonymity, concerns that are tackled in the contributions of both Helene Snee (Chapter 10) and

Yvette Morey and colleagues (Chapter 11). Snee's research on the 'identity work' of young people who take an overseas gap year was based on analysis of a sample of gap year blogs. A key issue for Snee, as for many other researchers working with online material such as blogs, is whether such material should be considered as public or private data, and accordingly, whether the requirements of informed consent associated with 'offline' data generation should apply in online contexts. For Snee, attempting to draw a distinction between bloggers as *either* human subjects *or* as authors provided a key to resolving this issue: concluding that a blogger is a human subject implies that traditional notions of informed consent should apply, whereas concluding that a blogger is an author implies that their blog entries can be treated akin to any other publicly available text. Morey and colleagues raise a similar set of concerns in relation to online content generated by Web 2.0 technologies, but argue that the application of traditional rules-based ethical guidelines concerning consent and anonymity may be outdated in the context of the contemporary practices and expectations of Internet users, linked to 'a radical *erosion* of the boundaries between the public and the private, and the move to active participation in, and creation of, online content' (emphasis added). In other words, researchers may be holding themselves to higher standards of consent and anonymity than are expected by users of Web 2.0 technologies. The best ways to handle these sorts of issues are, then, still unfolding and subject to ongoing discussions among online researchers.

The use of mixed methods

If participatory research can be described as a 'new orthodoxy' in youth research, so too might the utilisation of mixed methods research designs. Nearly all of the examples of research included in this book were based on research designs involving a broad palette of (mostly qualitative) methods, rather than the use of a single method in isolation. In some cases this was in the spirit of a participatory, youth-friendly approach, in order to allow research participants to choose their preferred methods, as in Nadine Schäfer's use of a broad range of methods in her study of the everyday lives of young Germans (Chapter 8). In most cases, however, a wide range of methods were used in combination across a research project. Nicola Allett's research on Extreme Metal fans (Chapter 2), for example, involved the use of music elicitation as one of a number of techniques that she used across a series of repeated focus groups, alongside memory work and media elicitation techniques. She describes how 'each method was adopted to help produce and enhance different interactions' within the focus group setting.

As these examples suggest, a critical issue to consider when choosing to use mixed methods relates to the underpinning rationale for the specific combination of methods chosen. May (2010) identifies three common approaches to the use of mixed methods: triangulation, complementarity, and multi-dimensional explanation. The first approach is concerned with attempting to gain a more accurate picture of a phenomenon by scrutinising the *same* research object via the use of a number of different methods. In contrast, the second approach uses different methods to explore *different* elements of a phenomenon, on the assumption that different methods will answer 'a specific part of the problem' or because their combination 'might give a better sense of the whole' (May, 2010: 2). This second approach follows an integrative logic (Mason, 2006), and uses mixed methods 'to complement rather than validate each other' (May, 2010: 2). The third approach to using mixed methods builds on this integrative logic and is based on the assumption that all social phenomena are multi-dimensional and should be researched as such, rather than along a single dimension: 'This strategy allows researchers to ask distinctively different but intersecting questions about social phenomena, as well as to conceptualise what they are researching and what counts as knowledge and evidence in different ways' (ibid. 3).

Most of the mixed methods studies reported on in this book have, whether explicitly or implicitly, adopted approaches based on either complementarity or multi-dimensional explanation. Bagnoli's research on migrant identity (Chapter 5), for example, explicitly followed the integrative logic of complementarity in combining open-ended interviews, self-portraits and diaries: 'each different component was meant to provide one side of the phenomenon under investigation, either combining with other tools, enhancing what had already been collected, or supplementing them whenever any of the methods might just prove insufficient on their own to get a reflexive picture of the identities of these young people'. Similarly, Richard White and Anne Green's research on young people's attachment to place (Chapter 4) used a variety of different methods – a survey, focus groups, a mental mapping exercise, and individual face-to-face interviews – to complement each other and hence build up a more holistic picture of the way in which young people's attachment to place affected their opportunities and aspirations. These different methods each generated different types of data, which contributed to the whole. So, for example, the mental maps in particular unexpectedly revealed 'the prominence of social networks as a means of making and shaping [young people's] bounded horizons', while the mental maps also highlighted in graphic form the uneven nature of their research participants' spatial awareness, a finding which was complemented by interview data.

Most of the chapters in this book, then, provide very good examples of how different methods can be used in combination to enhance the quality of youth research. Youth research does, of course, have a rich ethnographic tradition, which has long combined a variety of different approaches within one study. What is striking about many of the examples in this book, though, is the way in which research designs based on the use of interviews and focus groups – methods that are also widely used in youth research – are being augmented and enhanced by creative adaptations, not infrequently through the inclusion of visual and arts-based methods.

Reflexivity and the social relations of fieldwork

A fourth theme running throughout the book is the importance of reflexivity in relation to the social relations of fieldwork. A major strength of accounts of research that foreground methodological rather than substantive issues is that they often provide intriguing insights into the everyday social relations of fieldwork as they actually unfold in real world research contexts. The reality of fieldwork is often a far cry from our initial hopes. Plan A is often quickly substituted for Plan B, the best laid plans not infrequently fall apart, and serendipity often provides us with some of our best research contacts and access routes. Most of the chapters in this book provide insights into the highs and lows of fieldwork. Our contributors have been honest enough to reflect upon some of their failures as well as their successes, on the things that did not work so well alongside those that did.

What is clear is that the quality of the research relationships that are established once in the field are often critical in this regard. In particular, who we are as individuals matters profoundly, particularly in relation to any claims we might seek to make in relation to insider or outsider status and the advantages and disadvantages that might flow from that status. Nicola Allett (Chapter 2), for example, conducted research with a group of young adults of which she counted herself a member. Her focus on the motivations for subcultural involvement among Extreme Metal music fans was as much about attempting to understand her own identification with this subculture as it was about understanding that of her fellow fans. Similarly, Anna Bagnoli's focus on Italian and English migrants (Chapter 5) arose out of her own experience of moving from Italy to the UK as a young woman, as part of what she described as 'a privileged group of '"global nomads"'. Both Allett and Bagnoli, then, were able to make valid claims to insider status, in contrast to many of the other contributors to the book who were, to varying degrees, situated as outsiders to the phenomena they were researching.

Charlie Walker, for example, considered himself an outsider in his research with vocational students in Russia and Lithuania (Chapter 12), as did Amanda Brown and Suzanne Powell (Chapter 7) in their research with university students in South India, although all three highlight other points of connection – a shared age, for example, or a shared gender – which at times seemed to override their differences in relation to ethnicity and nationality. In similar vein, Shane Blackman's school-based ethnography brought him into close contact with a group of female pupils, the 'new wave girls', and a group of anti-academic pupils, 'the criminal boys' (Chapter 13); Gemma Commane's ethnography of young women's involvement in BDSM (bondage, discipline, sadism and masochism), fetish and performance art cultures took her into a world with which she was largely unfamiliar (also Chapter 13); and Yvette Morey and colleagues in their digital ethnography of the marketing, branding and 'managed consumption' of music festivals and free parties (illegal raves) had to gain online acceptance among the free parties community, a group naturally suspicious of outsiders (Chapter 11).

In all these examples, trust had to be gained and reputations established as part of an ongoing process of establishing and maintaining credibility and rapport in the field. As our contributors ably demonstrate, the ability to reflect upon these issues, to think on one's feet and to respond flexibly to changing circumstances during fieldwork was vital to success or failure in this regard. In Chapter 13, Blackman and Commane provide some powerful examples of the importance of reflexivity during fieldwork, but also highlight that reflexivity is equally important in the process of writing up and interpreting data from fieldwork. They note that, 'although ethnography demands that fieldwork, analysis and writing all occur simultaneously, we want to draw attention to the fact that the ethnographer, when writing-up, returns to the field through the research imaginary, and encounters what we call the double reflexivity'. This 'double reflexivity' – the attention to reflexivity both in the field and in its representation – is apparent in many of the chapters in this collection, as the authors have, by virtue of contributing to this book, found themselves reflecting on both the social relations of fieldwork and the implications of those relations for the validity of their claims to knowledge. As we noted earlier, this is as much an epistemological concern as it is a methodological one.

Structure of the book

Having identified some of the common themes that emerge across the chapters in the book, we now provide a brief overview of what follows. The first part of the book focuses on a variety of creative methods which can be used to enhance encounters in interviews or focus groups. In Chapter 2, Nicola Allett focuses on her imaginative use within focus groups of music elicitation techniques as part of her research with Extreme Metal fans. Nicola breaks new ground in her development of this method and demonstrates how the powerfully evocative nature of music makes it a particularly appropriate – yet surprisingly under-used – medium for conducting research on young people's current subcultural affiliations. It is also apparent that this method has great potential for exploring many other aspects of young people's every-day lives. In Chapter 3, Nicola Ross and colleagues describe their use of walking interviews and car journey interactions as part of their research on young people in public care. Their choice of methods can be seen as a response to the 'new mobilities paradigm' in the social sciences, which has focused attention on how we make sense of the world through movement. As such, their chapter demonstrates how, in their own words, mobile research methods 'can be utilised to understand everyday experiences through embodied, multi-sensory research experiences, where journeys themselves become the focus of interest'. Ross and her colleagues highlight several of the advantages associated with their chosen methods, including the opportunity for young people to exercise greater control over the research process than in more conventional methods. In Chapter 4, Richard White and Anne Green provide an account of their research on young people's attachment to place and in particular provide an account of their use of mental mapping techniques within focus group settings. Green and White highlight some of the advantages of inviting young people to produce drawings of their localities and their movements through them as a complement to asking them to talk about their spatial awareness and complete surveys on this theme. In Chapter 5, Anna Bagnoli explores the analytic potential of using a mixed methods strategy for eliciting reflexive narratives. In researching the identity narratives of young English and Italian migrants, Bagnoli used a range of creative methods to enhance her one-to-one narrative interviews, including self-portraits, diaries and photo-elicitation techniques. She highlights how the different methods enabled a range of 'story types' to emerge, and explores the specific input of the different components. Bagnoli's chapter is richly illustrated with examples of the self-portraits produced by her research participants, while the chapter by Green and White is also brought to life by the inclusion of some of the mental maps produced by the young people involved in their research.

Chapters 6 to 9 focus explicitly on participatory research (although Chapters 2 to 5 are by no means untouched by these concerns). In Chapter 6, Dirk Schubotz explores the use of peer researchers in two projects related to young people's views of community relations in Northern Ireland. He raises the question of the validity of research conducted by young people, highlighting how on the one hand adult researchers and other stakeholders may be concerned that peer research will not be as rigorous as that conducted by trained professional researchers, yet on the other hand noting that the very nature of peer research may increase the validity of research findings, given that young people may be able 'to access the real life world of their peers more accurately' than adult researchers. He also highlights the importance of establishing realistic expectations on the part of peer researchers, and the importance of good quality training to this process. In Chapter 7, Amanda Brown and Suzanne Powell discuss their use of the 'Photovoice' approach in their research on young people and place in South India, an approach more commonly used in community health contexts than in youth research. Photovoice is specifically designed to 'give voice' to groups whose voices are seldom heard, and is a variant on photo-elicitation, based on participant-generated photography followed by group discussions. Brown and Powell used the technique in the context of walking interviews and describe how their research participants – undergraduate and postgraduate university students – initially found the method quite challenging, as they were used to adopting a fairly passive role in their usual classroom encounters. Nonetheless, the method succeeded in capturing their imaginations, as demonstrated by the examples of photographs included in the chapter. Chapter 8 is also based on the use of visual methods in participatory contexts, this time based on the use of video recording in Nadine Schäfer's research on young people's everyday lives in a disadvantaged rural area of what was formerly the German Democratic Republic. A key point in Schäfer's chapter is that we cannot always predict which methods will have appeal to young people. In her own research, she trained her participants in a range of visual methods, assuming that the use of videoing would be a popular choice, yet in reality very few young people opted to use this method. Schaefer explores some of the reasons for this, noting that the use of visual methods – despite their apparent 'youth-friendliness' – do not, in themselves, guarantee high levels of participation. She concludes that 'analysing young people's motives for using or not using specific visual methods provides an insight into young people's methodological sensitivity and might provide future youth research with valuable insights into young people's everyday lives.' The appropriateness of methods is an issue returned to in Chapter 9, in which Darren Sharpe reflects upon his involvement as a development officer in the Young Researcher Network of the National Youth Agency. Sharpe provides a personal view of some of the key lessons learnt from the work of the Network. He counsels realism in what we should expect from research led by young people but also points to the need for greater awareness of the diverse ways in which young people can be involved in research. As noted earlier, their involvement should not be viewed simply in polarised terms of passive research objects or active researchers: there are many possibilities in between which play to the strengths of young people, policy makers and adult researchers equally.

Chapters 10 and 11 are focused on online methods for youth research, methods made possible by Web 2.0 technologies. In Chapter 10, Helene Snee describes her use of blog analysis as a way of accessing a very rich vein of naturally occurring data on young people's construction of identity through their gap year experiences. She highlights a range of very practical considerations linked to this method, but also engages in a thought-provoking discussion of the nature of what is public and private in online domains. This is a theme continued in Chapter 11, where Yvette Morey and colleagues explore some of the ethical issues raised by their digital ethnography of festivals and free parties. They argue that existing ethical guidelines for researchers, even those targeted specifically at online researchers, have not kept pace with the nature of online interaction, and that in order to do so researchers have much to learn from young people themselves, as well as from bodies such as the Creative Commons and the Open Commons. These bodies are seeking to achieve universal open access to online material through providing an infrastructure that provides a balance between existing copyright laws and the reality of online communication. The importance of this is underscored by the lack of screenshots in Snee and Morey's chapters; despite having permission from the producers of individual web pages to reproduce some of their online materials, the conditions of copyright laid down by platform providers means that we are unable to reproduce them in this book.

Morey's focus on digital ethnography and some of the ethical challenges associated with it provides a nice link to Chapters 12 and 13, which take us back into the non-virtual world and into the realm of traditional ethnographic methods for youth research. In Chapter 12, Charlie Walker discusses some of the practical and ethical challenges of conducting ethnographic research in cross-cultural contexts, specifically in relation to a series of case studies addressing the changing nature of transitions to adulthood among working-class young people in Russia and Lithuania. Walker explores some of the classic ethnographic challenges of gaining and maintaining access and treading the path of insider/outsider status in fieldwork relations. In particular he highlights how, when approached as a form of 'cultural exchange', cross-cultural research can actually transform sources of difference into a vehicle for discussion, 'thus facilitating both the establishment of rapport with respondents and their own reflections on their lives.'

Finally, in Chapter 13, Shane Blackman and Gemma Commane reflect on the politics of friendship, fieldwork and representation within their respective ethnographic studies of young people: in Blackman's case, his study of school-based subcultures, and in Commane's case, her study of young women's involvement in BDSM (bondage, discipline, sadism and masochism), fetish and performance art cultures. They focus on risk, friendship and integrity as critical moments in fieldwork and point to the importance of ongoing critical reflection as a key element not only of fieldwork, but also of the processes of analysis, interpretation and writing-up, what they term 'double reflexivity'.

There is an interesting twist to Blackman and Commane's chapter: Blackman writes about his own doctoral research conducted over 20 years ago, while Commane writes about her very recent doctoral research under Blackman's supervision. It is instructive to reflect on the similarities and differences between the conditions and expectations of research practice between these two eras, both in very practical terms but also in relation to the more recent influence of different theoretical perspectives, in this case of postmodern approaches to ethnography. This raises a key question relating to the extent to which the methodological developments reported in this book are indeed 'something old or something new', a theme that we briefly revisit in the concluding chapter of the book. Our conclusion also considers the extent to which the methods described in this book might legitimately be considered to be 'youth-friendly' and capable of capturing the complexity of young people's lives. We also revisit the 'new orthodoxy' of mixed methods research, a phenomenon that is very evident within this collection.

Each of our contributors' chapters also ends with suggestions for further reading, organised under two headings: 'related methodological literature' and 'examples of related youth research'. Resources listed under the first of these headings will provide readers with an entry point into general methodological literature relating to particular methods, as well as some examples of their use specifically within youth research contexts. Resources under the second heading provide examples of recent youth research focused on cognate substantive areas, in some cases based on the use of similar methods. In combination, it is hoped that readers who are interested in a particular method or area of youth research will be able to extend their knowledge from these starting points.

2

'As soon as that track starts, I feel ...' Unravelling Attachments to Extreme Metal Music with 'Music Elicitation'

Nicola Allett

Introduction

Music is significant in many people's lives, providing a source of pleasure, escapism and identification. Music offers the listener an encounter with the body (which responds to rhythm and timbre), an encounter with the self (experiencing self-feelings and responding to familiar taste or unfamiliar 'noise') and in the case of live music, an encounter with the crowd. It may be of little wonder, therefore, that some people form their identities around music and identify collectively in their tastes. In undertaking research with Extreme Metal music fans, I aimed to reveal something of the everyday practices of the Extreme Metal fan and the distinct investments and attachments fans had to Extreme Metal as both a music genre and a music subculture. Such a focus demanded a qualitative method that aided the disclosure of Extreme Metal fans' experiences of listening to Extreme Metal music. I decided to integrate Extreme Metal music into research interviews in order to draw out descriptive accounts of experiences of, and attachments to, music and provoke in-depth discussion.

This chapter addresses my use of 'music elicitation' within semi-structured group interviews with Extreme Metal music fans. It reflects on my initial motivation to develop the method, its application within the research field and the data that emerged through its use. The chapter proposes that the inclusion of and experimentation with music in qualitative research, particularly through the music elicitation method, may produce valuable forms of rich and thick description and enable a new focus for youth and music culture research. The first part of this chapter gives an overview of the project and the context for my research. It then considers the existing uses of music as a methodological tool and the potential advantages that music elicitation could offer qualitative researchers. The chapter then discusses the data that emerged from my use of music elicitation with Extreme Metal fans. It highlights the particular benefits of using the method within a group context, and offers some considerations for researchers who wish to adopt music elicitation for their own research.

Extreme Metal fans and their subcultural participation

In this chapter, my discussion of the use of music elicitation draws on my research of a group of Extreme Metal music fans and their subcultural participation. Extreme Metal music consists of a collection of genres (i.e. Black Metal, Death Metal, Grindcore, and Doom Metal) that are distinct from one another, but can be largely characterised by their sonic extremity. This can be seen in their utilisation of extreme forms of tempo (both slow and fast), unconventional song structures, soundscapes of amplified distortion and vocal manipulations, and lyrical themes that include death, violence and the occult. The study had its roots in my own reflections on my activities and long-term participation in the Extreme Metal subculture. As an Extreme Metal fan and active in the UK music subculture since I was 18, I was interested in my own identification with and commitment to a music identity. I wanted to consider what was involved in investing in, performing and being an Extreme Metal fan and what were the distinct attachments and reasons for becoming embedded in a subcultural identity.

Between January 2007 and July 2007, I conducted recurring group research with six Extreme Metal fans. The participants, one female and five males aged 19–31, were friends who were active in their local Extreme Metal music scene as event organisers, musicians and fans. Recruitment for the research group started with my contacting the organisers of a monthly Extreme Metal club/live music night, one which I was aware of from my own activity, but in which I had not been previously involved.

I contacted them via their 'Myspace' social networking site, which advertised the nights, giving a short description of my research and a request for their participation or their help in giving me further contacts. On agreeing, my initial contacts then actively recruited the rest of the participants from among their friends who were Extreme Metal fans. The research was structured into ten semi-structured group interviews that were between two and a half hours and three and a half hours in length. These were interactive interviews in which my respondents often led discussions and asked the group questions, and I was involved as a co-participant (as an Extreme Metal fan). As co-participant, I took part as a research group member in disclosure, discussions and group tasks. My participation was, however, managed throughout the research as I switched between being a researcher who probed, questioned and directed, and a participant who had to be careful not to influence group talk. I used the qualitative methods of memory work, media elicitation and music elicitation within the group interviews in order to generate, enrich and facilitate the data. Each method was adopted to help produce and enhance different interactions. Memory work was used in six of the group interviews and involved writing a story for ten minutes at the beginning of the group session on a particular title I had chosen that would, also, be a focus for the rest of the session (e.g. 'remember a physical response to live Extreme Metal music'). This method was adopted to draw out memories of music experience and explore the construction and performance of identity and life stories. Media elicitation was used in one of the group interviews. My respondents were asked to bring examples of the music media (i.e. magazines and fanzines) that they liked and disliked to discuss with the group. Looking through the media as a group could trigger group discussion and generate individual and collective critiques of music media. Finally, music elicitation was used in two of the research group meetings to elicit descriptions of the music listening experience and the respondents' attachments to Extreme Metal.

I used music elicitation in the seventh and eighth group meetings. By this point in the research, the group and I had established ongoing rapport. In addition, members felt important to, and invested in, the research, resulting in their being more forthcoming in their answers and keen to self-evaluate. Music elicitation involved each group member choosing two recorded music tracks from their personal collections, having been asked in the previous sessions to bring music to the next meeting: firstly, a track they 'loved' and then a track that specifically drew out certain feelings or emotions. They did not ask for clarification of these requests, but during the music elicitation tasks, I asked how they interpreted such phrases as 'feelings', 'emotions' and 'love' in relation to music. The music elicitation tasks involved the group listening to each group member's choice of music. Participants were supplied with a notebook and pen, providing the option to record their thoughts and feelings while listening. After listening to a track, the group took it in turns to describe their thoughts about and reactions to the music, finally returning to the participant who chose the music to give an account of their reaction accompanied by an explanation for their choice. This was repeated with each participant and led to group discussion.

Context: Youth cultures and music

My methodological approach was motivated by my decision to focus on the fan/subculturalist's relationship with music genre. Music is a prominent feature in young people's lives and is often something with which they collectively identify. There exist numerous academic studies of youth participation in music culture, but few consider the relationship young people have with music itself. In the 1970s, the Birmingham Centre for Contemporary Cultural Studies (CCCS) was interested in musical subcultures, but the music was incidental and not a focus. Instead the CCCS placed emphasis upon subcultural style as symbolic class resistance (e.g. Clarke, 1976; Hebdige, 1976). Studies of music cultures continue to take into account seemingly everything other than the members' relationship to the music. For example, 'Riot Grrrl' (a music genre characterised by Punk riffs, female vocals and screams, and feminist politics) has been the subject of a number of studies, all of which focus on the lyrical content, spectacular resistance, feminist politics and its links to Punk culture (e.g. Leonard, 1997; Kearney, 1998; Piano, 2003). Yet such studies overlook the riot grrrl's attachment to and enjoyment of the actual music genre of Riot Grrrl. Similarly, with the rise of post-subcultural studies that emphasise the movement between cultures (Bennett, 1999) and the playful adoption of stylistic identities (Muggleton, 2000), the importance of music in individuals' lives and remaining in those lives is left unconsidered. Within fandom studies, the music relationship has also received little consideration. Instead, studies concentrate upon fans' relationships with their object of fandom. For instance, in his study on Bruce Springsteen fans, Cavicchi (1998) claims that the fan community is created through shared attachment to the figure of Bruce Springsteen and what he represents to them. Similarly, in studies that have considered Madonna there is a tendency to concentrate upon the powerful feminist values that could be attached to Madonna's image and songs (Kaplan, 1987; Fiske, 1989). Emphasis is placed, therefore, on the individual fan's attraction and attachment to the celebrity and the values that they supposedly portray. Yet, music fans have a distinct relationship with *music*. In researching Extreme Metal fans and their participation in music subculture, I wanted to consider the fan's relationship with music, to explore what kind of feelings are attached to listening to the Extreme Metal music genre and whether these are collectively shared.

Music elicitation

In order to explore the music experience and relationship, I needed a methodological tool to draw out affective descriptions of my respondents' experiences of Extreme Metal music. I recognised the possible difficulties in drawing out thick descriptions of experience and affect. Researching the relationship between music and feelings may be problematic. Negus (1996: 3) explains that although we may 'feel' and 'know' music, language fails us as soon as we try to communicate and share this experience: it cannot be easily explained or communicated. Furthermore, there could be some discomfort in the disclosure of feelings. When conducting qualitative interviews, researchers' questions may produce un-descriptive answers or their respondents may struggle to find the words to describe an experience or a feeling. A key concern in undertaking my research was, therefore, how to get people to 'open up' within the interview setting. By asking my respondents *why* they liked Extreme Metal I was likely to make them feel as if they needed to justify their taste rather than describe their investments and affective attachments. Indeed, Becker (1998) argues that researchers should avoid 'why' questions at all costs, suggesting that they should ask 'how' questions instead, which tend to solicit narratives rather than justifications. Yet, even by asking *how* Extreme Metal music was experienced, answers may be limited by respondents having to make generalisations about their feelings. Such questions need a point of focus: the music within the interview, to which respondents can refer and upon which they can base their claims. The difficulty in drawing out accounts of feeling with qualitative methods indicated a need, then, to innovate or adapt methods. I developed a use of music elicitation in the hope that it could access rich data about music attachments that may not emerge in a conventional group interview and stimulate group discussion. By introducing recorded music into the interview, I wanted to make music the shared focus of discussion and encourage my respondents to talk about their experiences, feelings, connections and judgments.

Music has been used in social research, but has not been discussed to the same degree as other media. There are particular uses of music worth noting. Music has been used in arts-based methods as data produced by respondents (Daykin, 2008; Leavy, 2008). Placing music as data, however, leads to difficulties in interpreting its meanings and may rely on the musical ability and knowledge of respondents. Although music may have particular uses as data, music also has the potential to be a methodological tool to gather data by eliciting dialogue and disclosure. Researchers have used forms of music elicitation across disciplines, but the method has not been examined in detail. For instance, in undertaking research on women's reflections of their mediated practices of everyday remembering, Keightley (2010) used photos and music within the individual interview. In his research on music fans, Hesmondhalgh (2007) alludes to using music in the interview to explore music fans' judgments of music and in researching the everyday uses of music. Anderson (2004, 2005) used music listening exercises with his respondents in order to consider the practices of memory and how music is judged in everyday life. Music has also been used to gather information about audience responses and associations. For example, Snyder (1993) used 'auditory elicitation' in his consideration of pieces of music associated with sport. In his approach, respondents wrote subjective meanings, which they associated with musical selections as they were played, to elicit meaning and emotions placed onto music. My development of a music elicitation method sought to use music listening within the group interview to draw out data about music fans' relationships with music, and to access their everyday experiences, uses, attachments and feelings that remain largely unspoken in the conventional qualitative interview.

The use of elicitation methods within qualitative interviews has the potential to uncover previously untold stories, contextualise research talk, and give respondents another means to express themselves. There are no rules on what can be used as an elicitation material. Rather, it is important to recognise that the characteristics of the material used to elicit have considerable impact on the research data. For instance, object elicitation is both visual and tactile because the object can be picked up, touched (even smelt) and viewed. Objects may hold memories and meaning and the presence of them in homes, in storage, in workplaces also means that they provide a connection between respondents and something about their lives (Hurdley, 2006). It is not only the ability to view these things/objects that can impact on the research encounter; additionally it is their materiality and respondents' sensory encounters with them that can aid the telling, remembering and disclosure.

Music elicitation, like other elicitation methods, uses a medium to enrich the interview data by gaining interpretations, stories and experiences that can tell the social researcher something (possibly different or more detailed) about respondents' lives and identities. Using recorded music as an elicitation device, however, offers particular qualities that differ from other elicitation methods. Music can exist in a material form, such as on a record, CD or iPod, and these forms may hold significance as objects, such as rare vinyl or a music compilation given by a friend, but music is always, also, a composition that is experienced as an auditory encounter. An auditory encounter is never the same, even when we listen to a familiar piece of music. Our encounters with music are temporal. Music unfolds with time, the song moves and changes and we experience it 'in the moment' of listening. The music encounter is also relational (Bull, 2001). It involves the relation between listener, sound, time and surroundings and the interactions of the aural senses, bodily sensations, affective experience and the listeners' understanding, expectations and judgment. Music elicitation creates a particular moment for the respondent(s) and researcher to share the music encounter. Although they may experience the music in very different ways as they listen together, they can reflect upon their perceptions and experience with the knowledge that they have shared music, time and situation.

In many respects, music has distinct qualities that make it closely related to our feelings. It gives a sensory experience through sound and vibration that can alter the 'feel' of a place, can engulf the listener and space, and can create place/space through transporting the listener into an atmosphere. According to DeNora (2000), it is the temporal, unravelling and communicative nature of music that is a central reason for its ability to stir the listener's feelings. Music may also create certain feelings because it is a powerful trigger of memories. Music can be imbued with memory (Keightley and Pickering, 2006). Furthermore, music can be consciously used to create or recall particular feelings and memories (Anderson, 2004). Music can be considered a device for memory retrieval, used to re-live and (re)constitute past experience (DeNora, 2006). Similarly, it can be considered a device for feeling and 'self' because often music is used to manage moods, gain desired states of feeling and is a resource for 'knowing how one feels' (DeNora, 2000). Music has, then, unique properties that can be utilised within research. Listening to recorded music could elicit respondents' feelings and affective memory because of the distinct experience music presents to the listener.

I developed a use of music elicitation, then, in order to gain descriptive affective accounts of music listening and fandom. Using methods that are original and creative in their use and application can produce exciting results. Yet, undertaking any methodological innovation comes with the risk that they will not work as anticipated. The method could fail to achieve the desired results or may not gain different research data. I did not know how successful music elicitation would be in practice and had no guarantee of what my respondents would reveal. The potential of the 'unknown' also has an element of danger. In using elicitation devices, there is a possibility that they may elicit unwanted feelings or negative/unwelcome memories that could cause upset to the respondent. This is particularly the case for music elicitation because of the connection between music, memory and affect. There is, therefore, a need for researcher sensitivity in undertaking the method and in dealing with any distress.

Using music elicitation with Extreme Metal fans

I have so far discussed music elicitation in relation to the possible advantages that the method can offer our research. I now discuss some of the data that emerged from using music elicitation in my research with Extreme Metal fans. I demonstrate that music elicitation gained accounts of my respondents' affective attachments and prompted group discussion, which gave valuable data about fan and subcultural practices. I also consider the impact of conducting music elicitation within group research on the successes of using the method.

Music elicitation was adopted in the hope that it would aid and prompt my respondents to describe their affective responses, experiences and attachments to Extreme Metal music. I found that using music elicitation within the group interviews was particularly successful in gaining rich descriptions of my respondents' feelings. During music elicitation they described the music listening experience and the impact the music had on their emotions, thoughts and bodies. For example, after playing my own choice of track, group member Ben described his reaction as he had listened to the music:

> Ben: As soon as that track starts [*Darkthrone's 'En As I Dype Skogen'*], I feel like this change comes over my body and I feel [pause] I feel totally powerful. I feel like I am standing on my own on a wind-swept plain, or something like that, and I feel like it brings out something. It puts me in a trance-like, almost psychotic, mood. There is something really primal in me, that [pause] it doesn't come out here. I'm not really an aggressive person but it makes me just [pause] I don't know, it's hard to explain.

Here, Ben describes the transformation he goes through while listening to the music. Ben's response is positioned as something 'primal', as an inherent response to the untamed power of music. Ben's feelings of power are also referenced against a backdrop of the romantic imagery of an awe-inspiring dramatic landscape, of the 'wind-swept plain'. In describing their feelings in such ways, my respondents were drawing on a cultural vocabulary available to them. In particular, they used romance and spiritual language centred on love and power to describe Extreme Metal's affect and their attachment to it. After listening to his song of choice, and receiving some negative comments about the music he played, Liam also drew on romance language to describe his response:

> Liam: I think it [*Ensiferum's 'LAI LAI HEI'*] is one of the most beautiful songs I have ever heard. It is going to sound like bollocks to you guys, because you [the research group] just heard it and thought nothing of it, but, I really like the start with the folk [a reference to the use of acoustic guitar, melody and clean vocal]. It's really earthy and it's singing in another language and I think it is quite evocative of like, oral tradition. And the actual guitar itself, there's a bit about two minutes in where they are playing a melody and one of them just plays a kinda off note and I think that's awesome. But the bit towards the end, when he's just singing and it's just his voice rising against the music, it sounds, I think it sounds really vulnerable and really powerful at the same time. And, I just think it is one of the most incredible bits I have ever heard in a song ever. I've seen it live and it has so nearly reduced me to tears because it's just [pause] I just can't explain it. It just really provokes something.

Realising that his feelings had been different to those of the rest of the group, Liam attempts to explain his attachment in relation to music's emotional effect and power. Liam describes the track as 'beautiful', expressing a love of, and aesthetic appreciation for, the song structure, tone and vocal; and also the sound, which he describes in relation to power and vulnerability, two extremes of feeling that can stir the listener to tears. The song's appeal is placed as 'awesome' and 'powerful'. Such words are used to represent the emotional charge that the music has for Liam. When Liam tries to describe the song's effect further, he struggles and then gives up ('I just can't explain it. It just really provokes something').

There were several other instances where my respondents had difficulty describing their feelings. At points, such as in both Ben and Liam's accounts above, they struggled and then gave up, but at other times they found their own vocal and physical expressions. For instance, in discussing the group's varied reactions to the music they had played, Liam abandons language to describe his feelings:

> Ben: Sometimes when I'm sad if I put on sad music I will feel much better, lifted out of it.
> Liam: I think you can't put sad music on if you are feeling incredibly happy and straight away be hit by, you know, an iron block of misery.
> Ben: Yeah? I don't know. That's how I felt when I put on the *Weakling* CD today.
> Liam: What, really happy then put it on and thought 'urrgh' [expressing negativity].
> Ben: Yeah.
> Liam: That is quite interesting. I still feel very 'arrgh' [expressing excitement/positivity] after having listened to my song, which you didn't like.

Liam used exaggerated facial expressions and sounds ('I still feel very arrgh') in order to express a particular set of feelings. Many feelings are unclear or untranslatable. Music elicitation may have opened up my respondents to describe their affective experiences of music, but language often got in the way. My respondents still struggled in many respects to put those feelings into words. Music elicitation did, therefore, have its limitations in uncovering feelings; but, on the other hand, without the music elicitation tasks these conversations and the felt attempts by my respondents to describe their feelings probably would not have emerged. The music elicitation tasks, nevertheless, elicited descriptions of the listening experience, affect and passionate attachment.

Music elicitation placed music at the centre of the group interview and in so doing made music the focus of discussion with little direction from the researcher. The method, therefore, played an important role in producing a wealth of information about music in everyday life. My respondents described their everyday uses of music, such as the mobile practices of listening to music in the car, and on the walkman/iPod. They also referenced using music to 'get ready to go out', to relax, and to create or reflect a particular feeling. Elements of the discussions that were triggered by music elicitation also gave insight into music fandom. For instance, after listening to Ben's choice [*Nachtfalke's 'Valhalla'*], Chloe described her dislike of the Black Metal 'badly produced' sound, a reference to lo-fi quality recording containing technical flaws such as limited frequency, distortion and background noise. This was originally a result of low cost studio production associated with the limited budgets of early Black Metal bands, but now many artists deliberately record in this way to achieve this Black Metal sound. Ben's reaction to her comment gives insight into the process of becoming a fan of the music:

> Chloe: Well, I prefer to hear my instruments, rather than wonder if my speakers are blowing.
> Ben: I think it is what you hear. The more Black Metal you listen to, the more badly produced music you listen to, the more your ears become attuned.
> NA: True. It's like you can hear beyond the initial fuzz.
> Ben: Same with Death Metal. The more you listen to it, it doesn't seem so extreme to you, but your mum would think 'oh my God. What's that noise?'

Ben describes the development of music taste through a process of 'learning to listen': to listen 'beyond the initial fuzz' and 'attune' one's ears, or acclimatise oneself to the music, which, in effect, reduces the extremity of the first listening experience. This suggests the constructed nature of taste, with taste dependent upon respondents 'developing an ear' for the music genre or band. This indicates something more of the fan attachment: that it is not only feeling, but also investment (i.e. through time and effort), to hear beyond the noise. Much of the data that emerged during and after the music elicitation exercises gave insight into fan practices and collective identity. Exclamations of likes and dislikes, and what was and was not considered Extreme Metal demonstrated how music was personally and collectively judged and how the group identified taste and authenticity among other music fans. Notions of 'good' and 'bad' music, and the judgments that decided this, often were revealed in the respondents' explanations for their track choice. Rob, for example, explained his choice in relation to what he felt was missing from current Extreme Metal:

> Rob: I love feedback, and that sort of thing, and drones but they [*Eyehategod*] use the sort of shit that most bands take out these days, especially with Death Metal, which is so clinical and over-produced to the point that it sounds really manufactured and lifeless. These guys were more of a punk aesthetic, they weren't fussed about production.

Rob's description of modern Death Metal as 'clinical' and 'lifeless' notably suggests it is something without feeling; or that it fails to interact with his feelings. His detachment from current genre styles and an alignment with the original styles and sounds of Extreme Metal genres' characteristics further seems to reflect his own identity as a long-term Extreme Metal fan. Music elicitation was, then, a valuable tool to engage respondents and to elicit varied and rich data. It not only gained access to the listening experience, but triggered discussion about music in relation to everyday life, fandom and subcultural participation that may not have emerged within the qualitative interview.

Undertaking music elicitation with a research group also gave me the opportunity to consider my own collective investments, judgments and attachments in relation to my personal music experiences. By taking part in the music elicitation tasks as a co-participant, I have seen my own experiences and attachments reflected by the respondents in the research group and, in effect, have realised the collective nature of aspects of my life that have before seemed personal and individual. For instance, although feelings appear private and personal, we have structures of feeling – a concept adopted from Williams' (1984) use of the term to describe a particular sense of life: the ways and experiences of community that are actively felt but hardly need expression – in common with others, seen in the similar ways in which we expressed the feelings we associated with Extreme Metal music.

Music elicitation had particular successes because it took place in the research-group context. Using music elicitation within the research group enabled my respondents to hear about other fans' perceptions of Extreme Metal and constructed a situation in which they could explain to one another, as well as the researcher, what they experienced when they listened to the music of which they were fans. The group listening experience was a shared moment in which attention was placed on the music. Music filled the room and the group listened intently, sharing the subtle physical reactions of the tapping of feet, nodding of the head, and the drumming of the beat on the leg. Talking straight after the embodied, sensory encounter may have made it easier for my respondents to explain their reactions. Moreover, because everyone had heard the music together, respondents were able to recall certain moments in the music that had effect and were able to refer to and compare their experience with one another.

As a fan, I also enjoyed listening to the music choices of the other group members, but if I had been unfamiliar with the genre, or someone who disliked it, I may have felt out of place in my negative or unaffected disposition, which may have affected the atmosphere of the group. As a member played their favourite song, they were opening themselves up to the group's scrutiny of their choice, disagreement about its effect and the sharing of their passion. Despite this, my respondents expressed their pleasure in finding out more about one another, and sharing their tastes. Their willingness to talk openly seemed aided by music elicitation creating a situation in which every member was taking part and sharing something personal. Music elicitation aided my respondents to disclose important attachments that they had never really talked about before. My respondents, of whom five out of six were male, may not have been used to talking about their feelings; yet, during music elicitation they openly spoke about their attachments to music, sometimes with embarrassment, but often with the determined goal to 'confess' what they experienced (and even the vulnerability they felt). A method like music elicitation, therefore, could offer a means to 'open up' young people, including young men, in the interview setting who may not normally wish to address the emotional and affective experiences and connections they have with music. Furthermore, music elicitation may offer one possible route to a discussion that could, in other circumstances, be difficult to have in the research field.

My undertaking of research with a group of fans meant that I needed to develop a structured way of carrying out music elicitation that enabled all group members to participate and feel included, while preventing members from dominating the task. The music elicitation tasks were an organised way of considering music in which everyone was given the opportunity to talk about their enjoyment, feelings and judgment. Such a structure did have limitations, because it prevented flowing dialogue and immediate reactions. To counter this I introduced the notebook and pen, so that thoughts could be recorded and held prior to speaking. In practice, not all of my respondents used the notebooks. When used, there was some jotting down of words that could be associated with affect in relation to the 'atmospheres' of music that were alluded to when they spoke to the group (see Figure 2.1). It is questionable how effective this technique was, but the task may have aided respondents in their recall of thoughts during music listening. By encouraging group discussion after the music elicitation exercise, members were able to reflect on their reactions and comments and further discuss their attachments to and judgments of Extreme Metal music.

Conclusion

There has been a distinct lack of consideration given to music and the relationship that the fan/subculturalist has with music in the academic study of music and youth cultures. My research was an attempt to address

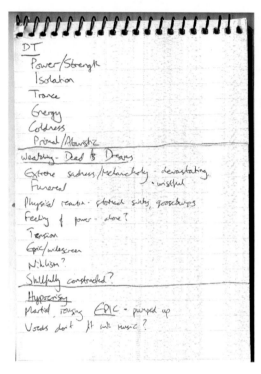

Figure 2.1   Example of notebook jottings during the music elicitation exercise

this, and music elicitation, as a method, was a means to gather data about the music relationship by focusing upon the affective music listening experience. In this chapter, I have highlighted the success of music elicitation in achieving my goal of gaining rich and thick descriptions of feelings, attachments to music and, moreover, data about being a music fan.

My use of music elicitation developed out of my curiosity about what the use of recorded music in interviews could produce. In some cases, it is only by altering and innovating methods that we can generate the data we are wanting from our research, and which will subsequently enable us to focus on aspects that have yet to be researched. Music elicitation, and indeed other forms of elicitation, are valuable devices within individual or group interviews to aid and focus the interview discussion, to trigger memories and feelings and to gain rich data from respondents. Music elicitation has particular value for social research because of the distinct qualities music offers the research process. Music is closely related to our feelings and memories and, therefore, could be used within our research to draw out data related to these elements. Moreover, music can create an atmosphere for research interaction because respondents experience the 'sharing' of something important in their lives and the auditory experience of music listening.

Music elicitation has many potential uses in youth research, because music is part of the everyday lives of young people. They are consumers of popular music, are often fans of particular music genres and also are subjected to music in their daily lives in shops, at home and through the media. Music elicitation could, therefore, aid the researching of not only attachments to music and youth cultures, but could be a route to examine the memories, attachments, relationships, identities and the everyday lives of youths. Music elicitation is particularly suited for research with young people, because it uses media that are prominent, and often important, in their everyday lives as a route to open-up and prompt the respondent about such things as their identifications, judgments, relationships, memories, thoughts and feelings. Music elicitation can change the research atmosphere and through the sensory encounter can create shared space between researcher and researched that may enhance the research interaction. There is, therefore, much potential and scope for the use of music elicitation by youth researchers.

Suggestions for Further Reading

Related methodological literature

- Batt-Rawden, K. B. (2006) 'Music – A Key to the Kingdom? A Qualitative Study of Music and Health in Relation to Men and Women with Long-term Illnesses', *Electronic Journal of Sociology* http://www.sociology.org/content/2006/tier 1/batt-rawden.html.

This article reflects on using a CD compiled by the researcher as a device in the interview.

- Keightley, E. and Pickering, M. (2006) 'For the Record: Popular Music and Phonography as Technologies of Memory', *European Journal of Cultural Studies* 9 (2), 149–65.

This article considers music's ability to hold memories and offer a route to researching memory.

- Duffy, M. and Waitt, G. (2011) 'Sound Diaries: A Method for Listening to Place', in *Aether: The Journal of Media Geography*, 7, January 2011: 119–36.

This article considers the use of audio elicitation using sound diaries (participant recorded sounds).

Examples of related youth research

- Laughey, D. (2006) *Music and Youth Culture* (Edinburgh: Edinburgh University Press).

This book gives a critique of approaches to music, youth and subculture and looks at how music interacts in young people's everyday lives.

- Malbon, B. (1999) *Clubbing: Dancing, Ecstasy and Vitality* (London: Routledge).

This book includes a consideration of the affective experiences of music and dancing in a music culture.

3
Meaningful Meanderings: Using Mobile Methods to Research Young People's Everyday Lives

Nicola J. Ross, Emma Renold, Sally Holland and Alex Hillman

Introduction

This chapter focuses on the use of mobile research methods in an ethnographic and participatory research project that explored the everyday lives of a group of young people in public care. It is informed by a broader emergent field within the social sciences – mobilities research, which focuses attention on journeys themselves as important in place-making practices, and discusses the affordances of mobile research methods in generating rich understandings of young people's everyday lives. Two different mobile methods employed in the research, 'guided' walks and car-journey interactions, are drawn upon to discuss the qualities of mobile research interactions. 'Guided' walks involved a young person walking with a researcher, leading the researcher through locales of significance to them that formed part of their everyday local geographies. The car journey interactions were generated as researchers and participants travelled together to and from designated fieldwork sites, journeys that formed part of the regular routines set up to facilitate young people's access to fortnightly project sessions. Research contexts, encounters and exchanges are explored in the chapter, and the value of utilising mobile methods is discussed in relation to the illumination of the ordinariness of the everyday when exploring young people's mundane geographies, everyday lives and localities, and in enabling young people to pace the sharing of their narratives in the exploration of more intimate or sensitive subjects.

The (Extra)ordinary Lives research project

The mobile methods discussed in this chapter formed part of the research design of a project that explored the everyday lives of a group of young people in care: '(Extra)Ordinary Lives: Children's Everyday Relationship Cultures in Public Care'. This was a demonstrator project carried out through Cardiff University's QUALITI research centre, part of the ESRC National Centre for Research Methods. Methodologically the project sought to explore the ethical and analytic issues that are potentially raised and challenged by enabling young people to choose and define their own modes of representation and authorship. Substantively it aimed to take a collaborative ethnographic approach to exploring the ordinary everyday relationship cultures, identities, social relations/networks (over time, in different spaces and contexts) of young people in care.

Young people in care, usually known in the UK as 'looked after children', are a group subject to much scrutiny, with aspects of their private lives regularly monitored and assessed. Given this context, the study aimed to create a highly flexible and creative research environment that would enable the young participants to shape research encounters, express themselves through multiple means of communication and exercise control over the representations of their lives which they generated and shared (see Holland, et al., 2008; Renold et al., 2008). Participatory methodologies were drawn upon to inform the research design (see Christensen, 2004; Gallagher and Gallagher, 2008; Holland et al., 2010).

The (Extra)Ordinary Lives project was conducted over the space of an academic year (October 2006–July 2007) and involved a team of four researchers working with eight young people, aged 10–20, six girls and two boys, all white and Welsh. Their care arrangements varied: three were in kinship care, three in foster care and two were care leavers. Contact with the young people was built around fortnightly project sessions called the 'Me, myself and I' project. It was envisaged that the 'Me, myself and I' project would involve up to 20 young people attending on a drop in basis, perhaps working with the team over a couple of months at a time. Unexpectedly, the young people who attended the initial sessions attended regularly and wanted to continue to do so. It was felt to be unethical to place limits on their attendance, whilst resource constraints meant it was not possible to expand the number of young people involved at any one time. The decision was therefore taken not to recruit more young people for the project after the initial sessions.

These sessions were designed to facilitate the development of each young person's multi-media identity project, with a range of activities made available to the young people, for example film-making, photography, music-making, drawing and craft based activities. The project sessions were supplemented by out-of-session contact, where individual researchers and young people engaged in various research activities, including 'guided' walks, trips to locations of past and present significance for young people, and research conversations held in a variety of settings, such as their homes, cafés, the university and, as will be discussed further in this chapter, in cars. An ethnography of the 'Me, Myself and I' project was simultaneously carried out, recording and exploring the possibilities and challenges of enabling the active participation of young people in the research process, from design through to dissemination.

Mobile research methods and the mobilities paradigm

Before focusing attention on the use of mobile methods to research young people's everyday lives, it is apt to firstly make brief reference to the new mobilities paradigm in the social sciences that informed their use (see Cresswell, 2006; Sheller and Urry, 2006; Büscher and Urry, 2009). The mobilities paradigm has focused attention on movement, networks, routes, flows and communications, of sensing and making sense of the world through movements, and to the ways in which mobile research methods can be utilised to understand everyday experiences through embodied, multi-sensory research experiences, where journeys themselves become the focus of interest. Journeys are constructed as dynamic, place-making practices, where movement, interactivity and the multi-sensory are foregrounded (see Thrift, 2004a; Ingold and Lee Vergunst, 2008; Ricketts, Hein et al., 2008; Fincham et al., 2010).

These current mobile research methods have connections to other earlier methods and approaches within the social sciences. For example, in childhood studies, Ward (1978) and Hart (1979) used walking with young people through their localities as a means of researching children's environments. Pink (2007a) has also discussed the practice of walking with others as a well-established technique in visual anthropology. In ethnographic studies, researchers have immersed themselves in the everyday lives of their research subjects, 'being there' and accompanying. However these earlier works often paid little direct attention to mobile research practices and the significance of the journey itself when reflecting on research contexts, unlike more recent research within the mobilities field, for example in relation to the practice of 'walking with' (see Lee and Ingold, 2006; Ingold and Lee Vergunst, 2008) or in relation to car journeys and cultures of automobility (see Bull, 2003;

Sheller, 2004; Thrift, 2004b; Laurier et al., 2008). The utilisation of mobile methods prioritises the productive effect of motion and experiential journeys in research interactions, and careful attention is paid to research relationships, contexts and engagements. It is argued that such mobile research interactions create enabling research environments, encounters and exchanges, generating time and space for participants and researchers to co-generate and communicate meaningful understandings of everyday lives (see Thrift, 2004a; Sheller and Urry, 2006; Binnie et al., 2007).

'Guided' walks

Within the social sciences of late increased attention has, then, been paid to walking within research practice as a means through which to perceive and understand research participants' everyday lives and localities (see Kusenbach, 2003; Anderson, 2004; Pink, 2007, 2008; Ingold and Lee Vergunst, 2008; Hall et al., 2008; Moles, 2008). In the (Extra)Ordinary Lives project the 'guided' walks typically involved a young person walking with a researcher, leading them through locales of significance to them that formed part of their everyday, local geographies. This allowed the young people involved to convey their movement through, and site themselves in, their everyday environments. The term 'guided' walk was used to make prominent the participant-led aspect of the research encounter but also to problematise the neat construction of one walker simply guiding another. These were co-generated research encounters, formed through, as Anderson (2004: p. 260) suggests, a 'collage of collaboration' between the participant and the researcher. These walks were usually filmed or audio recorded by the young people as part of the journey and recorded by researchers subsequently in their fieldnotes.

To illustrate the method two 'guided' walks will be referred to, one with Ryan and one with Megan, both aged 15. Each walk was located in the young person's local neighbourhood, and lasted between 45 minutes and an hour. The walks are described briefly in the following extracts from the researcher's fieldnotes written shortly after the walks were undertaken.

Experiential research interactions

Each of these journeys through the young people's everyday locales facilitated discussion of their local social and environmental relations, and of associations brought to mind by the places, people and things

'Guided' walk with Ryan

We walked across to the park and he headed for the skate park bit
of it first. A couple of boys about his age were there and we stopped
and watched them for a bit and Ryan chatted to one of the boys
he knew ... The park that we were at had a couple of open playing
fields with rugby posts up, the skate park and a children's play area
with play equipment ... We pass by a bus stop and he tells me this
is the spot where he meets his girlfriend ... As we talked about the
project and about the methods we'd used and he was saying filming
was the thing he liked best he started to tell me some more about his
own family ... He was going to see his nan this coming weekend ...
and he was looking forward to that ... Again it was the same thing,
he says a bit and then won't talk about it anymore, changing the
subject. This again I think illustrates a strength of the approach that
we're using – that as he gets to know me, he reveals details of his
family, what's important to him, what's current or changing in his
life etc. but knows he can reveal just as much as he wants to – and
that being on the move he has a ready supply of alternatives to talk
about or can orientate himself away from me to physically disrupt
the conversation. It's clear too that the things we pass on the way,
focus attention on aspects that wouldn't be discussed otherwise, or
perhaps not so readily – like the conversation about his girlfriend as
we passed the bus stop.

(Extract from Researcher's (Nicola) Fieldnotes 31st October 2006)

'Guided' walk with Megan

She checked with me about which way to go, but I said it was up to
her and that she could decide, so she said she'd take me up past the
park. We headed off again and whenever we passed anyone, she'd
tell me who they were if she knew ... She also pointed out places
she knew as we walked along, houses or areas where friends of hers
stayed, local shop, local pub, take away, old people's home, the
swimming pool, telling me where and when she was allowed to go to
these places and about restrictions placed on her use of her locality,
and fears held for certain places, the woods, the park at night. Much
of what she was saying seemed to be repetitions of messages she'd

taken on board from adults around her, often from her nan, about the woods being a dangerous place to play or to walk past because you don't know who might be there, especially when it was dark, the stranger danger fears evident, about getting older and not doing the same things as you do when you're younger ... As we chatted about these places and I asked her about the area and how long she'd lived there she started to talk more about her and her family. She talked about her relationship with her mum, saying she was both her mum's and her nan's daughter, and that she could see her mum whenever she wanted cause she just lives a few doors down the road. The two households seem quite fluid.

(Extract from Researcher's (Nicola) Fieldnotes 5th Jan 2007)

passed. The journeys allowed each of the young people to share various self-contained narratives with the researcher about their everyday lives and for the researcher to experience their localities. During the walk Ryan discussed details of his relationships with birth family, former placements, his girlfriend, activities he likes, places he hangs out and others he avoids, what subjects he likes in school, and what he thinks of the 'Me, myself and I' project and so on. Likewise for Megan the journey brought to mind narratives concerning the places she knows in her locality and her use of them, rules and restrictions placed on her negotiation of her locality, and about her relationships with her family. These research encounters were 'rooted' in the everyday present, yet they opened avenues for memories and imagined futures to be aired and explored. Through taking the walk the young people conveyed details of their negotiation of, and sited themselves in, their everyday environments. Those that undertook walks with a researcher ably communicated their intimate knowledge of their localities. Attention was drawn to favoured places, features, and to their social relations in their localities, meeting places, play spaces, friend's homes, local shops and so on, providing insights into young people's active, emotional and imaginative engagements in their localities. These were embodied, placed, and place-making interactions, research encounters on the move that heighten awareness of the experiential qualities of these journeys, the ways in which the journeys' sensory qualities communicated meaningful understandings of the young people's everyday lives and localities (see Sheller and Urry, 2006; Thrift, 2004a).

Meandering research conversations

The 'guided' walks had an unstructured, flexible format, responding to the direction and interests of the young person as they walked with the researcher through settings familiar to them. They were also characterised by various encounters, diversions and disruptions that comprised the experience of the walk. As a consequence the conversations held during the walks tended to jump around, meander, truncate, be revisited, rather than follow the set question and answer format of the semi-structured or structured interview. The free flowing movement of the walk and talk allowed the young people to share their narratives in a manner that resonated with the meanderings of everyday conversations, and importantly allowed them to pace the sharing of their narratives in an unpressurised way. Solnit (2001) suggests that the act of walking itself creates, through its pace, a passageway to perspectives, with thoughts generated in rhythm with walking, tumbling forth. The rhythm of the walk also offered potential for engagements and disengagements, walking in unison disrupted by quickening or slowing of pace, moving towards and away from each other.

The unstructured, meandering format of the 'guided' walks suited well the manner in which the younger participants in particular tended to share their narratives. It was noticeable that while Heather (aged 17) and Natalie (aged 20) were both keen and comfortable to provide long and detailed accounts of their life histories during ethnographic conversations held with a researcher, that this was not the manner in which the younger participants chose to talk with the researchers. The younger participants tended rather to provide their narratives in short bursts, and often were unresponsive to the more direct questioning that is characteristic of more formalised interviews. The older participants were much more concerned with reflecting on their life history and its significance to their current identity, providing retrospective accounts of their care history, education, relationships with family and friends and so on. The younger participants often recounted the present, sharing the immediacy of their everyday experiences and embedded talk related to their histories within this, rather than providing more coherent or chronological accounts of their lives. The method thus avoided some of the difficulties that have been encountered when using one-off interviews to research the lives of young people in care, namely a reluctance on the part of the young people to talk, to only give brief responses, or to change the subject (see McLeod, 2007).

The unstructured nature of the walks also suited well Megan's ways of communicating. She has learning difficulties and tended not to relate her narratives in a linear fashion, instead jumping from one topic to another through connections that various circumstances, events and feelings had brought to mind, providing a snapshot view of her world through what could be at times somewhat confusing, splintered narratives (see also Holland et al., 2008). The experience of the walk and the people, places and things passed, provided a framework to which Megan, and the other young people, could attach their narratives. In the following extract, from the transcript of the audio recording of the walk, Megan talks about her relationship with her mum, family stories and remembered events, interspersed with talk relating to the journey being made.

Megan:	I spend more time with my cousins than my mum, my sister and my mum's ex-boyfriend, weird yeah? But our mum's our nan's daughter.
Nicola:	Yeah.
...	
Nicola:	So does your mum live close by then?
Megan:	Ah. Yeah ten doors down.
Nicola:	Oh, that's handy.
Megan:	Yeah, whenever I want my mum I just run straight over. What's it, when I was a little baby yeah, I'll tell you a story about me. Just go straight across there and we'll just come up onto the other pavement. I'll tell you a little story about me yeah. When I was little I was in bed crying, yeah, cause I wanted to get out and there was nothing else to do. I didn't have anything on me, yeah, to put in my mouth. No, just walk around this, go this way. What was it? And then after that my nan gave me some for my mouth to shut me up. I still wasn't (inaudible) so I thought, this was when I was about two, started to crawl. I thought get out of my bed. I fell out of my bed in the morning. Get out of my bed, next minute downstairs I go. Next minute out of the door and over to my mum's. My nan phoned my mum 'Is Megan there?' 'Yeah, she's fast asleep.' Me up on the settee asleep. Cause I was crying all night. I still won't forget that. Another thing, Jodie got bit by a swan.

Nicola:	Really?
Megan:	Trying to give it bread (inaudible).
Nicola:	Watch the cars.
Megan:	(Inaudible) There's another story that I was going to
Nicola:	So do you never use the underpass for crossing the roads then?
Megan:	No. I use this but the only thing when I get caught I can't use it
Nicola:	Yeah.
Megan:	Cause my nan won't know (inaudible).
Nicola:	So why don't you use the underpass then?
Megan:	Can't be arsed to walk up hills.
...	
Nicola:	And watch for the cars. Yeah, we'll just wait here until it's passed. Okay, we can cross over now. Do you want to cross now?
Megan:	No, 'cause I'm walking down here.
Nicola:	Ah, we're walking on this side.
Megan:	Don't worry about that side! We'll get home alright, don't worry.
	(Transcript of extract from audio recording of guided walk)

Disruptions and diversions

Towards the end of the extract shown above from the walk with Megan disruptive interventions by the researcher become more apparent, curtailing narratives that Megan wants to share, as the researcher increasingly raises safety concerns regarding the route being taken. At this point they were walking on a grassy bank that ran alongside a busy main road, very muddy and wet after a heavy downpour. The researcher's perceptions of immediate risks impact on the research interactions, closing down the narrative being shared by Megan, and leading to a questioning and redirecting of the route being taken. However, Megan, alert to the researcher's anxiety, counters this by drawing upon her knowledge of her local area to reassure the researcher that she is familiar with their route and that they will get home safely. The mobile research encounters were interspersed with such disruptions. Space for narratives to be shared was opened up, closed down, diverted, and revisited in response to the negotiation of these shared experiential journeys. This led to certain narratives being lost, although the disruptions also served to divert conversations towards other topics, here road safety, and discussion of rules which Megan's family had laid down, and as demonstrated, were often not adhered to by Megan.

As is evident in this extract, these were not encounters recorded in the quiet of indoor, private spaces, but the conversations were situated within the commotion of the journey, and recordings of the soundscapes of the route sometimes made inaudible the conversations held. Lack of clarity regarding what was said on occasion was characteristic of the recordings, although some of these narratives lost in the audio recordings were noted in the researcher's fieldnotes written shortly afterwards. However, as will be discussed later in relation to the car journey interactions, the recordings of the soundscapes of the routes taken generated insights into the young people's everyday environments, and should not be viewed simply as noise pollution (see also, Hall et al., 2008).

Car journey interactions

Continuing the discussion on the qualities of mobile research encounters, attention is now focused on the car journey interactions that took place as researchers transported the young people to and from the fortnightly 'Me, Myself and I' project sessions. These journeys were not originally envisaged as being part of the data generation stage of the project, but just a necessary means of enabling young people to attend the project sessions. However, relatively quickly, it became clear that these journeys were important in themselves not only in terms of the sharing of information of relevance to the substantive aims of the project, but also in terms of research interactions between researchers and participants.

Unlike the 'guided' walks that were generally undertaken only once with each young person, the car journeys took place on a fortnightly basis, with set routines established over time. One of the researchers would usually arrange to collect and drop off the same young person for each project session. These routines repeated over time, meant that closer relationships were formed between certain of the young people and researchers during this one-to-one contact time, each becoming increasingly familiar with the other. Laurier (2002) has referred to car journey conversations as 'copresent immersion' where the researcher is there with the participant within the mode of movement and employing a range of observation, interviewing, and recording techniques. When the importance of the car journeys to the (Extra)Ordinary Lives project was recognised the young people were invited to audio record the journeys if and when they wished. It is important to note here that it was the young people who controlled the digital recorder, switching it on and off as they wished, sometimes listening back to and even deleting recordings made during the journey. These journeys, as with other research interactions, were also recorded in researchers' fieldnotes written up shortly afterwards. The audio recording of these journeys became a routine aspect for some of the young people. These interactions were characterised by narratives of the near and present, centring very much upon what was going on in the young people's lives at that moment, such as events that had occurred in school that day. Yet the conversations were also interspersed with memories and thoughts that were brought to mind by the people, places and things passed during the journey. The experiences of one young person, Cerys (aged 13), will be drawn upon here to further discuss the method.

Moving between the mundane and the personal

It was evident that talk of interest to our substantive research themes was set within the more everyday car talk of routes and directions, the mundane talk of driving and passengering. Given that the main purpose of the car journey was to transport the young person, and not to hold an interview, the car journey offered a choice to the young person, on when to talk and share details of their everyday life with the researcher, from extended accounts, to snippets of information. Generally the shortest or most easily negotiable route was taken between pick up and drop off points (usually young people's homes/schools and the project session location), but while en route there were opportunities for the young people to share their knowledge of their city with the researchers. There was scope for some diversions to be made, passing by places of importance to the young person. Illustrative of this, is the following extract from the transcript of a car journey conversation with Cerys and a researcher. Cerys has led the researcher to believe she knows a short cut to take on the route home. Instead she capitalises on the researcher's lack of knowledge of this part of the city to direct them past a care home that she used to live in.

Cerys:	We are going up there.
Emma:	Where?
Cerys:	Up there.
Emma:	Are you sure?
Cerys:	Yes.
Emma:	Oh right I trust you. I have got no maps, if we get lost we are completely lost.
Cerys:	We are not going to get lost, I used to live by here.
Emma:	Oh right. Are you sure?
...	
Cerys:	Keep going, oh my god I haven't been by here before in ages. There is my house, that is my house there, on the left. Who is in my room please? Hold on. Who is in my room? Go on a minute, I want to see if anyone is in my room ... Can I call in? That's my key worker.
Emma:	No we can't really.
Cerys:	Right, I'll shout then. There is my room now, there, WHO'S IN MY ROOM? GET OUT OF MY ROOM, get out of my room. Just go.
Emma:	We can come back again though, we just haven't got time tonight.
Cerys:	She is in my room, someone is in my room, they are in my room, Em, They are in my room now, Em. I am going to kill them.
Emma:	Now where the hell are we?
Cerys:	Just go straight.
Emma:	Will it take us back out to that road?
Cerys:	Em, they are in my room, Em they are in my room, Emma.
Emma:	Do you still see it as your room?

Cerys:	Yes, they are in my room Em, Em (laughs) No! Right we are going up and then right, R I G H T, right, we are going right now. Now you can find your way?
Emma:	This is the main, is this back on that road again?
Cerys:	Yes.
Emma:	Are you sure?
Cerys:	Let's just go
	(Transcript of extract from audio recording of car conversation)

This sequence was later adapted and formed part of a short animated film, *Place in me* (Soyinka, 2008), made by a local film maker who worked with the research team. It addressed the theme of geographies of belonging, looking at young people's attachment to place. As the still from the film demonstrates (Figure 3.1), this was one technique used by the research team to relate the young people's narratives to a wider audience in an engaging, yet non-identifying manner, a topic that will be discussed further later.

The car journey allowed Cerys to visit a location of significance to her and share some details about what this journey meant to her with the researcher, in the moment. At the time the researcher thought that Cerys wanted to re-visit and re-connect with her past. However, following the sharing of further information by Cerys at a later date, the significance of the journey to Cerys' situation at the time became more apparent. Cerys was at risk of being permanently excluded from school and if she had been excluded this would have jeopardised her foster placement. The journey past Cerys' former care home then became more meaningful, as somewhere to which she may have to return, a subject which was then revisited and elaborated on further during later conversations between Cerys and the researcher. The car journey interactions were characterised by such disjointed narratives, that were reflected on and made sense of by the researcher afterwards when reviewing the recordings made and in subsequent discussions held with the young people involved. The longevity of the project, taking place over an academic year, facilitated this process, allowing the individual narratives to be linked and creating more detailed insights into the young people's everyday lives.

Figure 3.1 Still from 'Place in me' (2008) Copyright 2008 Bambo Soyinka

The productivity of motion, commotion and distractedness

It was apparent that the need to be an attentive driver necessitated that the researcher be a distracted contributor to the conversation at times. As the extract shown above demonstrates, the researcher's concern with driving, not getting lost and the route being taken, intersperses with the dialogue that Cerys is sharing about her former care home, the experience of the journey informing and disrupting the conversation. While curtailing exploration of the topic in that moment, such lack of an intense focus on the talk itself, unlike the context of more structured interviews held in stillness in a fixed location, was key in enabling the young people to share their stories at their own pace. Such distractedness made disengagements from a research conversation simpler. The car setting also meant there was little direct eye contact as participant and researcher sat side by side, rather than facing each other as in more traditional interview contexts. Physical distance could be created by orientations of the body, looking out the window, leaning forward to use the in-car stereo, looking down to play with a handheld game or mobile phone, and so on.

Others have also noted the context of car journey interactions as having a beneficial effect on the holding of conversations that may be difficult or awkward to articulate in quieter, fixed locations, where the gaps and pauses in dialogue may appear too weighty (see Ferguson, 2008; Laurier et al., 2008). The noise, movement and the multitude of visual stimuli, and other sensory cues that comprise embodied shared journeys can be used to productive effect to aid the sharing of intimate narratives, the ready availability of alternative sounds filling the void created by the ending of a conversation, avoiding any potentially awkward silences (see Ross et al., 2009; Hall et al., 2008). In this manner, motion, commotion and distractedness proved productive elements of mobile research encounters and supported well the project's participatory aims, of working collaboratively with the young people to allow them to generate, in their own time, their own representations of their everyday lives.

Guarding the personal

Careful attention was given to the different ways in which the young people communicated their engagement and disengagement with the research project, particularly given the informal nature of many of the research interactions and the resultant slippage between research context and social context (see Hillman et al., 2008; Renold et al., 2008). We were keen to ensure that the young people were mindful that they were participating in a research project, and that what they shared with the research team in more informal moments was intended to be recorded, either by audio-visual equipment used or in researcher's fieldnotes. For example, during the car journey interactions Cerys revealed much about her everyday life. Indeed she sometimes appeared somewhat blasé about the sharing of information about her life and this was at times a concern for the researcher who had formed the closest bond in the project with her. The concern was that Cerys was not reflecting on, nor placing limits on, what she was revealing of herself and her life to the research team during the car journeys. However, when this issue was raised and discussed it was evident that Cerys was consciously drawing a boundary around what she shared and what remained private, as the extract overleaf from the researcher's fieldnotes discusses.

At other times Cerys used more diversionary means to avoid subjects she was not prepared to discuss, through for example playing music at volume during the car journeys, changing the subject, physically distancing herself from the researcher, or simply by ignoring the question. While a loss for the substantive concerns of the project, such markers were positive indications that the young people involved were able

> I bring out the transcript of the car conversation to show Cerys what we are doing with the conversations we do have in the car. She reads it and begins to comment on some of the things we said. 'oh I remember this' – she doesn't add much, but seems to enjoy reflecting back ... Interestingly, at this moment the issue of privacy is raised again ... we talk about Cerys writing song lyrics and I say I'd love to see them (in the car conversation – I think). 'Some things are just private tho' she says and relates this to personal bits of her life that she doesn't want to share and I have to say, that this really comforted me, because I have been concerned at times, that Cerys lets me read her life like an open book – I actually think now that she reflects quite a lot on what exactly she'll let me and other know about her and her life and she is very considered in this.
> (Extract from Researcher's (Emma) Fieldnotes 25th April 2007)

to assert and define their own limits to engagement with the project, supporting the project's participatory ends.

Mobile methods, multi-sensory data and multi-media recordings

At this point in the discussion of methods used in the mobile research, it is pertinent to focus attention more directly on the recordings of these research encounters. As mentioned, a range of different recording means were used. The young people generated various audio-visual recordings; transcripts were derived from these, researchers generated fieldnotes of research interactions, and notes were taken of analysis and discussion as a team of the various data records.

The excerpt from the researcher's fieldnotes shown in the previous section draws attention to an important aspect in the ethical approach used – that of transparency. It is illustrative of interactions with the young people regarding the data being generated. All of the data recordings were generated with the young people's consent, many recorded by the young people themselves, and regular reference was made to the existence of these data records, the different media within which they existed, and to how these were utilised, as a team.

The different means of recording drew attention to what is captured, and to what is lost when representing research experiences in data records. The multi-sensory data of the field, the sights, sounds, movement, rhythm, emotion and feel of these research encounters, and the affordances of the media in translating these into data records were all of interest (see Dicks et al., 2006). However, in the transcribing process much of this multi-sensory data captured in the audio-visual data records was overlooked. For example, transcripts of the mobile research interactions centred attention on what was said during the conversations that were held, omitting reference to much of the soundscape within which these conversations were set, and the attributes of the voices in conveying meaning, the pitch, tone, intonations and so on. However as Hall et al. (2008) remind us, in eliminating these everyday soundscapes we eliminate the sounds of the place and the potential of sound to inform qualitative inquiry (see also Bull and Back, 2008).

In the outputs from the (Extra)Ordinary Lives project attempts have been made to integrate the different media and to utilise innovative ways to address ethical concerns that using participant-generated audio-visual material creates. For instance, maintaining the anonymity of participants and research locations is problematic when using visual material. There are issues to consider regarding the format in which images can be presented and the different audiencing of them. The fleeting glance that is gained during a presentation is a very different context to the more lasting imprint of images in web-based or text-based resources. In the (Extra)Ordinary Lives project, specialised software was used to create cartoonised versions of some of the visual material to protect the anonymity of participants. As mentioned, a local filmmaker also produced a series of short films and animations based on some of the young people's narratives that have been used in dissemination activities. Further stills from one of these films, *Place in me*, are shown below (Figures 3.2 and 3.3). These represent another young person's narratives, on belonging and attachment to place, accounts derived from a 'guided' walk undertaken around places she valued in her locality. The experience of the walk conveyed the importance of nature, wildlife and animals to her, her strong attachment to the family dog, and her locally based social relations that her kinship placement had been able to maintain.

These approaches to dealing with confidentiality and anonymity proved popular with the young people involved in the study, and were more engaging and playful than other means of anonymising material, such as blurring, pixelating or blacking out of faces, actions which can sometimes engender negative or criminal connotations. They allowed representations of the young people's lives to be aired publicly while creating visual or narrative distance from the individual young people involved in the project (see Wiles et al., 2008).

Figure 3.2   Still from 'Place in me' (2008) Copyright 2008 Bambo Soyinka

Figure 3.3   Still from 'Place in me' (2008) Copyright 2008 Bambo Soyinka

Conclusion

The mobile methods used in the (Extra)Ordinary Lives project proved productive both in terms of data generation in relation to the project's substantive aims and in supporting the participatory aims of the research. As the discussion of the two methods demonstrates, though different in format the 'guided' walks and car journey interactions held similarities. Both centred research engagements in the everyday present of young people's lives and localities, generating insights into their local geographies and identities. The journeys allowed each of the young people to share various self contained narratives with the researcher about their everyday lives and allowed the researcher to experience their localities. They were well suited in particular to the ways in which the younger participants related their narratives, their unstructured, meandering format providing a plethora of stimuli for conversations and allowing topics to be changed readily. They generated much rich material on young people's everyday lives, the walks contributing espe-cially to understandings of the young people's social and environmental relationships, and the car journey interactions providing much on what was current in their lives. In these mobile research encounters motion and commotion were used to productive effect, as the shared journeys, as perceived and experienced, generated assemblages of connections, understandings, closeness, distance and diversions. This context aided the development of research relationships by allowing young people to control the pacing and sharing of their narratives about their everyday lives, and in defining their own limits to their engagement with the project, supporting well the project's participatory ends.

The substantive and participatory aims of the project as a whole were subject to scrutiny through the ethnography undertaken, reflecting not only on the material generated, but also paying attention to the con-texts in which it was generated, to relationships between researchers and young people, and to young people's group interactions. Important to the participatory approach used was that the young people not only exercised choice over how they created representations of their lives through use of the different activities on offer, such as film making, photography, music making, craft-based activities, 'guided' walks, car journey interactions and interviews, but also that they exercised con-trol over the use of their outputs by the research team during analysis and in the wider audiencing of materials. Thus the young people's involvement was not limited to data generation, it continued through to analysis and dissemination activities. The methods used facilitated a rich understanding of the young people's everyday lives and provided insights into the ethics and power relations of participatory research of this kind (see Holland, et al., 2010; Renold et al., 2008). The research did not seek to make generalisations about the lives of young people in care. Instead, by focusing in-depth, over the course of a year, on the experiences of a small group of young people, the research provided nuanced accounts of the intricacies and complexities of these young people's lives.

Suggestions for further reading

Related methodological literature

• Fincham, B., McGuinness, M. and Murray, L. (eds) (2010) *Mobile Methodologies* (Basingstoke: Palgrave Macmillan).

This edited collection covers key debates within the mobilities paradigm and mobile research practices.

• Ingold, T. and Lee Vergunst, J. (eds) (2008) *Ways of Walking: Ethnography and Practice on Foot* (Aldershot: Ashgate).

This is an edited collection of ethnographic work on walking as research method with discussions on embodiment, place and materiality.

• Ricketts Hein, J., Evans, J. and Jones, P. (2008) 'Mobile Methodologies: Theory, Technology and Practice', *Geography Compass*, 2 (5) 1266–85.

Ricketts Hein et al. provide an overview of mobile methodologies, mobile research methods, and discussion of new technologies for the field.

Examples of related youth research

• Chase, E., Simon, A. and Jackson, S. (eds) (2006) *In Care and After: A Positive Perspective* (London: Routledge).

This edited collection brings together a number of studies exploring the experiences of young people in care and of care leavers.

• Holloway, S. L., and Valentine, G. (eds) (2000) *Children's Geographies: Playing, Living, Learning* (London: Routledge).

This is a collection of studies on the geographies of children and young people, which emphasises spatialities in childhood and youth studies.

- Luckock, B. and Lefevre M. (eds) (2008) *Direct Work: Social Work with Children and Young People in Care*, London: BAAF.

Luckock and Lefevre's collection discusses experiences of working with children and young people in care.

4

The Use of Mental Maps in Youth Research: Some Evidence from Research Exploring Young People's Awareness of and Attachment to Place

Richard J. White and Anne E. Green

Introduction

The rising interest in children's and young people's geographies in recent years has led to broader and deeper insights being made into their lives. These insights have further unravelled the complex meanings, frameworks, identities and subjective relationships that children and young people have in relation to place and space (see James, 1990; Matthews and Limb, 1999; Young and Barrett, 2001; Ross 2007). The additional emphasis on exploring the subjective as well as objective relationships that young people have to space and place has been recognised as highly significant; not least as it promises to reveal a more holistic understanding of space and place. As Reay and Lucey (2000: 410) observe: 'Experiences of places and spaces are structured in all sorts of ways by broader social power relations, which include race, class and age as well as gender.' From a methodological perspective, the focus on exploring and understanding young people's relationships with space and place has seen a range of innovative and mobile methods and approaches being employed to complement or replace more traditional approaches to research (such as questionnaires, interviews and focus groups). Many of these 'new' approaches have focused on utilising young people's written, oral and visual skills. Some of the most notable research in this field has incorporated mapwork exercises, self-directed photography, writings, drawings and commentaries (Ross, 2007); mental maps, thematic and non-thematic drawings, photo diaries and daily time lines (Young and Barratt, 2001); and qualitative applications of geographical information systems (GIS) (Dennis, 2006). Against this

58

background, and drawing critically on a recent research project undertaken with young people in the UK, this chapter explores the relevance, implementation and findings that can be derived from mental mapping. We argue that this method should be seen as an important tool of enquiry in youth research focused on urban spaces.

At the outset it is worthwhile trying to establish a working understanding of what mental maps are. In much of the literature, the concepts of 'mental' maps and 'cognitive' maps are used interchangeably (Murray and Spencer, 1979; Soini, 2001) and can 'be thought of as a marriage between spatial and environmental cognition' (Kitchen, 1994: 1). Similarly, Ley (2009: 455) considers mental maps to be 'mental constructs that were seen as intervening between geographical settings and human action'. Elsewhere Soini (2001: 226) finds it appropriate to define mental mapping by considering the qualities that distinguish this technique from concept mapping. She argues that 'mental mapping always has spatial connections, whereas concept mapping is purely related to conceptual structures and processing of landscape'. Downs and Stea (1977: 6) consider cognitive mapping as abstractions of a person's spatial environment:

> Most importantly, a cognitive map is a cross section representing the world at one instant in time. It reflects the world *as some person believes it to be*; it need not be correct. In fact, distortions are highly likely. It is your understanding of the world, and it may only faintly resemble the world as reflected in cartographic maps or color photographs.

The drawing of mental or cognitive maps of particular spaces and places can be traced back to the 1960s (e.g. Lynch, 1960; Gould and White, 1968) and 1970s (Goodchild, 1974; Gould and White, 1974; Lee, 1970; Pocock, 1976; Murray and Spencer, 1979). More contemporary examples of research that have included as part of their wider methodological approach the technique of mental mapping are also evident. For example Leonard (2006: 1120) in focusing on the story-telling process of teenagers growing up in North Belfast, asked her respondents to 'construct geographical maps of their typical movements in a typical week' and used these to inform some of the content that was considered within focus groups. Elsewhere Reay and Lucey (2000), in a study focusing on children in inner city council estates, sought to uncover the spatial imaginings, which inform about children's relationships to local geography, their orientations to mobility and associated spatial horizons.

However, despite some further notable exceptions (e.g. Smith and Ford, 1985; Quinn, 1986; Kitchen, 1994; Green et al., 2005), the use of mental mapping is still under-used in the broader design, conduct and analysis of social-science research generally, including in research focused on young people. This oversight is unfortunate on many levels. Whether used as a standalone method, or more powerfully (as argued here) as a complementary one, mental maps can be used effectively to add considerable depth and clarity to research focused on young people. The method is particularly revealing for understanding the subjective relationships (e.g. perceptions, attitudes and experiences) that people have towards the objective spatial world(s) they inhabit, and which shape their behaviour. It may well also lead to exciting and innovative methodological developments. Dennis (2006), for example, suggests that mental maps do not have to be simply employed as methods to 'reveal' apolitical spatial representations of place and space, but they could be employed to inform policy and practice at the local level. To this end Dennis (2006) explicitly desires the incorporation of young people's qualitative appraisals of their environment into forms amenable to a neighbourhood-indicator GIS. In this way the use of qualitative GIS

> may open up an important space for youth participation in politi-
> cal processes beyond their immediate community, with important
> implications for their civic engagement.
>
> (Dennis, 2006: 2041)

However, the *appropriate* use of mental maps demands an awareness of some of the limitations associated with the method. Gillespie (2010: 19) argues:

> Many of the disadvantages of mental mapping are based on the diffi-
> culty of portraying a three-dimensional landscape in two dimensions.
> Drawing measures more than just the sketcher's spatial understand-
> ing of the environment ... It is also a physical and creative process
> that involves many variables and potential drawbacks in transferring
> one's mental map to a piece of drawing paper.

Elsewhere Pocock (1976: 493–4) suggests that the simplicity of approaches to mental mapping mask over what is a quite complicated and complex undertaking:

> Although the respondent is invited to undertake a free recall, a map-
> ping exercise, in fact, imposes a general filter on the individual's
> information store. In short the response is constrained to physical

attributes of the environment, and even then – annotation apart – to those items which are *mappable*. Moreover although the technique minimizes intrusion by the researcher, it is important to realize that the instructional set determines which aspects of the mappable information are elicited or emphasised. Even the size or shape of paper, for instance, can induce bias to the result.

These limitations, however, when adjusted for, do not undermine the significance, relevance, or 'added value' that mental maps – incorporated within an expanded methodological repertoire – can bring to youth research. The use of mental maps can be seen as an effective end in itself, or as a means to other complementary ends; for example, in encouraging individuals or groups to reflect in more detail about their attitudes, aspirations and behaviour in relation to places or institutions.

Reflecting on a range of relevant experiences and outcomes that emerged through harnessing mental maps within a specific recent UK-based research project, this chapter critically addresses the design, implementation and outcomes of the method and outlines how it was used to help inform and direct the principal findings of the research. The aims of the research project from which the evidence is derived focused heavily on exploring the horizons, in both social and spatial terms, of young people from three deprived New Deal for Communities (NDC) neighbourhoods. In addition to considering the ways mental mapping techniques added a more innovative and creative dimension to the research, the chapter also problematises the technique before presenting some conclusions and implications.

The 'attachment to place' research project

Overview

There has been a longstanding desire within academic and policy-making communities and among practitioners across a range of domains, to engage successfully with the complex intersections of people and place, particularly in the context of high levels of economic deprivation and social exclusion. In seeking better to understand the relationship between people and place, a key objective of policy has been to transform the prospects of disadvantaged places through appropriate policy interventions. Such normative thinking brings the role of *geography*, and how geography plays a central role in influencing the decision-making process of individuals, families and communities, firmly into the foreground. For example, in what ways might a young person's geographical knowledge influence the jobs or further education opportunities they perceive to be appropriate and accessible to them? This question in turn draws attention towards the problematic relationship between objective and subjective factors of influence, and how they operate to influence an individual's decision-making processes. Are subjective values and aspirations more likely to constrain, or enable, the behaviour of young people? How are aspirational and geographical horizons constrained, and how do these close down or open up the range of opportunities people consider relevant to them? And, more fundamentally, what do people's perceptions of space look like and how do they match up with reality?

These, and similar, questions have been seen as particularly important ones to explore in the context of young people, and there is evidence of some researchers having used mental maps to respond to these themes. For example, through focusing on school leavers in Birmingham, Quinn (1986) demonstrated how the perceptions of young people were a central influence when deciding where opportunities to work existed. In Quinn's research, focusing on knowledge of bus routes in Birmingham, mental maps indicated that perceived job opportunities were a subset of actual job opportunities.

This chapter is focused on the evidence and experience that was gained from a research project commissioned by the Joseph Rowntree Foundation: *Attachment to Place: Social Networks, Mobility and Prospects of Young People* (Green and White, 2007). Our research was guided by two main aims: (i) to investigate the role of social networks and attachment to place in shaping the attitudes, aspirations and behaviour of young people from deprived areas in accessing post-compulsory education, training and work; and (ii) to identify whether young people's horizons need spatial/social widening, and what opportunities and policies would be helpful in 'widening horizons' in order to improve their prospects as people in deprived places. This research aimed, then, to provoke deeper insights into the relationship between the relative (im)mobility of young people and the role of place attachment. More explicitly, the research explored how social networks and attachment to place shape young people's attitudes towards education, training and work opportunities. The young people at the heart of this research were aged between 15 and 23 years, and came from three regeneration areas in Hull, Walsall and Wolverhampton. The choice of these three specific deprived neighbourhoods allowed the research to compare and contrast the relationships that young people's aspirations had within broadly similar geographical and socio-economic contexts.

The rationale for focusing on young people in the study was that the decisions and actions they take (or are likely to take) concerning education, training and/or employment at this early stage will have tremendous importance in shaping their later trajectories. The young people who were part of the research had a wide range of experiences, 'starting positions' and 'life-worlds'. Some were in the final stages of compulsory schooling, while others were continuing at school post-16, or were studying at college (full-time or part-time) for further qualifications or were in higher education. Other young people were involved in employment, apprenticeships or work placements. Finally, some of the young people were NEET (ie not in education, employment or training).

The findings emerging from the research were used to explore the scope for interventions to help 'widen horizons' to enhance access to opportunities for further/higher education, training and employment for young people, and discuss what form such initiatives should take in order to do this successfully. Hence, it was deemed important to engage with young people from 'where they were at' and to understand how they see their locality, the wider urban area and the opportunities available to them.

The place of mental maps in the overall research design

As noted above, the central focus of the research in the three case-study neighbourhoods was to explore the subjective attitudes, aspirations and experiences of young people towards attachment to place and its relationship to current or future education, training and labour market prospects. Mental maps were employed as a *complementary method* and used in conjunction with survey, focus groups, and individual face-to-face interviews with young people. Given the focus of this chapter, the survey approach and interviews are outlined in brief to set the broader context of the research methodology in its entirety, while the mental map exercise, which was introduced and carried out as part of a focus group exercise within the three neighbourhoods, is elaborated in greater detail. These approaches were supplemented by additional one-to-one interviews with key stakeholders in the case study areas.

The survey of young people

A guided, structured self-completion questionnaire was completed in each of the three case study areas by approximately 60 young people. These young people were recruited purposively via schools, colleges, youth groups and community workers in each of the neighbourhoods.

Around half of respondents were in their final year at school or were in their first year of post-compulsory schooling. In each of the three areas just over half of the respondents were male. The ethnic mix of interviewees broadly reflected the ethnic mix of young people in the neighbourhoods concerned: nearly all of the respondents in the Hull and Walsall neighbourhoods were of White British origin, while in Wolverhampton the ethnic mix of respondents was much more diverse. The questionnaire collected information on individual characteristics, current economic position and future intentions, patterns of mobility and use of transport, links to and attitudes towards the local area, job search and sources of information, job locations and employment aspirations. The survey provided extremely useful illustrative information on broad baseline patterns across the case study areas and, importantly, was complemented by much more detailed qualitative information harnessed by other methods, particularly individual face-to-face interviews and focus groups.

Focus groups

The mental mapping exercise was introduced and undertaken as part of the focus group element of the research project. As such, the conduct of the focus groups is explored in more detail following this overview of the main methodological approaches used in the project. Four focus groups were held in each case study area, each having between four and eight respondents. The main contribution of the focus group was to explore in more detail the key subjective perceptions and experiences that young people had toward their neighbourhoods and the wider urban environment. This included a focus on their attitudes toward the local area; their attachment to the local area; their knowledge of local employment opportunities; an exploration of the key factors that influenced their job search behaviour; the key barriers (if any) to mobility that they faced; what they felt were the dominant employer attitudes towards their age group and their local area; what future plans they had towards education, training and employment; and whether they felt that 'getting on' meant 'getting out' of their local area. The participants in the focus groups were recruited from those who were involved in the young people's survey.

Individual face-to-face interviews

In order to gain a rich and detailed analysis of social networks, and the attitudes, perceptions, experiences and future plans of the young people, at least eight individual face-to-face interviews were undertaken in each case study area. The interviewees were selected mainly from the focus groups. A particular commitment to include older respondents with more post-school experience was exercised here, in order to bring their greater knowledge, experiences and insights of life beyond full-time education, to complement the views of those who were younger – especially those who were still at school, college or on training courses.

Other key sources of information

The information gained from the survey, the focus groups and the individual face-to-face interviews with young people was supplemented with around ten one-to-one interviews with key stakeholders in each case study area. Those interviewed included local employers, public transport providers and community organisations, representatives from the education sector, providers of youth worker training, as well as representatives of Jobcentre Plus and associated delivery organisations. These interviews explored a diverse range of relevant topics, including the changing nature of the employment market; recruitment/selection practices and whether these might disadvantage young people from deprived neighbourhoods; and the main barriers to employment faced by the local population.

   In our final report, we argued that, taken together, the different methodological techniques which were adopted provided rich insights into how subjective behavioural factors intermesh with objective opportunities in influencing choices made by young people about whether and which education, training and job opportunities are sought where, when and why (Green and White, 2007).

Drawing mental maps as one element of the focus group discussions

An aide memoire was used to ensure that each focus group was approached in a consistent and transparent way. Following a welcome to all respondents, a brief introduction to the researchers and to the Joseph Rowntree Foundation was made, and the aims of the project were presented in a clear and accessible way. The respondents were told that the researchers were interested in (i) how attached individuals feel to the place where they live and whether they would like to move elsewhere; (ii) whether their family, friends and other people they associate with are all from the local area; (iii) what people know about other parts of the city and other places, and whether and how often they go there; (iv) what (if anything) stops them from travelling further afield; and (v) their prospects of finding employment locally/elsewhere. It was also stressed to the respondents that all (their) opinions, perceptions and experiences were valid, and counted equally (i.e. there were no right or wrong ways in which to answer the questions).

In order to provide a gradual introduction to the focus group session and to encourage the respondents to gain a sense of familiarity and confidence early on, as well as to allow the researchers appropriate insight into the background of the participants, the researchers went around the group asking them to say their first name, where they lived, how long they had lived there, and one good thing and one bad thing about the area (writing the 'positives' and 'negatives' on a flip-chart). The focus group discussion was then based around a series of pre-determined themes and questions. The first section drew on perceptions of the local area (neighbourhood) and the city, both of local residents and people from outside the local area, and whether local residents were likely to suffer area discrimination in accessing employment. Participants were also asked what area they thought of as the 'local area'; what they knew about other parts of the city; and what other parts of the city they went to, and how often. The second section focused more specifically on jobs in the local area, including what they expected to get from a job; the sorts of jobs available in the local area and wider city, and whether these were jobs they wanted to do; barriers local people faced in getting work, and what qualities they thought employers sought when recruiting young people.

Importantly, though the suggested content helped to achieve a level of consistency between the focus groups in Hull, Walsall and Wolverhampton (in order to facilitate comparisons between the areas), it was not introduced in a fixed and dogmatic way. Rather, allowance was made for the possibility of 'new' additional insights and questions to be suggested that were relevant from within the focus group, and were not addressed or accommodated by the guiding framework.

Having established and explored the opening selection of themes highlighted with the group, it was felt that it would be refreshing from a strategic perspective to introduce a break from the routine question-and-answer dialogue at this point, and it was here that the mental map exercise was introduced. It was important to give the respondents clear and consistent instructions for undertaking this method. Having provided each participant with A3 sheets of paper, and a selection of pencils and pens of different colours, the researchers addressed the group and asked participants to attempt to draw a rough sketch map of Hull/Walsall/Wolverhampton as they knew it. Starting with their own area (and marking their home), respondents were asked to include as many areas and as much detail as they could possibly draw. Anticipating the wide spectrum of artistic ability and inclination, it was stressed from the very beginning that this was not an art exercise, and that we were not expecting perfect drawings; rather the interest was in the 'content' and not the 'beauty' of the maps. This reflects the instructions offered in previous exercises in which individuals have been asked to draw mental maps.

The participants were asked to sketch on their map, and to label, their school, college and/or place of work, the services that they used (e.g. shops, youth clubs, sports grounds), and anything else that helped them find their way around – for example, generally well-known landmarks, roads, paths, rivers or districts of the city. So first of all the participants entered what Lynch (1960) termed the 'skeleton phase' of drawing a mental map, in which most of the important information, objects, direction, names and paths are recorded. Using coloured pens or by writing notes on the map the respondents were also invited to make distinctions between the areas that they knew well, and identify any areas that they felt were unsafe and/or that they would fear to go to. This marks Lynch's (1960) second phase of drawing a mental map, which puts the flesh on the sketch by linking between memories with information and description, so enriching the maps.

During this process the researchers took the opportunity to go around the group and speak with the participants on a one-to-one basis about their emerging maps. This interaction was an important part of the exercise, and added value to the role of the maps not simply as ends in themselves, but as a valuable means to allow the researchers to develop a more nuanced and detailed understanding of the participants' relationships to their map. Where relevant, participants were asked to clarify aspects of their map; talk about how they knew about certain areas/jobs/opportunities; why they felt areas to be unsafe; what kind of transport they used to get around; what kind of experiences they had had in relation to employment, training, and/or further education, and where these were (on the map). At this stage participants both added to their maps and also adjusted and critiqued them.

Once the maps had been completed, with the names written on the back, the maps became a focus for general discussion in order to generate wider conversations and debate within the group. The participants were encouraged to talk about and compare their sketch maps, perhaps by focusing on some of the key similarities/differences between the mental maps; their contrasting knowledge of the city; and what areas they thought they would like to work in (or live in).

The focus group then turned to consider three remaining themes: getting jobs in the local area and beyond; exploring limits of travel-to-work; information sources used for job search; and future residential mobility intentions. They were concluded with an invitation to the participants to highlight anything else which they felt to be of significance that had not yet been reflected on during the course of the discussion, or that they felt needed to be considered in more detail. The researchers made a brief and focused summary of the areas and arguments which had been introduced and discussed within the focus group, and thanked everybody for attending.

Collectively the research methods adopted provided valuable insights into objective and subjective opportunity structures and their impact on the choices made by young people about further education, training and employment. The drawing of mental maps made an effective and rich contribution within this methodological approach. The next section details just how this approach enriched and coloured the findings of the research project.

Exploration of methodological themes and issues

The use of mental maps offered the researchers considerable insight, both as a complementary method (when interpreted alongside the information returned by the survey, face-to-face interviews, and the focus group discussions more generally), and also when assessed on its own strengths. Certainly the mental maps proved an excellent visual tool for use in comparing not only internal differences *within* Hull, Wolverhampton and Walsall but also differences *between* these three cities and the case study neighbourhoods. The maps themselves varied in accuracy of scaling, orientation and technique. Irrespective of these differences what is ultimately important to recognise is that all of them conveyed something that was relevant, meaningful and appropriate to the individual who drew them. The map acted as a highly visual way of reinforcing the finding of Reay and Lucey (2000:414), drawing on Massey, that

> while children living in the same area shared many common perceptions and experiences of their surroundings, there was no 'single sense of place that everyone shares'.
>
> (Massey, 1993: 60)

This section explores the methodological themes and issues arising from the use of the mental maps with reference to the broad themes of interest to the project, and in doing so explains what key findings were extrapolated from the maps themselves. It is structured around three main themes: 'the importance of social networks', 'variations in spatial awareness' and 'identity'.

The importance of social networks

The mental maps of many young people, particularly in Hull (more so than in Walsall and Wolverhampton), drew attention to the importance of social networks, and demonstrated how influential their extended family networks and friends were, in informing how they saw their local area. The prominence of social networks as a means of making and shaping their bounded horizons, and conveying a sense of attachment to place was extremely interesting and significant, particularly as there had been no explicit instruction or guidance given to the young people to make reference to the locations of wider family, friends or neighbours when designing their mental maps.

Figure 4.1 is an excellent example of this social embeddedness, and conveys a very strong sense of place attachment. The respondent – a student in full time education – had an extremely accurate sense of scale focused around part of East Hull, and this detailed spatial knowledge is clearly captured in her mental map. The map itself contains several key reference points to houses of friends, and these houses generally work to frame the bounded horizons of the area represented. Remarkably, in Hull some of the mental maps could be fitted together by orientating the maps toward these non-kin reference points. So, for example, 'Emma' would indicate 'Sarah's house' and 'Rachel's house' as lying toward the north and south edges of her own mental map. When looking at Sarah's (or Rachel's) mental map, she would have placed her own house at the centre of the map, and indicated the other friends' houses. This unexpected commonality – conveying a sense of social embeddedness through spatial representation – added a rich layer of interpretation to the research, and is something that could be addressed and developed more actively in similar research in future. At a more general causal level, it could be observed that those who had influential social networks that were more geographically widespread generally created much broader mental maps (see Figures 4.1, 4.2 and 4.3).

Variations in spatial awareness

The maps broadly indicated a negative relationship between the amount of distance and detail covered (i.e. the greater the geographical perspective

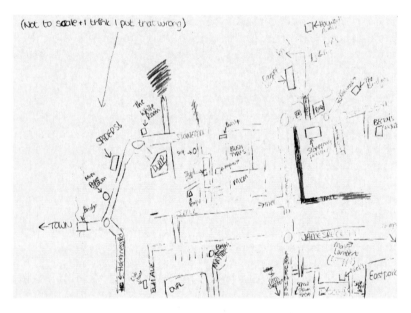

Figure 4.1   Hull (white female school student, 15 years old)

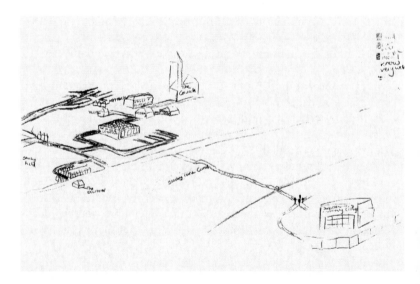

Figure 4.2   Walsall (white male school student, 16 years old)

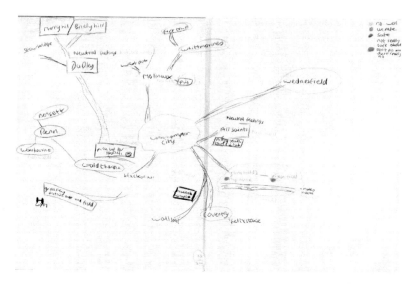

Figure 4.3 Wolverhampton (white male at college, 16 years old)

the less detail was conveyed). The four maps reproduced here quite clearly captured the uneven nature of the spatial awareness that the respondents had. Figure 4.2 for example is simplistic in concept – the student chose to mark their journey from home to their college, and identified several key landmarks. This individual adopted a 3D perspective.

When the maps were taken in conjunction with the wider individual- and group-based discussion harnessed by the focus groups, it quickly became apparent that many participants rarely, if at all, left the local area and thus had very little understanding or awareness of other locations outside their immediate area. This was especially apparent in the Hull focus groups, and is exemplified by Figure 4.1. For example, the map identifies the general direction of the city centre (identified as 'town') by means of an arrow pointing westwards. This approach – to offer vague direction toward the city centre of Hull and West Hull – was evidenced elsewhere by other participants in the East Hull focus group.

The consequence of having a limited spatial awareness given the focus of the research was obvious, and clearly demonstrated that in the context of access to employment, training, education and transport, geography matters. One of the key findings was that perspectives about possibilities differ significantly not only between case study areas, but also equally importantly *within* case study areas. Spatial awareness has a central role in informing what opportunities young people see, or choose to see, as relevant and available to them. Thus those who have a limited spatial awareness will also have a narrower subset of opportunities available to them. Other young people 'transcend' space and embrace a much broader range of potential opportunities that were perceived to be of relevance to them.

Focusing on the content analysis of the mental maps, there was some evidence that the maps portrayed a larger geographical area with age, though it is important to reiterate that this was a very general observation. This may be because older individuals have richer life experiences outside of the immediate school and home environment, perhaps afforded by being more independently mobile.

In Wolverhampton the mental maps were generally less geographically constrained than Walsall or Hull. Figure 4.3, which extended over two A3 sheets, was drawn by an individual who was an experienced and confident user of public transport. The map certainly captures a wide geographical perspective which includes Wolverhampton (the NDC area and the city) but also the broader sub-regional context. Notably, this individual indicated in discussion that he had amassed a good deal of knowledge of the city through participating in various sports and travelling to fixtures in different areas.

Identity

When encouraged to talk about their mental maps, both on a one-to-one basis with the researchers and in the focus groups more generally, the powerful connections that an individual has in relation to place and identity were made clear. For example, in Figure 4.4, the comments made on the map emphasised a strong place attachment and undisguised hostility toward other areas, identifying home as being 'the only place I like ... all rest shit [*sic*]'. This illustrates how, for some individuals, pride in their neighbourhood was something tangible to cling on to, at a point in the life course when there may otherwise have been uncertainty in other aspects of their lives, and especially with regard to longer-term employment prospects. It is also illustrative of the role of place identity in territorial behaviour among young people (see Kintrea et al., 2008), although in this instance it did not take on negative overtones associated with gang culture.

Other participants indicated pride in their local area when talking about their mental maps while not making derogatory comments about

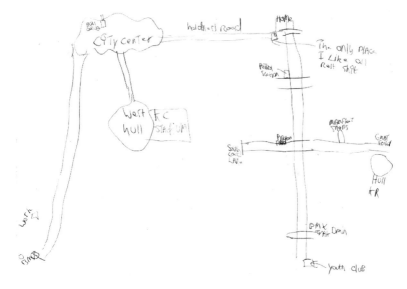

Figure 4.4   Hull (white male with weekend job while at College, 18 years old)

other neighbourhoods. The familiarity of relatively long residence in the area and the presence of friends and extended family close by were cited as positive attributes. Those individuals who had more experience of travelling outside the local area often indicated, from their experience, that their neighbourhood was not as bad as outsiders claimed. Among the minority of respondents who spoke about going into higher education and where there was often a likelihood of moving out of the area, some spoke of 'coming back' afterwards, whereas others felt that better opportunities would mean that they would only be visitors to the neighbourhood in future, implying that with greater spatial mobility their place identity would be weakened.

Interestingly differences in the maps were not evident by gender, and the only real impact that gender may have had on the design of the maps could be discerned in relation to young women being less likely than young men to include and orientate their maps around sports facilities. The location of sporting facilities, venues and stadia another prominent feature within the identity of respondents – and in particular their strong allegiance with local teams. This strong sense of local identity and parochialism was more evident in Hull than in Walsall or Wolverhampton.

Discussion and conclusion

The use of mental maps made a valuable and unique contribution to addressing the key aims of the research project foregrounded in this chapter. The new insights that mental maps made into the roles of attachment to place and the spatial and social horizons of young people in deprived areas can be discerned in two key ways. First, they permitted broad comparisons *between* the three case study areas to be made, and helped to develop an understanding of the uneven nature of social networks and attachment to place that the young people had, as well as how their subjective attitudes impacted on their 'objective' decision-making actions relating to education, training and employment. Second, the maps also allowed the individual young people to contribute something unique to each of them. This contribution certainly encouraged the research (and the recommendations it made to practitioners) to be sensitive to diversity within particular communities, and not to try to overly homogenise the subjective impressions of young people by filtering out *differences* in order to create an uncomplicated and sanitised policy response to the socio-economic issues that interventions are seeking to address. The uneven relationships that were uncovered and represented in the mental maps are complex. This point was reinforced in our final report, which emphasised the importance for policymakers to keep in mind that, despite some obvious commonalities, not all neighbourhoods or all (young) people are the same. Where they are located, their history, their socio-demographic and economic characteristics matter: place-specific factors are crucial in understanding how and whether interventions work, alongside who is involved in their delivery (Green and White, 2007).

There are numerous ways in which mental mapping could be applied to youth research. For example, it would be interesting to develop research which focuses explicitly on how and why mental maps may vary in terms in gender, class, ethnicity, age, ability and experience. Such a contribution to the literature on young people would provide insights into their perceptions, experiences and attitudes, and the ways in which their actions are influenced by these subjectivities. Looking ahead, one avenue of likely future expansion is the incorporation of mental maps in GIS, with increased interest in qualitative GIS (Cope and Elwood, 2009) and participatory GIS (e.g. Cinderby, 2010). These techniques offer ways not only of more thorough technical analysis of mental maps and comparisons with objective reality, but also of recording young people's views and harnessing their participation in the design of communities of the future. Likewise, the use of mobile methodologies and 'walking interviews' may offer further elaboration of some of the key features of mental maps and their meanings to the individuals concerned. Nevertheless, we argue that there is considerable merit in a more reflective mental mapping exercise which involves individuals in selecting what is important to them and portraying how they see their neighbourhood, city or some other geographical unit. Moreover, for many policy makers such subjective insights may have greater impact than objective images of the places depicted in mental maps.

Another interesting and related application of mental maps could be achieved through bringing together the subjective and the objective worlds of young people by, for example, overlapping the mental maps on Ordnance Survey maps of the place in question. An excellent example of this innovative approach can be seen at http://www.flickr. com/groups/mentalmap/. The juxtaposition of mental maps with 'real' maps has been undertaken at the Centre for Advanced Spatial Analysis, UCL. A particular application is 'mental maps of daily commuting', the findings of which can be explored on the blog site Urban Tick (http:// urbantick.blogspot.com/).

To conclude, given the broad appeal and relevance of mental maps for youth research, there is a strong argument for using them more than is currently the case. The use of mental maps can be envisaged either as effective ends in themselves, or as means to other complementary ends (in encouraging individuals or groups to reflect in more detail about their attitudes, aspirations and behaviour in relation to places or institutions, for example).

Suggestions for further reading

Related methodological literature

- Gould, P. and White, R. (1986) *Mental Maps* (2nd edition) (London: Allen and Unwin).

This is the second edition of Gould and White's seminal work on mental maps. It provides a comprehensive and accessible introduction to the topic.

- Lynch, K. (1960) *The Image of the City* (Cambridge, MA: MIT Press).

This influential account in the literature on mental maps examined contrasting perceptions of Los Angeles by social class, ethnic background and location. Some residents' mental maps were more limited to their immediate vicinity than others.

- Downs, R. M. and Stea, D. (1973) *Image and Environment* (Chicago: Aldine Publishing Company).

This edited collection brings together a number of contributions examining aspects of urban perception, cognitive maps and spatial behaviour.

- Pocock, D. C. D. (1976) 'Some Characteristics of Mental Maps: An Empirical Study', *Transactions of the Institute of British Geographers, New Series*, 1 (4), 493–512.

This article reports on a mental mapping exercise conducted in Durham and discusses different styles of mental maps.

Examples of related youth research
- Green, A. E., Shuttleworth, I. and Lavery, S. (2005) 'Young People, Job Search and Labour Markets: The Example of Belfast', *Urban Studies*, 42 (2), 301–24.

This article reports a study undertaken among young people in the context of a divided city: Belfast. It examines the perceptions and behaviour of young people from Protestant and Catholic communities in inner and outer areas of the city. It shows that areas associated with the same community tend to be better 'known' than those of the other community and that some parts of the city centre are perceived as 'neutral territory'.

- Kintrea, K., Bannister, J., Pickering, J, Reid, M. and Suzuki, N. (2008) *Young People and Territoriality in British Cities* (York: Joseph Rowntree Foundation).

This study focuses on disadvantaged areas of British cities, and examines the manifestations and impact of territorial behaviour among young people. This reference is of relevance to studies of gang culture among young people.

5
Making Sense of Mixed Method Narratives: Young People's Identities, Life-Plans, and Time Orientations

Anna Bagnoli

Introduction

Mixing methods has become more popular in recent years, and in research with young people an increasing number of projects are nowadays making use of a range of research tools, often within a participatory framework. As Brannen (2005) argues, mixed methods can enhance creativity, by offering a range of ways of addressing research questions. Mixing methods does however have its risks and it is not unproblematic. The logic and purpose with which methods are combined in a study should be made explicit by researchers, since they will inform the ways in which data are brought together analytically (Mason, 2006). Corroboration is only one possible strategy for combining results from different data at the analytical stage: others include elaboration or expansion, initiation, complementarity and contradiction (Brannen, 2005).

This chapter will focus on the process of making sense of multimethod data, drawing upon a project on identities that involved the active participation of young people from two European countries. It will look at the justification for its qualitative mixed method design, which included open-ended interviews, diaries and visual methods, and at the rationale behind the choice of the different components. The chapter will reflect on the analytic map that was followed for linking data from different sources, to provide both a categorical and a holistic reading of data based on a scheme elaborated from the literature on narrative studies. Identifying the different narrative tones and time perspectives in the data was one leading strategy in the process of organising and making sense of these young people's stories. By offering a view of the different story types that emerged from the data, the chapter will discuss the advantages brought by the use of a mixed method design as well as the specific input contributed by each component of the approach, pointing out how multiple perspectives were combined to form a holistic picture of the identities of the participating young people.

Young people's identities and mixed method autobiographies

This research project was a mixed method investigation of young people's identities that I carried out as part of my Ph.D. programme at the Centre for Family Research at the University of Cambridge[1] (Bagnoli, 2001). In this autobiographical project that I defined on the basis of my own experience of migrating from Italy to England as a young woman, I looked at identities in relation to a case study of migration. The young migrants involved in the study had moved between England and Italy and had stayed in their host country for at least 6 months. A privileged group of 'global nomads', they could be considered a vanguard among their generation, actively making use of the new possibilities for internal movement within the European Union (Bagnoli, 2007). The research was carried out in Cambridgeshire in England and in the Provincia di Firenze in Italy and involved a total of 41 young people, aged 16 to 26, and equally divided by sex, nationality and between migrants and locals. Participants came from different socio-economic backgrounds and were recruited so that in both countries the samples could be comparable in terms of background and experiences.

Young people's identities were investigated with a relational model, which I called 'self+other', based on recent dynamic theories of the self: Hermans and Kempen's 'dialogical self' (Hermans and Kempen, 1993), and Markus and Nurius's 'possible selves' (Markus and Nurius, 1986). In this dialogical model, identities are constructed in the dialectics between self and other, and different and even contradictory self-representations contribute to shaping them as ever changing narrative constructions (Bagnoli, 2007). In order to appreciate identities dialogically I constructed a mixed method approach, which, through the use of different qualitative components, aimed to encourage reflexivity in participants.

A first open-ended interview started by eliciting a self-description and asked the young people about the most important events and others in their lives, as well as any expectations they had about moving. I then deployed an arts-based technique of my own design, the self-portrait, whereby I presented the participants with a blank sheet of paper and coloured felt-tip pens with the input: 'I would like you to show me who you are at this moment in life', then followed by 'please also add the people and things that are important to you'. The task was not specifically asking for a drawing, but left it to participants to interpret the request. After the interview, participants were assigned a one-week diary, which, through a three-prompt structure asked them to record the most important events, the people they spent time with, and the people they thought about. They were, however, instructed to fill in the diary in the way they preferred, without necessarily following the input provided. The young people were then asked to provide a photograph of themselves that they particularly liked. We subsequently met for a second and final interview that was guided by all the materials collected.

These methods were designed to offer young people the possibility to express themselves in their own ways, and were intended as a supporting frame that could be elastic enough to adapt to their needs without being too rigid or constraining. For this reason, I tried to avoid being too prescriptive or structured in my instructions. The young people's responses to this approach were enthusiastic: they were actively involved with high levels of participation. All 41 of them filled in their diary, 37 keeping it for a week according to my instructions, three for seven non-consecutive days, and one for three days. Only one person dropped out after the diary and was not re-interviewed. All but one took part in the self-portrait task and 29 brought some photographs to share with me in the second interview. Even though the self-portrait did not specifically ask for a drawing, but more generally for a visual representation of who participants were at that moment in time, many young people did produce a drawing in response, perhaps because being given felt-tip pens led them to construct the task this way. Overall, the portrait styles went through a continuum from drawing to writing, which included intermediate formats like drawing stick people or symbols and writing keywords in a list or map (see Bagnoli, 2004 for a more detailed description of the methods).

The reasons for designing this mixed method approach were therefore, first, promoting the collection of reflexive narratives, which might make a holistic and dialogical investigation of identities possible, in the assumption that the interview instrument on its own might reveal insufficient insights for this purpose. Second, offering a range of formats was meant to enhance participation, allowing young people to express themselves in the ways they found most congenial, and which might not necessarily involve talking to an interviewer, ultimately giving them a chance to assume a guiding role in the research process. The diary task also allowed a more complex picture to emerge, granting the possibility to expand the research time, with the inclusion of participant-guided data collection over their daily lives for one week. Finally, a longitudinal element was introduced via an inbuilt delay between the first and final research encounters.

The logic behind this mixed method design was an integrative one (Mason, 2006), in which each different component was meant to provide one side of the phenomenon under investigation, either combining with other tools, enhancing what had already been collected, or supplementing them whenever any of the methods might just prove insufficient on their own to get a reflexive picture of the identities of these young people. It was intended as a flexible approach, to be applied with the young participants in mind, to whom these methods aimed to give a voice, and to offer them a guiding role in the research process, respecting and adapting to their different styles, times, and expressive preferences.

Making sense of mixed methods narratives

The use of diaries and the inclusion of the visual element in the research design – two choices motivated by the aim of engaging participants in reflection – significantly shaped the process of data collection, and also informed the quality of the verbal narratives that were collected contextually. On the analytical level the multifaceted nature of the method demanded a multilevel reading that could appreciate the complexity of the different components of the approach: visual, verbal and written. Different source data were analysed in relation to each other and interrogated in terms of the narratives that were being told (Lieblich et al., 1998). Narrative analysis was aided by Atlas.ti computer software (Muhr, 2007), which allowed a categorical reading of textual and visual data under the same coding system as well as the creation of hyperlinks between documents of different types.

In order to get an overall sense of the perspective that these young people had over their lives, the key story that they were telling about themselves and who they were, I aimed to appreciate the ways in which their narratives were unfolding over time. This exploration of identities in relation to the dimension of time was conducted by looking at the data from a holistic/form perspective (Lieblich et al., 1998), which allowed a structural reading of narratives and helped in delineating moments of transition, signalled both by answers to specific questions and by the participants' own use of key terms such as 'turning point'. This reading enabled a mapping out of the young people's life-projects with their corresponding narrative tone.

McAdams (1993) speaks of narrative tone as the 'most pervasive feature' of the personal myth that we create about our own lives. Narrative tone gives us an indication of the worldview that we express in the stories we tell about our lives, by re-elaborating our past in view of some imagined future. The form in which stories are told is crucial for an appreciation of their narrative tone. McAdams (1993) and Gergen and Gergen (1988) make use of literary studies' distinction between four narrative forms – comedy, romance, tragedy and satire – pointing out the optimistic narrative tone of the first two, as opposed to the pessimistic tone of the latter two. Gergen and Gergen (1988) further identify three basic units that are used to compose narratives of higher complexity: these rudimentary narratives are identified as 'progressive', 'regressive' and 'stable', on the basis of the subject's evaluative position in respect to the attainment of their goal state. Thus, in a complex story such as romance, the main character will face a series of challenges and struggles, from which she or he will end victorious with a progressive narrative. In contrast, a tragedy will display a subject who very rapidly descends from an initial high position through a regressive narrative.

In my adaptation of Gergen and Gergen's model I introduced two distinct modalities in place of what they call 'stable stories', linking these to the Eriksonian notion of 'moratorium', and distinguished between 'prospective', 'retrospective' and 'moratorium' stories, the last further differentiating between 'apparent stability' and 'trial and error' (Figure 5.1).

The concept of moratorium, adopted from Erikson's theory of identity development (Erikson 1980), refers to a period of uncertainty and change in one's life. Two different possibilities were here associated with the moratorium phase: an apparently stable trajectory which may in fact correspond to an intense period of search within the individual life-course, or a 'trial and error' route, characterised by rapid oscillation between short-lived and heterogeneous experiences, undergone without commitment. By evaluating the narrative tone of these stories my intention was thus to identify the ways in which people establish links between events in their lives, and to trace a corresponding life trajectory. Narrative tone gave an indication of each participant's dominant attitude towards his or her overall life story at the time of the research. These four units should however be thought of as abstractions, since all life trajectories will in fact be made of a complex arrangement of ups and downs plus relative moments of stability. These were heuristics employed to appreciate, with the dominant tone of each narrative, the particular outlook that participants seemed to have over their lives at the time of research and the key around which they were making sense and telling these lives as a story.

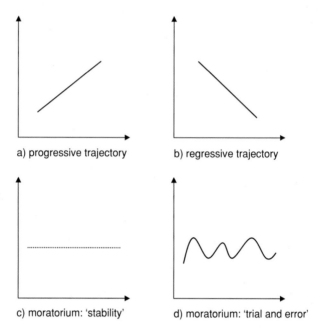

a) progressive trajectory   b) regressive trajectory

c) moratorium: 'stability'   d) moratorium: 'trial and error'

Figure 5.1 The dominant narrative tones. Adapted from Gergen and Gergen (1988)

The experiences which the participants themselves mentioned as standing out and which were associated with some significant change in their lives were a staple in the time analysis of narratives. Many of these turning points could be considered 'fateful' (Giddens, 1991) or 'critical' moments (Thomson et al., 2002), when the course of events was altered in some major and consequential way, and an effective turn was impressed upon on their life trajectory.

The holistic framework followed in the analysis made reference to the visualisation of the young people's present selves, which emerged in their self-portraits alongside the textual reading of their verbal and written narratives. As I have argued elsewhere (Bagnoli 2004, 2009b), the portraits possessed a 'condensing' quality that could narrate complex stories about young people's plans, dreams, dilemmas and emotions. Self-portraits gave an insight into the metaphors through which the young people were making sense of their lives and identities in relation to the dimension of time and were often very useful in guiding the contextual analysis of the multilevel data. This reliance on visual imagery took on a guiding role in the analysis process, thanks to the well-known evocative power of images (Weber, 2008). Attention to metaphors, as well as to other rhetorical devices commonly used in speech, was thus another important analytical tool, on a categorical/form reading of data as highlighted by Lieblich et al. (1998).

The following examples illustrate the three main story types – *prospective*, *retrospective*, and *moratorium* (stability, and trial and error) – that emerged with regards to the temporal organisation that these young people impressed upon the narratives about their lives. The discussion, organised around the three story formats, will highlight how different source data concurred in the process of making sense of these young people's time orientations.

The journey of life: Prospective accounts

The majority of these young people's life stories are embedded in an implicit developmental view, which conceives youth as inexorably advancing towards adulthood and maturity. In these stories the main character displays a clear agency, keeping in control of events and advancing in life with a deliberate effort to grow up. Images of growth, often referring to a repertoire of natural symbols, are recurrent. These two aspects have been found also by other studies investigating young people's perspectives on time (Gillies et al., 2000). In this project the use of the self-portrait technique, as already pointed out, favoured the collection of images, also leading the analysis towards a visual under-standing of the whole data set. Reflecting on these growth metaphors routinely used in everyday language can help us establish wider connections to the cultural assumptions and social representations (Moscovici, 2000) by which we anchor our life experiences in relation to time. The following three self-portraits exemplify how young people narrate their lives through images of growth.

A 'prospective' outlook on life emerges neatly in the self-portrait drawn by Pamela, a 24 year-old Italian travel agent living in London (Figure 5.2)

> AB: So, you have drawn the grapes ...
> Pamela: Yeah, because before I used to be here ... and now I see the fruits (...) That is when in the end you are waiting for the harvest ... for that I have drawn the grapes.

Just as the grapes ripen in the vineyard, so the young individual matures into an adult: this is the ancient symbol of the tree of life, an image

Figure 5.2 Pamela's self-portrait. The writing translates as 'Family; Success; Health'

which appears in the mythologies of many different cultures (Warner 1989). As such, the tree has been defined by Jung as an archetype, a symbol bearing a collective meaning for humanity. Even with all the possible phenomenological variations, it is with the concepts of growth, life, nourishment, solidity and rootedness that it is most commonly associated (Jung 1967). The tree is a symbol of wholeness, which connects human existence to the wider life cycle of the earth. Pamela sees her own present as the result of her past, the events of her life being connected and integrated into an organic whole.

With a different image, Ernesto, a 19 year-old Maturità student (studying for the Italian equivalent of A levels), conveys another way of looking at life within a framework of natural development, with a forward looking attitude (Figure 5.3):

> Ernesto: It is a road, a river, anything that can lead me to the sun (...) Well then ... How do you draw the wind? I don't know (...) I am

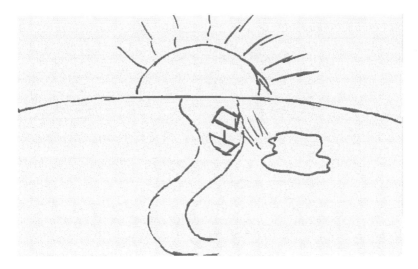

Figure 5.3 Ernesto's self-portrait

thinking in general, everything that is around me, and that, yes, from which I get positive energies, shall we say.

Here a river is running towards the sun, giving an optimistic picture of life. Navigation is made possible by the wind: an appropriate metaphor for the change and dynamism which is often associated with youth. The representation of life as a journey is another well-established metaphor in Western civilisation. Throughout the sample, there are many references to life journeys of various kinds, but William's self-portrait best illustrates this metaphor, through its image of the path of life (Figure 5.4):

AB: OK, this is Cambridge ...
William: Starting in ... yeah, it's a kind, it's a sort of a ... this is the path of life ...
AB: Yes.
William: And ... from, come from home, and that's me and Vicky, and Cambridge, the sun is supposed to be something nice ...
AB: Yes! Because ...
William: Because I'm enjoying it, and ...
AB: Yeah ...
William: So, yeah, it's nice. Em ... the hurdle ... the hurdle of finals.

Figure 5.4   William's self-portrait

AB: Finals ...
William: ... And the wedding, and, hopefully ... ordination.
AB: Aha ...
William: Em ... then these are ... em ... people I'll meet on the way, em ...
AB: So people ...
William: ... Friends ...
AB: ... That you don't know yet?
William: Yeah, mm ... and then ... I don't know where it's going but, somewhere nice!
AB: Alright, that's very good! And ... what is this symbol?
William: That's em ... (indicates on his neck) supposed to be ... a collar.

William is a 21 year-old modern languages student at Cambridge whose life is at the moment dominated by the thought of his impending finals. The future he pictures for himself is an optimistic one: the possible others (Markus and Nurius, 1986) he imagines to meet along the way have a smile on their faces, the sun is shining over his path. But it is also a future which is clearly mapped out, where the different stages he will go through are already defined: the hurdle of finals, the two interlinked rings of his wedding, and the collar for his ordination, since William wants to be a vicar. As a student of Italian he spent one year of his degree on placement, working in the administration of an Anglican church in Rome, a position he found after another job failed to materialise. This is how he recalls that experience:

> William: When the job that I had organised in Florence fell through and suddenly I was ... there was this opportunity to work in a church in Rome I did feel that that was a ... very much a ... a sign, really ... em, that this is something to think about seriously, here's an opportunity for me to see exactly what is involved and what life is like for a vicar. Em I think during the year I realised that it wasn't quite ... that wasn't quite the case, because it wasn't a typical, it wasn't a typical church, he was ... he certainly wasn't a typical vicar, em he certainly wasn't a typical priest, em ... I began to think that I couldn't do it, that it was too stressful, it was too ... that perhaps if it was a sign it was a sign to turn me off it rather than ... to change my mind.

The placement year is interpreted as 'a sign': it acquires its meaning as standing for something else, in relation to what is the transcendent plan. The traditional view of life as a pilgrimage on earth is a social representation that permeates our culture and is behind the widely used metaphor of the journey. In William's narration, there is a clear awareness of the religious significance of this symbolism. He thinks of his chosen vocation as a calling, which informs the whole of his life journey. The self-portrait helped visualising this journey as a clear-cut path in William's expectations. As a social representation, the image of the journey often appears in the words and images of young people, even without any awareness of its religious content. Most of these young people, however, are not able to project their future lives in the form of a clear-cut path ahead of them.

One recurrent narrative pattern involves presenting one's life in terms of the progressive construction of an expertise of some kind. Such narratives are clearly prospective, their plot is shaped by the subject's achievements, yet they lack detail about the contours of the future. One such example is provided by the story of Michelangelo, a 26 year-old engineer and high achiever, who migrated from Italy through an Erasmus project, and eventually stayed in England after getting a job at an electronics firm. 'Growing' is for Michelangelo a key concept, which appears on the top left of the self-portrait that he draws as a map (Figure 5.5).

By the notion of growing, it is not to a repertoire of natural symbols that Michelangelo refers, but characteristically to the scientific/technical culture of his discipline:

> Michelangelo: I have changed a lot, because before I used to have only 10% or 0% social life, and now instead I have totally ... too much, even too much. Actually I say that 'I have to reach the peak', since I had never done it. Now I reach the peak, I exaggerate, and then I start to get into the reverse gear.

The comparison of his life to a graph, the use of percentages to illustrate his varying degrees of commitment, the reference to getting into the reverse gear: Michelangelo tells his life story in the same scientific/ technical script he uses in his job. The 'reaching the peak' metaphor in

Figure 5.5   Michelangelo's self-portrait

particular is recurrent throughout his narrative. Here he describes what he thinks has been the main experience in his life:

> Michelangelo: It would mainly be the choice and the experience of going to *ITI* [*Technical Secondary School*], because that was a personal challenge. Few people were counting on that, I wanted to try, and eventually I was successful. And afterwards even more the challenge with university, wanting to start university. Because, coming from a small village that was even more of a challenge, and few people were suggesting you to do that.

Studying has been a personal challenge, at the end of which he has been able to 'raise himself up', moving upwards from his low social class and away from the village in which he was born. The 'reaching the peak' theme reappears in relation to another important life experience: the trips he would periodically take to the Alps, which have taught him how to strategically plan for a challenge and how to cope with difficult situations, making it possible, quite literally, to reach the peak. Growing and reaching the peak now means for Michelangelo making up for all the years when time was only available for studying, and accordingly widening the definition of his identity. Michelangelo enjoys living abroad, and he plans to continue travelling through his job:

> Michelangelo: The way I see my future is to go on travelling every two-three years, change country ... Travelling maybe until I'm 30 (...) I would like to do it, though I am also a bit afraid at the idea of travelling too much and never stopping.

The future prospect of travelling for work is appealing, yet it is also accompanied by an underlying fear, as Michelangelo is not at ease with the thought of such indeterminacy in his future. For the moment, that fear is put at bay by setting 30 years of age as a threshold for the end to his travelling.

Flashback: Nostalgic narratives

In the methodological design of this study the diary had a key role in the collection of reflexive accounts of lives. This instrument offered young people the possibility of guiding the process of reflection over their lives, allowing them to choose what could be the topic of research, and even to note things that might have slipped from the preceding interview.

To some participants the diary acquired a confessional nature, and recorded thoughts and reflections that perhaps would not have emerged so easily in a face-to-face interview. In such cases the diary could register the importance in everyday life of the memories of significant others who had passed away (see Bagnoli, 2004), or collect narratives in which the young people were expressing self-doubt, questioning their life priorities, and generally painting a candid and not particularly positive picture of themselves.

Although many of the young people talked about the significance of negative experiences in their lives, only two stories could be categorised as marked by a retrospective narrative tone, in which with the passing of time the main characters appear to be led backwards by the unfolding of events, while also losing any agency or ability to control their life plan. These stories were told by two Italian students in England who were mutual friends, and show several points of contact. Travelling on a language study trip after the break-up of a relationship, these two young people had found new partners, for whom they decided to move to England. They then enrolled at university, where they had also made friends with each other. At the time of the research both their relationships were going through a difficult phase. I will focus here on the story told by 26 year-old Alessandro in his diary, which faithfully recorded his internal questioning, thus proving a key source for identifying the retrospective character of his narrative.

In this first diary extract, Alessandro comments about an evening at the cinema:

> We watched 'Sliding Doors', a romantic comedy, which made me feel some emotions which I had not felt for a while. It seemed like I had gone back in time, to when I was watching these mellow romantic films and I was hoping I would fall in love like that myself, too. Strange, because actually I am already in love, or maybe not?
>
> (15 May 98 – written on Monday, 16 May, 23.00)

Movies may allow us to relive and experience our past anew in the changed circumstances of our present, in the very same way as myths do, by changing their meaning in relation to varying contexts (Adam 1990). Watching a romantic movie, Alessandro comes to doubt the feelings he has for his girlfriend. His diary records his desire to call his former girlfriend, with whom he never lost touch, who is soon to leave her student flat in Venice:

> I cannot even imagine what will be of me then. She has always been a reference point, a secure place where I could take refuge from

everything and everybody. Soon that place will disappear and I do not know what I will do.

(28 May 1998, 22.00)

The thought of his ex girlfriend provided Alessandro with a scenario to which he felt he could always return, either for real, or in his mind. In a similar way to what was happening in the movie he had been watching, this scenario made it possible for him to imagine alternative stories for his life. A nostalgic view of Italy as a dreamland offers an escape to the migrant who is facing a troubled daily life abroad. However, with his ex girlfriend's imminent move things are changing rapidly, and Alessandro is afraid of the future. Seeking refuge in memory, and fatalistically waiting for events to happen, he pessimistically views his entire life as 'running away'.

Reconstructing identities: Moratorium narratives

The multi-faceted nature of this methodological approach proved able to capture the complexity of young people's identities, being sensitive to their multiple dimensions, changing features, uncertainties and contradictions. The extent to which these methods were able to register the fluid character of some of these young people's identities is especially evident in the moratorium narratives, which are presented in this section. Erikson described the moratorium stage as an exploratory time when the self is allowed, or even sanctioned by institutions, to try on different identity options in a non-committal way (Erikson, 1980). Erikson associated this stage with adolescence: the time when the question of identity had to be resolved. However, with the life course becoming destandardised (Brannen and Nilsen, 2002), boundaries between life stages are increasingly fluid and periods characterised by exploration and uncertainty may be found across the life course. Moratorium narratives may be compared to what Beck describes as a 'choice biography' (1992): these are life plans in which at every turn possibilities are left open for alternative self-reconstructions. The two stories that follow correspond, respectively, to each of the moratorium formats introduced earlier in Figure 5.1: 'apparent stability' and 'trial and error'.

Emma, a 26 year-old English travel agent living in Florence, drew a self-portrait that pictured well the situation she was living in at that moment (Figure 5.6):

Emma: The ocean is all around me so I am finding it a bit difficult to get out and I've got my mum and my sister, who I've said are

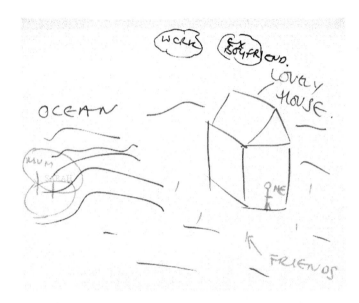

Figure 5.6   Emma's self-portrait

obviously the people who were close to me, but they are there, but they are not ... they are on an island sort of separated from me. And then I've got my friends that are around, but they are not ... I mean they are there, but they are still only friends. And then we've got two black clouds, which are obviously black clouds ...
AB: Because they're like ...
Emma: They are hanging over me horribly and they need to be sorted out and become nice coloured clouds again.

The ocean, which is around her 'lovely house', is a good metaphor for the uncertainty Emma is experiencing in her present. The two black clouds highlight two areas of her life that she wants to address: Emma has just come to the realisation that she wants to leave her job as well as wanting to get over the thought of her ex boyfriend. The self-portrait effectively shows Emma's own understanding of her need to impress a change in her life: this is a moment of transition for her. Even though from the outside she may just be seen as carrying on with her life as usual, psychologically she is experiencing a period of moratorium, and beginning a process of internal search towards a different possible future.

An apparently more complex 'trial and error' story is that told by Bianca, a 22 year-old Italian au pair in Cambridge. At a moment in her life that she hyperbolically defines as 'total depression', Bianca decided to follow her mother's suggestion and travel to England to study the language, something that she resolved to do with a fatalistic attitude:

> Bianca: I said 'yes', I don't know why. I simply said 'yes'. But inside of me I was convinced that something would happen and I would not leave. (...) When I eventually got on the plane I started crying and said: 'Here I am: nothing happened. What am I doing now?'

As noted by Adam (1995), with the experience of a flight we can neatly separate the temporal dimension we live by between a 'before and an 'after'. In narrating her move to England, Bianca contrasts the temporal dimensions of her Italian and English lives. If time in Italy seemed to be standing still, her intense and eventful English life has made her develop 'a different point of view'. Back in Italy for the holidays, she realised she could no longer relate to her old friends:

> Bianca: I went back (...) and they were still the same, as if time had stopped. And many things which used to make me laugh before, things we would say and do, which I would always be the first to say and do ... Now they are still doing them, and to me they are nothing.

Bianca is feeling 'distant' and estranged from the people who used to be important to her, and does not think that she will ever be able to 'reintegrate' with them. Her spatial move has also been a temporal move: whereas her old friends are still 'wasting time' and behaving as if 'time had stopped', her experience in England has put her on a route of changes from which she neither can, nor wants to, return. The photograph she showed me,[2] a portrait of herself from an earlier time in her English stay, is to her an important reminder of the recent turns in her life:

> Bianca: This photo was taken at a moment of intense reflection, and in fact I eventually did reflect and I changed my life and (...) That is what I like, because I have changed my life since then!

Bianca notes in her diary her need for reflection, in her words her need for 'an introspective journey' (see also Bagnoli, 2009a). Her recent experiences have taught her a new flexibility, which she extends to future possible 'mistakes':

Bianca: If it all ends up in a bubble, there are planes everyday.

Just as a flight enabled her to change her life before, there is no reason why it should not do so in the future as well. The exploratory phase of varied experiences and rapid changes, which started with Bianca's move to England, is ongoing and the future looks open for the construction of a choice biography.

Discussion

This chapter has shown the ways in which I framed my analysis of the mixed method narratives that I collected in a participatory project exploring the identities of young people in England and Italy. My aim here was to explore these young people's narratives in relation to the dimension of time. One of the most common ways of telling one's life story is to organise events through a temporal structure. By relying on classic work by Gergen and Gergen (1988) I aimed to identify the narrative tone of the stories participants had told me about their lives, through a contextual and holistic reading of what was emerging from their words, drawings, diary notes and photographs. The way events seemed to concatenate over time within the narratives, and the characteristics of agency and control – or their lack – which distinguished the narrators were important markers, which helped single out the narrative tone and time orientation of these stories.

The majority of stories told the prospective narrative of an agentic main character in control of events who was advancing towards increasing independence and maturity. Growth metaphors, with images drawn from the natural world, and occasionally from scientific jargon, were common. Another recurring metaphor was that of life as a journey. The plots of these narratives made a frequent, more or less explicit, reference to the social representation of the path of life. However, although immediately resounding with meaning, this metaphor is not tenable to most nowadays, as the world has been made inhospitable to the pilgrim (Bauman, 1995). Tracing one's life according to a well-defined path is a difficult task in a contemporary society dominated by uncertainty and with an apparently increased range of choices available. For the majority of people life is lived in the present in a one-dimensional and fragmented way, with very little possibility to go beyond the immediate future and trace any long-term plans. The typical reaction to this uncertainty involves constructing an expertise of some kind, following some training or course of studies. Such expertise becomes the key around which the whole of life is experienced and structured, thus making it possible to impose some 'purified' sense of identity (Sennett, 1996). In narratives of a retrospective kind, it is by looking backwards in one's memory that some security is found. Narrators relinquish control over their lives and take refuge into the past in search of an escape, and a chance for thinking a different possible future. Moratorium narratives are told at moments of intense questioning of life priorities and aims, and are characterised by either an apparent 'business as usual' attitude, or a series of the most varied but discontinuous initiatives. Their characteristic flexibility seems to fit well with the 'choice biographies' described by Beck (1992). However, the extent to which young people may actually be able to redesign their life plans and engage with new opportunities will be very different on the basis of their position in the social structure, despite the apparent widening of options emphasised by the rhetoric of choice (Brannen and Nilsen, 2005).

The cases that I have presented here as illustrating these three story-types show how the different qualitative components in the approach together contributed to an appreciation of the time dimension in these narratives. The introduction of a visual element in the study design was particularly important in shaping the data collection process and the subsequent analysis. The inclusion of an arts-based method of simple data collection like the self-portrait within the first interview was very consequential for this project, and ended up guiding the analysis along a visual route from an early stage. Even as data were being collected, the researcher's sensitivity was being focused on those visual images which we routinely use in making sense of our lives, often in a taken-for-granted way and without much awareness of their possible meanings and interpretations.

Through their evocative power, images could then be an important lead in the analysis process, offering the creation of 'in vivo' codes directly arising from participants' own visualisations of their lives, as well as from the interpretations drawn by the researcher herself. Both these levels, the researcher's and participants' own interpretations of images, were therefore taken into consideration in the analysis. If the researcher looked at the cultural repertoires evoked by the images in the portraits, participants' own meanings emerged from the narratives with which these young people engaged in the production of the self-portrait, or responded to visual elicitation in the second interview.

The longitudinal design of this project made it possible to use the self-portrait for visual elicitation at a later stage, in addition to the photo-elicitation task based on the photograph brought by participants. Most young people were re-interviewed only two or three weeks after the first meeting and usually confirmed their portraits as valid narrations of who they were. More interesting was the case when more time had passed before the second interview took place. The lucidity with which they had visualised their lives in the portraits came sometimes as a surprise to them (see Bagnoli, 2009b). Occasionally things had changed so much that the portraits had lost any meaning. Participants' interpretations of the portraits should therefore be considered as contextual to the interview situation, which was relational and included researcher input as well.

The longitudinal element in this project was a feature of the methods employed, which were constructed on the basis of repeated interactions between researcher and participants. However, this study did not set out to run for a prolonged period of time over successive waves of data collection. The longitudinal application of the self-portrait in the context of this project does however suggest its potential for elicitation purposes when applied in studies that may prospectively aim to run over a longer time span. The self-portrait was indeed one of the methods that I chose to employ also in the first two waves of the Young Lives and Times study, a prospective qualitative longitudinal investigation of a cohort of young people that aims to run for 10 years[3] (Bagnoli, 2009b).

The photographs that participants chose for the study were similarly treated as visual documents in their own right in terms of the stories that were being told, the context, and style of their production. The narratives with which participants talked about the significance of these photographs in the photo elicitation task provided information about the meanings that they attached to them. The case of Bianca presented here shows how the analytical importance of a photograph may lie not so much in what it actually shows, but in what it evokes in the participant, in the associations it triggers, in this case the experience of change. Even though I was not able to publish Bianca's photograph in this chapter, I can still share what was her interpretation of this photograph, its significance to her, as recorded in the interview.

The stories presented in this chapter show how, notwithstanding the driving role it had in the analysis, the visual was considered in context with the textual data, emerging from the oral and written narratives collected through interviews and diaries. Attention to images meant, on this level, attention to the metaphors, and other recurring linguistic features and rhetorical devices, such as hyperbole, which appeared to distinguish the narrative styles of these young people.

In the diaries, participants usually wrote retrospective accounts of their lives, telling about events that had already happened, although in the writing of the most confident diarists, 'in progress' records also emerged, registering events as they were happening. Indeed, the research documented diary writing to be a very common activity among these young people, who in fact might have self-selected for participation on the basis of this very interest. Other stylistic features which typically appeared in the writing of those participants who were diarists also in their everyday lives are the use of devices to accentuate some parts of the text, such as underlining and punctuation in order to express emotions, and capitalising or breaking the text so as to highlight the different voices speaking, with an effect similar to speech bubbles, conveying the effect of a 'close to life' writing. This 'diarese' (Symes, 1999) made an abundant and, to a great extent, self-defined use of such devices, as well as of shorthand codes, and contrasted with the more formal style of other writers.

Through three prompts designed to be rather broad and inclusive, participants were asked to record in their diaries the most important events and the people they had seen and thought about, therefore soliciting accounts that spanned from the factual to the imaginary. The extent to which, in addition to recording the minutiae of day-to-day living, diaries could also be reflexive instruments registering participants' imaginary worlds varied. One example of a reflexive diary is that by Alessandro, which I have discussed in these pages. Here the diarist engaged in providing a candid account of his inner thoughts, shedding light even on his own self-doubts and those sides of his life that did not paint a particularly successful or endearing picture of himself. The kind of reflexive accounts collected through the diary were key to identifying the general retrospective outlook on life that distinguished Alessandro at the time of research. More generally, it can be argued that diaries as a method allowed participants to share with the researcher even the darker sides of their existence, if they so wished, in their own time and on their own terms (see also Bagnoli, 2004). Perhaps revealing any such self-doubts or unappealing self-image would have been more difficult in the context of a single face-to-face interview. The use of a method so closely associated with a confessional mode of thinking might definitely have encouraged the collection of such revealing accounts, just as the use of self-portraits led researcher and participants to communicate and read the data through visual metaphors.

In combining these methods I was aiming to get a holistic picture of identities, a picture that could be rich, multilayered and reflexive. I was also aiming to give participants a range of possibilities for telling their stories. The process of analysis in this study responded to a logic of integration, which was inherent to the study design and saw different types of data as each adding a dimension to the whole. The data were read contextually, without assuming any component of the method as dominant. Diary data could thus add dimensions that other methods had left obscured, and visual data could take on a leading role in making sense of these stories, sometimes portraying deep-seated and perhaps not entirely self-aware images which these young people had of themselves. This model of analysis, however, might be more difficult to apply in a team, where people with different backgrounds and skills might have diverging views on the analytical approaches to follow, or the importance to be attached to different types of data. This does point to the need for research teams to reflect on and discuss their approaches to analysis, clarifying how different competencies of the members may best be involved in a project.

In this chapter I have shown how I made sense of these young people's identities in terms of the temporal plot that could be traced in their stories, drawing from textual and visual data alike. This reading came as an attempt to synthesise complex biographical materials into one dominant picture for each individual case. I was therefore deliberately focusing on the main lines of these stories. Other readings might have been developed, looking for discrepancies and ambiguities in the data, such as those that emerged with the longitudinal application of the method, which on some occasions rewrote the story that had previously been told, or the contradictions sometimes arising between what participants were saying and my own interpretation. But this might be the subject of another paper, and perhaps another study.

Suggestions for further reading

Related methodological literature

* Hesse-Biber, S. (ed.) (2010) *Qualitative Inquiry*, special issue, 16 (6).
* Bryman, A. (ed.) (2006) *Qualitative Research*, special issue, 6 (1).

These two special issues are dedicated to the theory and practice of mixed methods research. Most articles focus on designs mixing quantitative and qualitative methods, but a few contributions also specifically address qualitatively driven mixed method studies, such as Mason, J. (2006) 'Mixing Methods in a Qualitatively Driven Way', *Qualitative Research*, 6 (1), 9–25; and Hesse-Biber, S. (2010) 'Qualitative Approaches to Mixed Methods Practice', *Qualitative Inquiry*, 16 (6), 455–68.

- Riessman, K. C. (2008) *Narrative Methods for the Human Sciences* (London: Sage).

This book discusses various approaches to narrative analysis, including research carried out with visual methods in which visual data are analysed as narratives.

- Prosser, J. and Loxley, A. (2008), 'Introducing Visual Methods', ESRC National Centre for Research Methods, NCRM Methods Review Paper, NCRM/010 October, http://eprints.ncrm.ac.uk/420/1/ MethodsReviewPaperNCRM-010.pdf.

This NCRM review paper gives a background introduction to a range of visual methods, reviewing early visual research; approaches making use of images created by researchers; approaches using participant-generated images; research design; and visual ethics.

- Luttrell, W. and Chalfen, R. (eds) (2010) *Visual Studies*, special issue, 25 (3).

This special issue of *Visual Studies* discusses the use of participatory visual research, including the complexity of the notion of 'giving voice' and the ambiguities and different dimensions in the analysis of images.

Examples of related youth research
- Bagnoli, A. (2009) 'Beyond the Standard Interview: The Use of Graphic Elicitation and Arts-based Methods', *Qualitative Research*, special issue, 9 (5), 547–70. Also published in A. Coffey and T. Hall (eds) (2011) *'Researching Young People. Volume 2: Engagements'*, Sage Fundamentals of Applied Research (London: Sage), 2, 343–65.

This article discusses advantages and disadvantages of applying various visual methods in the context of participatory and mixed-method research with young people, drawing examples from two different studies.

- Henderson, S., Holland, J., McGrellis, S. and Thomson, R. (2007) *Inventing Adulthoods: A Biographical Approach to Youth Transitions* (London: Sage).

This 10-year qualitative longitudinal study investigated young people's transitions in five different geographical areas of the UK with a mixture of methods.

Notes

1. The project was awarded an EC Marie Curie Fellowship (1998–2000), an EP Ramon y Cajal Scholarship (2000–2001), and an ESRC Postdoctoral Fellowship (2002–2003).
2. When I contacted Bianca for consent to publication of her photograph I could get no reply. I am therefore unable to include the photograph here.
3. Waves 1 and 2 of the Young Lives and Times study were funded by the ESRC under the NCRM Real Life Methods Node (2005–2008). The study was subsequently funded as part of the ESRC 'Timescapes' qualitative longitudinal research initiative.

6

Involving Young People as Peer Researchers in Research on Community Relations in Northern Ireland

Dirk Schubotz[1]

Introduction

In the last decade or so, social research into children's and young people's lives has been increasingly concerned with the issues of participation and consultation. While the consultation of children and young people for policy making challenges our perception of how much say and involvement we should afford young people in society in general, working with young people as lay researchers also confronts us professionally as social researchers, regardless of the context and environment in which we are based. Involving young people as peer researchers challenges us methodologically and epistemologically. It challenges our views on how we generate knowledge, to what extent we trust accepted and tested methodologies and our willingness to develop and apply new innovative ways of collecting data. Working with young people as peer researchers confronts us also with the question of how much interpretive power we are prepared to surrender to the young lay researchers who have not gone through the lengthy process of acquiring the methodological tools and personal maturity that allow us to be confident about the way we work in our field and the way we generate knowledge that stands up to methodological scrutiny among *our* peers and those who use our research.

The main objective of this chapter is to explore the benefits and challenges of working with young people as peer researchers using the example of two recent participatory projects I was involved in. However, this shall not be done without at least attempting to address some of these more generic and epistemological questions that arise from participatory research with young people in the first part of this chapter.

Focus and main aim of the research projects

The two specific research projects, discussed in more detail later, were both broadly concerned with community relations in Northern Ireland – that is, the relations between young people from different religious and ethnic backgrounds. Methodologically, both projects utilised mixed-methods approaches, consisting of a survey – the annual Young Life and Times (YLT) survey of 16 year-olds (ARK, 2003–09), interactive focus groups and one-to-one interviews. In neither project were peer researchers involved in the quantitative elements of the study and their input on the design was limited to the development of qualitative instruments. However, it was the suggestions received from 16 year-old YLT respondents on what topic areas should be covered by future surveys that contributed to the design of the two studies in the first place.

The first project focussed on 16 year-olds' experiences of cross-community contact schemes in Northern Ireland (Schubotz et al., 2008). We were interested in finding out what motivated young people to attend such projects outside the school context where cross-community projects are part of the compulsory curriculum, even though it is basically left to the schools *how* they teach this. We were particularly interested in finding out to what extent young people were actively involved in the running of these projects and at what level there was a mandate for the cross-community work from the local communities, which were often socially and religiously segregated. Finally, we wanted to find out about the motivations of the project leaders to organise and run such initiatives.

The second participatory research project was concerned with young people's attitudes to, and experiences of contact with, people from minority ethnic and migrant backgrounds in Northern Ireland. This was a joint research project undertaken by ARK and the National Children's Bureau in Northern Ireland (NCB NI). While religious and national identities (whether someone identifies as Catholic and/or Nationalist/Irish or as Protestant and/or Unionist/British) are key markers of identity in Northern Ireland's divided society and central to its socio-religious conflict, until recently the issue of attitudes towards minority ethnic and migrant groups has been a relatively under-researched topic. This can partially be explained by the fact that due to sectarian conflict and violence, Northern Ireland had been a 'net-export country' in terms of population migration until the early 1990s. Although Northern Ireland has had established Chinese and South

Asian communities for some time, their concerns were for a long time overlooked. It wasn't until the European Union opened its borders eastwards when, fostered by the Northern Ireland Peace Process and the all-Irish 'Celtic Tiger' phenomenon which brought substantial, albeit evidently short-lived economic growth, mass-immigration to Northern Ireland challenged and changed the social *status quo* in the country, which encouraged us to undertake the *'Attitudes to Difference'* project (NCB NI and ARK/YLT, 2010).

Young people – our future?

Time and time again, I have read in open responses to the annual YLT surveys (ARK, 2003–09) from the 16 year-olds that they felt they were 'the future'. Often they related this statement to their ambitions to improve the society left to them by their parent's generation – whether this is with regard to social division and socio-religious segregation, in relation to the environment or regarding political decision-making. Clearly, this is evidence that a large number of young people have internalised the inscribed subordinate status of children and young people as 'citizens in waiting' rather than decision makers of today. At the same time, this is also evidence for the appetite of young people to improve the world around them. Thomas (2007) links this existing subordination to Bourdieu's concept of *habitus* as well as his ideas of *social* and *cultural capital*. Both of these are important theoretical considerations when thinking about the motivations for and consequences of, involving young people in decision-making and participatory research, as Thomas explains in his article.

However, there is also an increasing recognition of children and young people as social actors who are capable of presenting valid opinions on their lives. This changed perception has contributed to young people taking a more active role in social research itself. Recently Brownlie (2009) reported that she and her team had been contracted to undertake a feasibility study of involving children and young people in research by the Scottish Executive in 2005. When this study was completed, they had counted more than 50 such ongoing research projects in the UK alone.

Using the Scottish example, Borland et al. (2001) explore how research has been *on* children and young people, *with* children and young people, and more recently, how there have been empowering approaches *to* children and young people. The authors argue that an advanced level of participation can only be realised through research that encompasses this last approach. This agenda of empowerment and participation has been significantly informed and fostered by the legal context of the United Nations Convention on the Right of the Child (UNCRC, 1989). According to Articles 12 and 13 of the Convention, children and young people have the right to express their views and to seek and receive information of all kinds through any media of their choice.

In Northern Ireland, the specific local policy and legal context that recognises the right of the child or young person to be listened to, and which is of particular interest for this chapter, is centred around the Children (NI) Order 1995 and on *Our Children – Our Pledge: A Ten-year Strategy for Children and Young People in Northern Ireland 2006–2016* (OFMDFM, 2006). Similar to the Scottish example discussed by Brownlie (2009), a multi-agency feasibility study on the establishment of a consortium to support the involvement of young people in public decision-making took place in Northern Ireland (Northern Ireland Youth Forum, 2005). As a result, in 2006 the *Participation Network* was established in order to provide training and consultation to the public sector on involving children and young people in decision-making processes with the aim to create '*a culture where the views of our children and young people are routinely sought in matters which impact on their lives*' (OFMDFM, 2006, p. 13). It is in response to these initiatives and legal frameworks that a culture of participation with children and young people has started to emerge.

Children and young people are increasingly respected as part of the 'here and now' rather than just as 'future citizens'. However, a policy recognition of the need to seek the view of young people in social policy making in itself does 'not necessarily bring about changes in practice', as McAuley (1998, p. 165) notices. Roberts (2000, p. 238) also points out that 'listening to children, hearing children, and acting on what children say are three very different activities'. Furthermore, while the consultation and participation agenda is now established in the social policy arena, involving young people in scientifically rigorous data collection and analysis – that is, to recruit and train them to become young researchers – does not automatically follow from this. Nevertheless as Greene and Hill (2005) write, there is now a pragmatic interest among researchers to develop appropriate methods to access those voices. However, this raises the question of scientific rigour, namely whether the employment of peer researchers results in qualitatively better research, a question which Darren Sharpe also considers in Chapter 9 of this volume.

Methodological reflections on the involvement of young people as peer researchers

According to Boyden and Ennew (1997) no research is inherently participatory, regardless of the participatory agenda senior researchers may have. However, as YLT responses and comments show, there is a real and growing appetite among young people not just to participate in research, but to make a difference as well. If seen in the social research context, Hart's famous 'ladder of participation' (Hart and UICD Centre, 1992) illustrates how peer researchers can meaningfully take part in research that is with, or empowering to, other children and young people (Figure 6.1). The ladder illustrates that there are different levels of participation for young people, from being informed but not actively involved at the first (non-participatory) level, to being leaders in a research project at the highest level. The way social research is governed and funded, it is sometimes neither possible nor practical to involve young people at the highest level of this participatory ladder. Funders of social research may have quite firm ideas of what research they would like to have undertaken and what methods are to be used. More often than not, applicants for research funding are requested to determine their research methodology at the point of application – that is, before the stage at which an involvement of young lay researchers is meaningful – and they are then tied to this. Finally, some research questions lend themselves to particular methodological approaches. So, while some

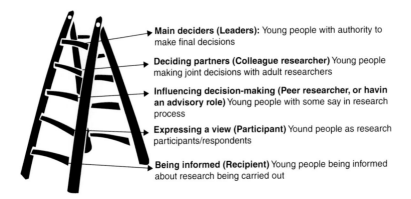

Figure 6.1   Hart's ladder of participation, adapted for participatory research with young people
Adapted from Kirby (1999)

research projects exist in which young people are initiators and leaders (Educable, 2000; UKYP, 2007), more often young people are recruited to either have an advisory role or to become co-researchers with some decision-making powers. Thus, the task of the lead researchers is to negotiate as much of a meaningful and honest participation by young people as is appropriate and sensible.

Despite its usefulness from a rights-based approach to young people's participation, Hart's ladder does not directly deal with the issue of scientific rigour, which every researcher has to address. Central to this question of the rigour of social research is an understanding to what extent feelings, views and knowledge of research participants are accessible and to what extent these are important for our understanding of the world around us. Empirical researchers, whether they work with qualitative or quantitative methods or a combination of the two, seek to access these views and feelings.

Regardless of whether we believe that macro-societal properties or symbolic interactions between individuals at the micro-level are responsible for the social cohesion or the conflicts within society, empirical social researchers rely predominantly on the responses of interviewees, focus-group participants or questionnaire respondents in order to answer research questions asked. Symbolic interactionism has greatly contributed to the insight that social researchers have limited access to the social world of others. That social expectations influence the way respondents answer questions even in anonymous postal questionnaires in the safety of their own homes is now an accepted fact, even among the majority of quantitative researchers. Feminist researchers such as Janet Finch (1984) have also increased our understanding of power relations in interview situations. Recent publications on focus group methodologies (Halkier, 2010) have also acknowledged the enactment and dynamics of focus groups that significantly influence their content and overall outcome. Thus, empirical social research regardless of the method used, is now a lot more reflective about the role of the researcher and the power dynamics in the field than it used to be.

The question is therefore not whether or not subjectivities exist in social research, but rather *how* we account for this and how we make sure that we gather data that represent the real life world that we investigate as accurately as possible. In relation to research concerning young people's issues, the question is then whether young people themselves can help us to access the real life world of their peers more accurately and assist us in better understanding some of the dynamics and enactments in the interactions they have with each other and with other adults. In terms of the actual research fieldwork, we need to ask whether young people can help social researchers to formulate questions and to interpret responses more appropriately and accurately.

As far back as 1967, the advocates of grounded theory (Glaser and Strauss 1967) promoted multi-disciplinary teams for data analysis, and they emphasised that the involvement of laymen and women in these teams would not be a hindrance but rather an advantage due to their intrinsic knowledge, which is 'unpolluted' by social theory. It is no coincidence that the formulation of *natural codes* is the first step in the data analysis procedure of grounded theory. Glaser and Strauss argue that it is this first step of coding data that expert social researchers have most difficulty with, because they may be preoccupied with the baggage of social theory that they have acquired over years. Ultimately they may overlook or misunderstand issues that present themselves in the empirical raw data collected. Lay researchers do not carry the burden of theoretical preoccupation. Rather they are more likely to be focussed on the issues as they emerge and present themselves.

Alderson (2000) supports the involvement of peer researchers in research concerning young people from an epistemological rather than rights-based perspective. She argues that, similar to research about women, which 'has become far more insightful because women are involved as researchers' (p. 253), research involving young people as researchers has helped us to gain a better insight into their lived experiences. Young researchers are more likely than adult researchers to share common experiences and a 'common language' with young research participants. This includes local shared meanings and references associated with words, which is also seen as one of the main benefits of peer research with children and young people by Kirby (1999). Warren (2002) also argues that bringing an insider perspective to the research process can help generate a fuller understanding of the topic that supports the development of data collection methods.

In summary then, the involvement of young people as peer researchers in social research should primarily be informed by the attempt to produce qualitatively better research. As I have argued elsewhere (Schubotz and Devine, 2008) the main purpose of undertaking social research is first and foremost to deliver academically sound findings. To my mind, there is no doubt that young peer researchers can help us to design better research instruments and help us to get access to hard-to-reach groups of people and information. The fact that social research can now take place in an arena which is much more perceptive towards lay participation is helpful. Finally, young people's interpretive capacity that is relatively free from theoretical pre-occupation is a further asset that can significantly shape the outcome of a research project.

Benefits and challenges of involving young peer researchers – empirical evidence

Undeniably the involvement of peer researchers has both practical and methodological limitations and creates additional challenges. However, there is also no doubt that young people themselves may benefit significantly from working as peer researchers. In this section of my chapter I will address some of these benefits, challenges and expectations using the examples of two recent participatory projects with which I was involved.

Background to the research projects on community relations in Northern Ireland

The first of the two projects focussed on the experiences of 16 year-olds in cross-community projects in Northern Ireland (Schubotz et al., 2008). The other one was a joint project undertaken by ARK and the National Children's Bureau in Northern Ireland (NCB NI) and investigated young people's attitudes to, and experiences of contact with, people from minority ethnic and migrant backgrounds in Northern Ireland (NCB NI and ARK/YLT, 2010). Both projects had in common that they were mixed methods projects, which included quantitative large-scale surveys and qualitative follow-up studies. In both studies, peer researchers were only involved in carrying out the qualitative elements of the research, namely interactive focus groups (or 'Talkshops', as they are termed by NCB) and one-to-one interviews – in one instance with project leaders of cross-community projects, and in the other instance with young people from minority ethnic backgrounds.

The project on participation in non-school-based cross-community schemes was a direct follow-up project to the 2007 YLT survey. Funding came from the special EU Programme for Peace and Reconciliation in Northern Ireland and the Border Regions of Ireland (PEACE II Programme) and was for a mixed methods project, involving a module in the 2007 YLT questionnaire and a follow-up with focus groups and one-to-one interviews. YLT is an annual postal survey undertaken in Northern Ireland based on a random sample of 16 year-olds drawn from the Child Benefit Register. Respondents to the survey were asked a number of questions about their experiences of cross-community schemes. Those who said they had taken part in such schemes outside of the school context – 40 per cent of the 627 YLT survey respondents said they did – could tick a box in the questionnaire if they were interested in becoming a peer researcher to investigate this further. The questionnaire contained a small paragraph saying:

> Later this year, we would like to *explore* young people's experiences of taking part in cross-community projects *further*. If you are currently involved in such a project anywhere in Northern Ireland, we can give you the *exciting opportunity* to work alongside us on this. You would receive some basic research training and would get the chance to talk to other people involved in projects like yours. We would also *pay you £250 and give you a certificate* if you are getting involved.'
> (http://www.ark.ac.uk/ylt/2007/YLT07quest.pdf, emphases in original questionnaire)

All respondents who had reported experiences of cross-community projects *and* who were interested in becoming a peer researcher (n=34) were sent letters with further information about the project and a basic application form, which asked them why they were interested in the project; what, if any, related experience they had; and what other commitments they had that might interfere with becoming a peer researcher. Eight 16 year-olds applied to become peer researchers, which coincided with the number of peer researchers sought for the project. Only one male applied compared to seven female 16 year-olds, but apart from this gender imbalance the eight peer researchers came from diverse backgrounds. Some attended academically orientated Grammar schools, and others comprehensive secondary schools. Two attended religiously mixed planned integrated schools (schools which are mixed both religiously and academically, an unusual combination within the Northern Ireland school system where the selective grammar school system prevails and where religiously divided schools are by far the norm). Half came from Northern Ireland's two main cities, but the other half from small towns or rural areas. In terms of the cross-community projects they were involved in, some were sports-based, some arts-based and others were youth work/drop-in centre-based.

Drawing on material from Kirby (1999) and Worrall (2000), a one-day training session covered research ethics and confidentiality and then concentrated on the practical skills required for facilitating focus groups (see figure 6.2). Time was also set aside to discover more about each young person and the project or activities with which they were involved. An hour-long session was spent considering the key research questions drawn from the 2007 YLT survey. It was also important to spend some time discussing the practical details of undertaking the fieldwork and to draw up a checklist of the next steps the peer researchers needed to take once the training had been completed.

Peer researchers set up the focus groups and interviews, wrote the field notes and met for another day to analyse and discuss the collected data together once data collection was completed. While the bulk of the report writing was left to the two senior researchers involved, the peer researchers contributed to this and were the main presenters of the findings at a research seminar. The qualitative element of the project that the peer researchers were involved in was completed within seven months. At the end of the study, peer researchers received a certificate and were paid a nominal fee (plus expenses) that reflected their input in the project. Their names have been mentioned as co-authors in all publications arising from this project and are included at the end of this chapter too.

While *Attitudes to Difference* (NCB NI and ARK/YLT 2010) has many similarities to the previous project, there were also some significant

Figure 6.2 Cross-community schemes: Some participants in training day. Photograph by Dirk Schubotz

differences. The starting point of this project was again a module in the YLT survey. However, the bulk of the fieldwork of the *Attitudes to Difference* project, which was funded by the Office of the First Minister and Deputy First Minister of the Northern Ireland government, was planned to take place in a purposive sample of post-primary schools across Northern Ireland. Peer researchers were recruited through the schools which had agreed to take part in the project. We asked teachers of the respective year-groups to advertise the project among their pupils and ask those interested to apply to become a peer researcher. We received 20 applications for ten available peer research posts. All 20 candidates went through a similar recruitment and training process as in the previous project, with the exception that training, designing and piloting of fieldwork instruments took place on two Saturdays rather than just one (see Figure 6.3).

It was made clear to the 20 applicants from the start that only ten young people could be selected and that several quota had to be applied (gender, the school they attended, ethnic background) subject to a satisfactory completion of the training. By being frank from the start, expectations of those participating in the training about being selected were realistic. However, it was still challenging for the team to manage

Figure 6.3 Attitudes to difference: Participants in training day 1. Photograph by Dirk Schubotz

the selection process and to communicate this to the young people. The greatest difficulty was that all participants were enthusiastic and clearly capable of undertaking the work. By way of rewarding and acknowledging engagement and the skills they acquired, all young people who completed the research training received a certificate, regardless of whether or not they were then chosen to work as peer researchers. We also offered other ways of how the young people could use their new skills, for example by becoming an active member in Young NCB, a lobbying group of young people within NCB. Some took up this opportunity, yet only those who then became peer researchers in the *Attitudes to Difference* project co-authored arising publications and were paid for their input in the study.

In common with the previous project, teams of two peer researchers worked alongside two adult researchers. Again the young researchers were responsible for facilitating the focus groups, conducting the interviews, taking field notes, feeding into report writing and contributing to the presentation of the findings. A data analysis day was again held in order to aid the report writing.

Establishing realistic expectations – the challenges of working with peer researchers

One of the first tasks during work with young people is to establish realistic expectations. The completed applications forms give senior researchers a first idea about young people's motivations to become involved. In the first project we undertook on cross-community schemes peer researchers' applications reflected a range of different motivations for their involvement, ranging from career-related aspirations:

> I am interested in becoming a lawyer or social worker, I would like to specialise in children's law. Also I was a victim of bullying at school and I would like to stop this happening to others.

personal development;

> I would like to broaden my perspective of the other side of the community but I feel that my values, beliefs and morals should also be respected as my beliefs will remain unchanged.

and a desire to action social change;

> I believe that young people [should be] consulted and well-represented when important issues are raised and I would be thrilled

to be part of this and to collect their opinions, giving them a voice in society. I think it is important to hear what we have to say because we are the future decision-makers and it's best if what we say is fair to all.

Applicants were also asked to consider why they felt they would make successful young researchers. Again they explained their desire to be involved quite differently. Their reasons related to personal and career development or social action but some also considered it an opportunity to build on their existing qualities, revealing a distinct confidence in their own skills and abilities which could benefit the project:

> I have the capacity to learn, I do not wish to grow up living a prejudiced life.
> I am patient, articulate and easy to talk to. As a survivor of bullying, I believe I could help a wide range of people. I also feel that Northern Ireland is now changing and feel that it is up to the young people of our society to seize this opportunity denied to our parents to develop a kind society.
> I'm interested in furthering my knowledge in all aspects of cross-community. I'm also studying Business Studies at AS Level and I feel it would mutually benefit the project by using my researching and analytical skills and put them into practice.
> I have a rapport with my peers and I enjoy putting my leadership skills to good use. I always make sure that everyone's opinion is heard in conversation and I would love to be a part of something that will so greatly impact the future – making life better for everyone.

The applications from peer researchers to the *Attitudes to Difference* project revealed a very similar range of motivations.

In order to channel and discuss expectations in the whole group, we would normally start the peer researcher training with an ice-breaking activity which allows the young people to voice their expectations. Everyone is requested to respond to five questions on a flip chart, and the answers are later displayed and discussed. These five questions are:

1. Why do we involve young researchers?
2. What can young researchers contribute that we cannot?
3. What are the expectations of young researchers?
4. What are the risks of involving young researchers?
5. Are we (adult researchers) just too lazy to do the work?

Whenever we undertook this activity the responses to these questions have always revealed a great sense of methodological realism among young people. Peer researchers working on the above two projects felt, for example, that young researchers made the research less intimidating for all participants and that they related more easily to the young people being researched. It was argued that young researchers are able to provide an enthusiastic friendly face or attitude which other young people can connect with. Some felt that peer researcher involvement taught young people how to do research and to train them in becoming expert researchers. The provision of opportunities for young people – for example to have their voices heard – was highlighted, as was the ability of young people to suggest different methods of research. This was seen as being linked to young researchers' first-hand experience of young people's issues and attitudes which enabled them to understand and relate to participants in the research.

This ice-breaking activity also made it clear that young researchers not only have an expectation to learn new skills, but also expect everyone to have an enthusiastic approach to the work, to give their best to the project and to ultimately change misconceptions and attitudes, in this case towards people from different ethnic or socio-religious backgrounds. Peer researchers were sensitive towards potential risks, such as the loss of an interest in the project; the immaturity of peer researchers; the way that existing views and prejudices may influence the studies' results; and risks with regard to personal friendship circles which may be affected by the peer researcher role – either because peer researchers may be popular among adults but not their friends or the loss of friends due to time commitments attached to the research projects.

Generally, there was very little evidence of cynicism among young people about the adult researchers' motivations to undertake the research in a participatory manner. Young researchers genuinely believed that adult researchers wanted to have young people's opinions included and wanted to give young people a chance to be involved and to develop personal skills. They also felt that participatory projects contributed to the development of different research methods.

One of the first challenges then is to channel young people's idealism with regard to their social change agenda without compromising the initial enthusiasm that they have. Explaining that a research project is most likely to contribute to social change if it is methodologically sound in its approach, and consequently more likely to be seriously noticed by social policy makers, is an immediate task for researchers working with young people.

What is, however, most interesting in the young people's responses is their reflexivity about different power relations and potential weaknesses in their own research agency. One of the main challenges in undertaking participatory research is to find peer researchers who are close to the researched subject area but simultaneously distanced from the research field to enable reflective analysis. Jones (2004) found that some peer researchers in a study she undertook had such similar experiences to the young interviewees that they had difficulty separating out the issues.

The time scale (both the estimated time scale for the project's completion and personal commitments) and the consent of gatekeepers such as parents, schools, youth groups and so forth may ultimately decide who can participate in a project (McCartan et al., 2004; Schubotz and Sinclair, 2006). With regard to the projects discussed here, in the research on cross-community schemes, young people were contacted directly with no gatekeepers involved. In the *Attitudes to Difference* project, schools acted as gatekeepers and the project had the additional difficulty that we intended to recruit a diverse group of peer researchers and applied a number of quotas (gender, ethnic background, school attendance) during the selection process. We were clear and honest about the fact that not all researchers could be from the same school, nor could all be male or white. In fact, we were able to recruit ten peer researchers who were broadly representative of the school sample, which consisted of academic and selective grammar schools as well as secondary schools. We had a gender balance and also included three young people from minority ethnic backgrounds. Being clear from the start about certain quotas in our selection process helped us to prevent tensions and disappointments among applicants. Brownlie (2009) also refers to this need of being honest with the young people in order not to raise false expectations.

Some of the responses to the five questions above give evidence that one of the greatest risks of involving peer researchers is being unrealistic about young people's other commitments, such as school, part-time jobs and leisure time activities. Our experience is that research projects involving young peer researchers are most likely to succeed if they are relatively short (3 to 9 months seems a good rule of thumb) and do not over-burden peer researchers with tasks. The time it takes to train peer researchers throughout the process must be taken into account (McLaughlin 2005). While quality training is essential for the success of a research project, both in terms of team building and methodological soundness, the time spent on training young people must also be appropriate and proportionate in relation to the overall length of the project and the commitment and input required from peer researchers.

Lastly, different levels of ability among peer researchers should not be seen as an impediment to a successful completion of the project, but rather as an asset of the team, which broadens the horizon of the team overall. Both of the above projects consisted of mixed ability teams, and in the past we have worked with teams that included peer researchers from an even wider range of ability, ranging from young people with mild learning disabilities to academically high-achieving grammar school students (Schubotz and Sinclair, 2006). The challenge is again to find suitable roles and contexts in which the peer researchers can work to their full potential regardless of their background and ability. Our experience shows that the interactive character of our peer researcher training greatly contributes to the team building among young researchers and to a better understanding among young researchers themselves that diversity of experiences and backgrounds is likely to enhance the research results. While some young people may carry negative views and attitudes from the onset, well-organised research methods training will challenge these views, and the realisation will set in that young people from different backgrounds bring a multitude of skills which enrich the project and complement each other rather than compete with each other. In an interview we conducted with one peer researcher after the completion of a project, he reflects on his preconceptions, and admits that these were unfounded:

> There was a few people we thought that if they got picked the research project is doomed. A few of the people that did get picked actually turned out to be quite good at it. I must be honest; we did discuss a few of the people, in a very snobby way, to be honest.
>
> [Unpublished interview transcript]

Practical benefits of working with peer researchers

The merits of working with peer researchers have been extensively described (Burns and Schubotz, 2009). They broadly fall into two categories: (1) benefits for the senior researchers and the overall project outcome itself; and (2) benefits for the peer researchers involved. In terms of the latter, one of the main benefits is the potential emancipatory biographical effect that the project can have. This can be both on community and individual levels as Kirby et al. (2004) point out. Young people may have the opportunity to be involved in local authority decision-making processes or may be said to be participating more in civil society and becoming more critically aware of their community and its structure (Kirby, 1999). Peer researchers from both projects discussed here went on to take on responsibilities in a range of organisations (e.g. Young NCB NI and local cross-community projects).

Young people can also benefit from becoming peer researchers in terms of their personal development. Their confidence and sense of self-worth may increase, and they can develop their analytical, communication and teamwork skills as well as gain knowledge of research methodology, community issues and policy processes, which can be transferred to other settings (McLaughlin, 2005). The work experience can also be a stepping stone to future opportunities and career aspirations (Kirby, 1999). Furthermore, young people can form new bonds and friendships that can challenge pre-existing stereotypes (Fielding and Bragg, 2003).

From the senior researchers' perspective, benefits include a better rapport with participants/respondents, use of the appropriate language, access to hard-to-reach groups, utilising a first-hand experience of the subject matter that peer researchers provide, and generally the benefits of the different and additional perspectives that young people provide. As argued above, ultimately this may lead to qualitatively better research.

With regard to the two projects discussed here, *Attitudes to Difference* in particular gave evidence that participants in the research were less afraid of expressing views that are perhaps less socially expected on the issue of minority ethnic groups during the 'Talkshops' and interviews facilitated by peer researchers. Kirby (1999) also found that peer researchers can help children and young people to feel comfortable enough to say what they really think and discuss taboo topics.

Conclusion

For the annual YLT study that I direct for ARK, we agreed on four key objectives: (1) we aim to undertake academically sound research. We want this research to be (2) relevant to young people and (3) informative to social policy makers, but also (4) critical towards social policy (Schubotz and Devine, 2008). I suggest that this is a good principle when considering the involvement of young people as researchers in a project. As I have shown above, there are good methodological reasons to justify this approach. The growing participation and consultation agenda alone does not merit the involvement of young people in social research. Participation for the sake of it will ultimately lead to tokenism and disillusionment among the young people concerned.

The main benefits to the research project overall, as well the emancipatory effects that their involvement as peer researchers can potential have on young people themselves, have been highlighted above. However, these will only materialise if the key challenges are also recognised and dealt with appropriately. One of the main challenges to my mind is an agreement with peer researchers about realistic expectations. Of course those working with young people know that 'being realistic' often equals 'demanding the impossible'. If it was not for this approach, little social change would come about. In practical terms, however, young people should only be involved in areas of the research in which they can have a real impact and improve the outcome of the project. This includes an acknowledgement that there are some very technical areas in a research process, in particular involving the statistical analysis of data if quantitative methods are part of the project, which cannot be learned quickly and are therefore not meaningful to be tackled by young lay researchers. In our experience, young people realise this and would not expect anything else. Nevertheless, young researchers can of course contribute to the design of a survey questionnaire.

While a rights-based motivation alone does not suffice as a reason to engage young people as researchers, the minimum that is being achieved from an involvement is that young people learn to take responsibility as citizens. This in itself is a respectable outcome. In conclusion then, peer research, as an ethos and as a methodology, can offer many benefits to young people involved as researchers and as participants alike, to the adults who support their work and to the quality of the results. Empowerment and self-expression can be important outcomes of peer research for the young people themselves as the email message from one of the peer researchers involved in one of the projects discussed here shows:

> It has also been a pleasure working with you, being a peer researcher with YLT/ARK has opened many doors for me, I am now a lot more confident, and have made many new friends, and also being able to attend the Save the Children event and getting my face on the big screen and appear at the Mitchell Conference was great. Thank you very much for all your hard work with us. Thanks very much again, I will keep in touch.
>
> [Email message from peer researcher involved in Schubotz et al. (2008)]

However, the ultimate aim of social research remains to be academically sound and rigorous. This issue of scientific rigour brings us back to a more fundamental methodological and epistemological debate in the social sciences about the academic usefulness of the involvement of lay researchers. As Brownlie (2009) argues, the question of *who* is carrying out the research is linked with the questions about 'knowledge for *what*' and 'knowledge for *whom*', and ultimately the notion of what constitutes 'good research'. She reminds us of Gouldner's view that 'as sociologists we need to return to the people we are studying' (qf. Brownlie, 2009, p. 704), and contrasts this with an alternative approach which focuses on the skills-training of peer researchers in order to bring 'the lay researcher closer to the professional researcher' (ibid.). Brownlie notes that this difference in approaches overlaps to some extent with a qualitative and quantitative focus of research respectively. This relates the discussion on participatory research to the more fundamental methodological debate which is the 'elephant in the room': the dispute between quantitative-minded and qualitative-minded social researchers and between social theorists in their respective camps. As I have argued here, regardless of what methodological preferences we have or what methodological inevitabilities we follow in our research projects, whether or not we involve young people as lay researchers should be discussed in connection with the question of how this is likely to further our research overall and how this contributes to better research. In my view and experience, the involvement of young people as peer researchers often enhances the outcome.

Suggestions for further reading

Related methodological literature

- Fraser, E. et al. (eds) (2004) *Doing Research with Children and Young People* (London: Sage).

Fraser et al. explore from different angles the theoretical and methodological considerations involved in undertaking participatory research with children and young people.

- Lewis, V. et al. (eds) (2004) *The Reality of Research with Children and Young People* (London: Sage).

This collection discusses experiences of participatory research projects undertaken with children and young people.

- Worrall, S. 2000. Young People as Researchers: A Learning Resource Pack (London: Save the Children).

Worrall provides a very good practical resource book for participatory research with young people, which details practical activities and deals with potential challenges and difficulties.

Examples of related youth research

- Brownlie, J. (2009) 'Researching, not Playing, in the Public Sphere', *Sociology*, 43 (4), 699–716.

Brownlie links the notion of young people as actors in their own right to consequences for participatory research methods.

- James, A. and Prout, A. (1998) *Constructing and Reconstructing Childhood* (London: Falmer Press).

An analysis of the social construction of childhood and children's and young people's agency which connects well to participatory research methods.

- Thomas, N. (2007) 'Towards a Theory of Children's Participation', *International Journal of Children's Rights*, 15 (2) 199–218.

Thomas connects the notion that young people are 'citizens in waiting' to Bourdieu's concept of habitus as well as his ideas of social and cultural capital.

Note

1. **Acknowledgement**: Without the enthusiasm of the following young researchers who helped to bring the two research projects discussed here to a successful conclusion, this chapter could not have been written: Aaron, Ashleigh, Bróna, Felicity, Laura, Maria and Sinead (*Cross-community Schemes*); and Adrian, Aoifa, Caoimhe, Eryn, John, Jonathan, Leah, Nicole, Ruben, Samantha, Ruth and Vanda (*Attitudes to Difference*).

7

Multiple Facets of People and Place: Exploring Youth Identity and Aspirations in Madurai, South India

Amanda Brown and Suzanne Powell

Introduction

This chapter offers a valuable insight into the application of mobile-research methods within a participatory methodological framework. Drawing on empirical research on young people and place, we will consider the challenges of conducting such research in an international context, highlighting the importance of being critically reflexive in the application of our research design. As research 'newcomers' to the international research setting of Madurai, South India, we adapted the methodology of 'Photovoice' (Wang and Burris, 1997) as a means to investigate the influence of place on youth aspirations. A method of grounded enquiry and social action, Photovoice (Kenney, 2009) is an innovative mobile method that entails the use of photography generated by participants to explore their lived experiences. This method was chosen as a reflection of the international context and a concern that language may have posed a challenge to communication, thus making traditional research methods difficult to use. Our research purposely introduced this photography-based method to a set of participants who utilised it to identify the locally situated, place-related issues influencing their aspirations. Adapting the Photovoice method to develop a toolkit of participatory approaches enabled an engaging dynamic to be established in a very short time frame between researcher and participant , with the young participants being engaged beyond our expectations.

Photovoice as a method is extensively used in community health research (Hergenrather et al., 2006; Aubeeluck and Buchanan, 2006), within an international context (Graziano, 2004; Wang et al., 1996), and with young people in international settings (Strack et al., 2004;

Young and Barrett, 2001), with a small number of other examples found in neighbourhood projects. However, these projects are not typically about place and definitely not about aspirations, making our contribution of significance to this continually developing field. In their qualitative review of 31 Photovoice projects, Hergenrather et al. (2009) found that only eight involved young people, while the majority of the studies were undertaken in the USA, UK or Canada. This photographic approach to data collection has thus been under-utilised in research with young people and in an international setting. Overall, this chapter offers a critical reflection on the *process* of the research, drawing into the debate the common elements of Photovoice, its significant adaptability in the research setting, and the specific value it has for youth research. Following an introduction to the project, the chapter will firstly critically investigate the practicalities of applying a participatory photo-based methodological framework in research with young people in an international setting, analysing the research journey from engagement to debriefing. Secondly, it will examine the significance of the researcher–researched relationship in engaging and maintaining young people's participation in research.

Researching young people and place in Madurai, South India: An overview

> Over the centuries, Madurai has become famous for its temple complex. Rich in traditions, this ancient temple town has acquired its very own mythologies, evolving its own customs and festivals.
>
> (Devadoss, 2007: 10)

Madurai, South India, became the international setting for the research project because of established links between the institution to which we were both affiliated at the time of the research and the American College (www.americancollege.edu). This institution was the principal setting for the research and provided the means of accessing participants. At the time of the study we were both postgraduate research (PGR) students, and sought to combine our individual interests to explore how place was influential on young people's aspirations, using this visually stimulating participatory research method. This joint project expanded understanding of our prospective research areas into an international context, helped raise awareness of an established funded programme for undergraduates in Madurai, and highlighted ways for other PGR students to collaborate in professional and research development essential to the PGR process.

Research by Green and White (2007; also discussed in Chapter 4) underpinned important aspects of the design and direction of our study: specifically, that place and identity are powerfully connected. Notably, attachment to place is a very important factor in young people's life choices; where people live affects availability of education, training and employment opportunities, access to these opportunities, and their perceptions and horizons; and local, place-based social networks affect aspirations and behaviour. Thus, our collaborative research drew on literature involving young people, place and aspirations. A simple example of the effects of place upon young people's experiences is illustrated in Furlong and Cartmel's (1994: 9) study, which highlights the relationship between local labour market opportunities, the value young people place upon continued education, and subsequent occupational aspirations:

> [a]ny judgements [young people] make about the value of continued education need to be understood in relation to their occupational aspirations which are affected by their perceptions of their ability as well as by their knowledge of the sorts of occupations available in the local labour market.

This reflects the active role of young people who are engaged in a reflexive process; assessing the opportunities available in their locality, taking into consideration their own skills and competencies, and forming appropriate aspirations for education and employment. MacDonald and Marsh (2005: 143) also offer a succinct and insightful account of the relationship between place and developing aspirations, whereby 'local cultural knowledge and values bound individual choices and actions'. Furthermore, young people experience informal learning, particularly from friends and family and their own lived experiences, which shape their 'sense of future possibilities' (MacDonald and Marsh, 2005: 143). Essentially young people continue 'to define themselves through and against one another in the immediate and intense space of the "local"' (Nayak, 2003: 177). Indeed, the process by which place shapes aspirations is mediated by age: the young person accesses and moves among 'different economies of mobility' as they grow older, becoming more aware of how their own locality 'fits within a wider picture' and using 'whatever resources they are able to access' in order to realise their aspirations (Henderson et al., 2007: 106). Katz (2004: x) also emphasises this wider picture in her study of young people in New York and Sudan, acknowledging the effects of 'social, political, and environmental change', recognising the active role of the young person in realising their aspirations. In deriving knowledge from the location in which they live, young people 'expect that which is probable in their nearby environments' (Fernandez-Kelly, 1994: 89), thus their aspirations are circumscribed by their locality.

Visual methods

Visual images have been used in social sciences and social action since the nineteenth century, with documentary photography in particular highlighting and addressing the needs of oppressed and displaced groups (Green and Kloos, 2009). Photographic methods are increasing in popularity in contemporary qualitative research; the visual image is able to document social relationships between people and the spaces in which they live, as well as the relationships between people within those spaces (Joanou, 2009). More recently, the use of photography in research has been reconsidered and reformulated (see Pink, 2001, 2006; Green and Kloos, 2009); with the emphasis upon 'collaborative methods for constructing knowledge and understanding experience [...] the methodology and research process is grounded in the practices and culture of the informants' and thus is more likely to be success-ful (Green and Kloos, 2009: 461). Joanou (2009: 214) cites Collier and Collier's (1986: 99) description of photographs as 'communication bridges between strangers that can become pathways into unfamiliar, unforeseen environments and subjects ... [and] serve as a starting point for conversations in interviews', within which the interviewee moves from subject to guide, guiding the interviewer though their world.

The challenge for researchers engaged in the participatory youth-research agenda is to ensure the meaningful involvement of participants (Curtis et al., 2004; Lightfoot and Sloper, 2002). With a growing aware-ness that surveys and interviews, while useful, are less able to provide the insights of a participatory method approach (although see other chapters in this book, especially Chapter 6), Photovoice engages partici-pants as 'producers of images and words about their experience' to give 'voice' to people and issues often ignored by mainstream society (Green and Kloos, 2009: 462). We adopted Photovoice in our own research because it can be a particularly powerful tool for engaging young peo-ple as traditionally disenfranchised groups; benefits include its ability to develop rapport between researcher and participant, to generate and analyse data, and to understand the perspectives and experiences of participants (Joanou, 2009). As a form of participant-employed photog-raphy (PEP) (Hurworth, 2003: 510), whereby participants determine the subject and meaning of the photographs they take, Photovoice's origins are attributed to Wang and Burris (1994, 1997). Three elements make up the original Photovoice goals: 'to enable people to record and reflect their community's strengths and concerns, to promote critical dialogue and knowledge about important issues through large and small group discussion of photographs, and to reach policy makers' (Wang and Burris, 1997: 369).

Photovoice enabled us to demonstrate to the participants the potential of a 'new' way of researching, while gaining insights into what different places meant to them. The intention was not to create an action plan for change in the community, rather to develop a suite of photography-based research tools within a participatory framework from which other researchers could benefit. Our research design follows more closely the participatory photo mapping (PPM) of Dennis et al. (2009: 467). They used an 'integrated suite of digital tools, narrative interviews and participatory research protocols' to study the implications of place for the health of children, within which Photovoice was one of a number of photo elicitation protocols. Thus, in aiming to capture the visual, verbal and participatory approach offered by such a photo-elicitation protocol, Photovoice aligns with approaches to capturing the stories of participants. Participants' stories must be actively and methodically interpreted through the representations they share with researchers; in this sense, 'it is not possible to simply venture out into the field and directly access people's experiences'; rather people are able to 'indicate where experiences occurred (via maps), what experience looked like (via photos or drawings) and how experiences unfolded (via narratives)' (Dennis et al., 2009: 467–8).

The foundations of our research can be found in a visual methods paper by Young and Barrett (2001), based on their use of visual action methods in exploring the socio-spatial environmental interactions of street children in Uganda. This paper influenced us to create a flexible research design to explore the connections between young people's attachment to place and developing identity, their local networks, related availability of opportunities and subsequent impact upon aspirations for education and employment. Two projects were created; firstly to allow participants to develop an individual project without our specific participation, and secondly to facilitate a walking interview project with our involvement.

Research design and process

Both prior to and during the active research period, we were heavily reliant on the support of staff at the American College in Madurai, which had provided placements for student-volunteers from our home institution for several years. Liaising with the Indian coordinator over many months allowed us to develop an initial rapport over our intentions. Prior to arriving, we were able to establish that we wished to engage with two distinct groups of young people to undertake two different Photovoice tasks. The coordinator was actively involved in facilitating this process and found undergraduate students and postgraduate students from the American College willing to participate. The method for engaging the participants upon arrival in Madurai will be discussed later in more detail. The language of the research was English; this is the medium of instruction in India (an instructional language rather than the first language of participants). English instruction can be seen as a marker of imperialism and 'creating ruptures between the past and the future of upwardly mobile students in terms of their cultural understandings' (Faust and Nagar, 2001: 2878). However, the use of English facilitated a rich dialogue between the participants and us, enabling discussions on globalism and the current political and cultural situations in India, while recognition was made of historical influences.

Embarking on the research, we used participatory diagramming (or mapping) with all participants in the first instance (Pain and Francis, 2003) to collect data on their aspirations generally and insights into concepts of place. We then undertook walking interviews across the city of Madurai with two groups of undergraduate students (aged 18–19) with six to seven in each group, using a voice recorder and digital camera to capture their personal attitudes towards and experiences of the local area. With our postgraduate participants, we could accommodate a large group of ten people (aged 21–2); we set a photo-based project for each young person to complete independently. As solo researchers, they were each given a single-use camera to conduct their own personal photographic project about their locality and its influence upon their aspirations for education and employment, with the condition that they return to share and discuss their data in a focus group one week later.

This outline of methods represents the suite of participatory tools designed and applied by our co-researchers and us, to achieve triangulation of data. While the photographic images (still and moving) stood alone as data, the opportunity to interrogate these data during focus group discussions was essential to achieving the research objectives; both student groups were engaged in focus groups where we explored the multitude of visual data gathered, examining their perceptions of the role of their locality upon their aspirations. Conducting feedback sessions with participants offered an opportunity to verify the data collected, share emergent findings (including displaying visual data) and explore participant experiences of the research process (debriefing).

Having introduced the project, we now move on to critically investigate the practicalities of applying a participatory photo-based methodological framework in research with young people in an international setting, analysing the research journey from engagement to debriefing. Our discussion is organised into three 'P's; 'preparation', 'process' and 'post-study'.

Preparation

The international setting posed particular challenges for research preparation: primarily, establishing links and communicating to participants both our intentions and our research design. We explained that our purpose in using the Photovoice approach was to engage our co-participants in exploring their locality and how they felt this influenced their aspirations. We explained that the visuals were to help them express themselves in diverse ways and that they would elicit different information from different people (Morrow, 2001). However, our secondary aim was also to engage them in the use of tools that they could then take forward and utilise in their own studies.

It was essential to establish our own connection to the American College in Madurai before embarking on the research. We were fortunate enough to have an excellent counterpart in India to facilitate the setting up of the project who had long established connections with our University. We sent pre-study documents to the College outlining our research design, purpose and the requirements we had for participant interaction. From this and continued email contact, our Indian coordinator at the College was asked to find our volunteer participants and initiated the process of gaining consent from these participants. This ensured we had established communication over our intentions, ethical considerations were taken into account and a necessary part of the research process was well under way before we travelled. The opportunities represented by this project were to see how the characteristics of the young participants would influence the Photovoice process, to raise awareness with the participants of how they can research differently, and what they can do with the tool. We decided not to undertake a community action focus in using the tool for a number of reasons: the short time frame we had available; inability to make more than one international visit; and a conscious decision to use the tool as a challenging teaching and research aid. For the latter, we focused upon the engagement with young people to garner whether such a tool would be an inspiration to them in considering the wider implications of place upon their aspirations.

Figure 7.1 lists Hergenrather's ten common, yet not prescriptive, components of the Photovoice process (Hergenrather et al., 2009: 695). We have already identified that component one was not an aim for this research piece, rather a testing of the tools themselves and a means by which to explore place, aspirations and reflexivity with the participants. Component two, the recruitment of participants, may pose the most significant challenge to international youth research. For this, we were heavily reliant upon our established links with the American College as this allowed us to liaise with them over many months to determine how the research would be undertaken and to involve them in the process of participant recruitment. As it was, our participants had been selected from two different classes and were not volunteers, which we did not discover until our arrival. We therefore established that they would not be penalised in any way should they subsequently choose not to participate. This, along with other considerations, highlighted that flexibility is key in all aspects of youth research, including in our own research.

We explained that short introductory and training sessions would be needed to set up the study once we arrived. As part of our introductory process when we reached India, we used a presentation entitled 'Who am I?' in which we used images to convey who *we* were and what we wanted to do, not only because we were uncertain about the extent to

1.   Identification of Community Issue
2.   Participant Recruitment
3.   Photovoice Training
4.   Camera Distribution and Instruction
5.   Identification of Photo Assignment
6.   Photo Assignment Discussion
7.   Data Analysis
8.   Identification of Influential Advocates
9.   Presentation of Photovoice Findings
10. Creation of Plans for Action for Change

Figure 7.1   The ten common components of the Photovoice process
Source: Hergenrather et al., 2009. Reproduced by kind permission of the authors

which language might be a barrier but also to show how useful images can be in sharing ideas. Figure 7.2, 'Reaching for the Stars', represents one of these images of 'our place', Newcastle upon Tyne. This was an important aspect of component three, Photovoice training, as our training required the participants to be prepared to do this in their own research. The photographs we presented of our own locality were a source of amusement to the participants but also challenging in their appearance. For example, some participants believed a photograph of a church to be a gymnasium due to its utilitarian look, while they were fascinated by the piece of public art depicted in Figure 7.2. We were asked what this represented about our locality and how we felt about it. This in itself fostered a genuine interest in the photographic assignments we were asking them to do (component six). However, the freedom to research that we were offering the participants was cultur-ally a challenge in itself. Our participants revealed that they expected

Figure 7.2   Kenneth Armitage's 'Reaching for the Stars': Example of image of Newcastle shown to illustrate 'who are we?'

classroom instruction to be prescriptive and so at first they struggled with the concept of completing a project that was open to their own interpretation.

One of the most interesting difficulties we faced related to the equipment needed for our research (component four of Figure 7.1). For a photo-led project of any kind in the twenty-first century, it would be a reasonable expectation that digital equipment would be used. We found that this was an assumption some of our participants had. However, funding constraints did not allow 30 digital cameras to be obtained, insured and transported to India, and instead they were each issued with a disposable camera, a source of some amusement to our participants. The cameras entrusted to the participants allowed them to determine the subjects of their photographs; in this way, 'the research team gave up its power while enabling participants to gain control and set the agenda for the ensuing interview' (Castleden et al., 2008: 1398). This empowerment fostered trust between the participants and researchers/facilitators. Being able to determine the subjects of their photographs for themselves, albeit within our specified research remit, allowed participants the freedom to share their expert knowledge of their community and country.

Process

Photovoice assignments

As Photovoice 'uses the immediacy of the visual image to furnish evidence and to promote an effective, participatory means of sharing expertise and knowledge' (Wang and Burris 1997: 369), the research intended to use participants' photographs as 'a catalyst for eliciting oral description and information' (Young and Barrett 2001: 143). To achieve this, two projects were established (component six, Figure 7.1). The first Photovoice assignment was a solo undertaking by the postgraduate participants, conducted over the course of a week, in which they were tasked with conducting a project of photographing places that influenced their aspirations They were informed of the discussions that would take place to analyse this data in a focus group setting, accompanied by a debriefing we would undertake at the end. Setting up the photo assignment in the classroom with teaching staff present appeared to limit the participants at first. Fortunately, the postgraduates' initial reluctance to engage with us was tempered by their teaching staff departing, allowing them to work in a more relaxed small group setting. Two different groups of undergraduates undertook the second Photovoice assignment. We participated more actively in these assignments, though the overall aims were the same and participants were made aware of the analysis and feedback required. This assignment involved mapping walks, led by the participants to their chosen places, where they took photographs alongside us. This participatory diagramming tool of mapping (Pain and Francis 2003) was used as a base through which we gathered information on youth aspirations generally and initiated them in discussions about their concepts of place. Participatory diagramming (PD) is adaptable to most settings, effective in achieving inclusion and overcoming barriers to participation, and produces 'robust ... data in an ethical way' (Pain and Francis 2003: 46). Using a variety of PD exercises such as mapping, timelines, pie charts, matrices and cartoons can support participants to produce 'inclusive accounts using their own words and frameworks of understanding' (Pain and Francis 2003: 46). PD therefore allowed us to explore the students' plans and aspirations in a structured way, providing a useful prop by which narratives of place were generated.

Walking interviews

These mapping activities were utilised to plan walking interviews that the participants would lead. Walking interviews along with photography (Young and Barrett, 2001) allowed us to capture personal experiences of the local area. This interactive interview enabled participants to share their perceptions of place with us through the medium of photography. The participants accepted the single-use cameras, laughing at the basic technology we were asking them to use. Two participants decided to use their own cameras, one on a mobile phone and one digital camera. As Strack found under similar circumstances, 'the youths' own photos created a great sense of pride and ownership that contributed to their exchange of views' (Strack et al., 2004: 52). Undergraduates showed us significant places during walking interviews that they had not felt comfortable discussing in the classroom, which we believe is a reflection on the innovative approach of the Photovoice method. We recorded this journey using voice recorder and researcher photography. This interaction allowed us to collect a wide range of data and facilitated the building of a relationship between researcher and participant. As students took their own pictures, we took pictures and video of them engaging with the process. Field notes made from the walks recorded our journeys through streets, parks and their significant locales. The latter included coffee shops and temples at which we were introduced to the etiquette of the local culture. One note refers to the participants explaining that they called one of the group 'polar bear' due to his white skin, which led to discussions of our status as white females conducting research in India. On this matter, we did appear to be of some curiosity to the students but, rather than hindering engagement, the participants said they saw us as closer to their age and therefore it was easier to converse with us. We developed any pictures they took on the single-use cameras and returned them in the focus group discussion. Being present while participants invited us to share significant places in their local areas, recording them in their activity as research participants, enabled immediate discussion of why these places were significant, unlike the postgraduate project, which relied on still images alone being brought back to the group for discussion.

Focus groups

An important stage of the research process for both projects was interaction in focus groups, which enabled sharing of the photographs collected and allowed for in-depth discussion around the role of place within young people's aspirations. The photographs were the mainstay of the feedback process. The mnemonic PHOTO was used as a trigger for discussion: 'describe your Picture', 'what is Happening in your picture?', 'why did you take a picture Of this?', 'what does this picture Tell us about your life?', and, 'what Opportunities does this present you and how does this influence your aspirations?' The participatory analysis dictates a three-stage process of analysis: selecting, contextualising and codifying (Wang and Burris, 1997). The participants selected two photographs which were particularly significant to them and, in the process of the group discussions, they contextualised them. Codified themes emerged in a loose, participant-driven way as the group realised the common themes in their discussions. These ranged from the political and social to the cultural and environmental.

At first, a reluctance to speak openly in one large group led to a quick alteration to allow discussion in small groups. These smaller discussions then fed into the large group discussion. These 'group discussions are a critical aspect of the Photovoice process because they create opportunities in which participants can inspire each other' (Strack et al., 2004). As Green and Kloos (2009: 472) note in relation to their own work with students, the 'process of having the students select and discuss images was informative and helped to generate new questions'. Green and Kloos nonetheless found this process of reflection a hindrance when undertaken in a classroom-like setting. Indeed, following our initial introductory session with participants, we were able to anticipate that the classroom setting would be obstructive in the process. Culturally, the participants strongly identified the classroom environment with formal instruction rather than the freethinking and participant-led research that we were suggesting. However, the group sessions lent themselves to many settings so we chose one the students were clearly more relaxed in, in this case the campus cafeteria.

Overall, although not embracing the goals of Photovoice in their entirety, this research encouraged its participants 'to reflect on and record aspects of their own identity and experience'. By giving a camera to the participants, they took these photographs 'to amplify their place in and experience of the world' (Booth and Booth 2003: 432). Photovoice plays a key role here by

> challeng[ing] the established politics of representation by shifting control over the means of documenting lives from powerful to powerless, the expert to the lay-person … Photovoice is all about point-of-viewness: it sets out to capture and convey the point of view of the person holding the camera.
>
> (Booth and Booth 2003: 432)

Data analysis

For the data analysis process (component seven of Figure 7.1), the participants determined what each photograph said about their chosen places and their aspirations. This participant-focused process allowed them to expand upon their narrative as encapsulated in the still images. In Figure 7.3, for example, the participant's chosen photograph and accompanying quote highlight the development of some of the focus group discussions. This place of significance for the participant led her to discuss the local political influence upon her own aspirations to study at postgraduate level, and how this would increase her options in the future both economically and socially.

A particularly insightful aspect of the research related to that which participants showed us once they were out of the classroom setting. The methods allowed the building of a working trust between the participants and facilitators; on walking interviews, participants showed us places which they told us they would not take adults to, or that they would leave if adults were there. The success of these discussions can be illustrated by the image and accompanying narrative in Figure 7.4, which shows the bridge that 'divides' Madurai. The postgraduate students photographed the bridge and described it as a divide, while the undergraduates took us on a tour beneath the bridge, where there were

Figure 7.3   Discussion of place and aspirations
'This is one famous politician in Madurai. He is the leader of Madurai. This photo was taken for his birthday. He's a very big criminal [all laugh]. India is very dominated by politicians; they are enjoying the wealth – 90 per cent of wealth. Poorer are very much poorer; richer are going richer and richer.' (Female Postgraduate).

coconut sellers, children playing and animals grazing, and discussed it as a place to 'hang out'. This insight would not have been garnered from the postgraduates' still images alone. This illustrates the significance of the different perspectives Photovoice can produce.

Discussions allowed some common areas to be identified regarding the hopes, concerns and aspirations of the undergraduates and postgraduates. Nearly all participants commented that global changes were significantly affecting their environment socially, culturally and economically. The global influence of information technologies had impacted on the participants' locality; participants explained, for example, that the burgeoning IT industry was housed in shiny new buildings developed on the periphery of the city. They felt disconnected from these developments and believed they were, in part, increasing the marginalisation between the rich and poor.

Photovoice allowed us to develop group and individual work assignments and offered an important flexibility in approaching this research with young people. Figure 7.5 depicts the outcome of this journey. These contrasting images are ours. The first photograph depicts the

Figure 7.4   The bridge that divides Madurai
'I took this picture because whenever I think of Madurai, I would like to [show] this picture. Because this bridge has really separated the city from one community and other community – in this area, most of the upper community people are living and this is the area where the really oppressed and the marginalised [live]; all these communities are living in these areas. So this bridge actually means to bring them together but has actually separated those communities. So this picture is really important to me in Madurai city.' (Male Postgraduate)

Figure 7.5   Outcome of the research journey, establishing interaction

classroom setting where the project was established; the formality can clearly be seen in the student reactions.

The second photograph shows a clear change in this. The student is engaged, smiling and clearly proud of the photograph he is displaying to the group. To the bottom right of the photograph, another participant is holding our voice recorder like a microphone. By this stage in the research process, the participants were comfortable enough in our company to use and engage with the equipment we had with us as part of their own focus group experience.

Post-study

Post-study is a critical element of the philosophy of Photovoice. It refers to the period following completion of the photo assignments, including the debriefing, and allows for numerous innovative ways of further engagement. Such active research produces a variety of outputs that can, and should, be revisited with participants. Component nine in Figure 7.1 for us included the post-study data we shared with the students and our intentions to disseminate our findings to the wider research community; component ten was adapted to focus upon what the students learned about the Photovoice tool and participatory means for research that we discovered in the debriefing. Action plans for change, again adapted to our research aims, became opportunities for our participants to consider their developing aspirations and the potential use of research tools, and for us an identification of our missed opportunities. Participants were also asked to comment on the Photovoice process itself, with the opportunity to comment upon it built into our use of the method; participants were able to comment while conducting Photovoice, to re-visit it with us at any time, and it formed a significant part of the group discussion. This formed one of the most enjoyable aspects of the feedback process as participants delighted in taking part and expressed their gratitude. A few commented that the process had made them consider new ways in which they could conduct their own research and some expressed the wish that this could be used in their next College assignment.

It is important to state that the participants were not promised any outcomes or outputs following their participation, aside from their images. In addition to these images, we wished to create a reminder to the participants of their engagement, and to this end, we used our own photographed images and created a visual booklet of the research. This booklet incorporated a large number of quotes from the participants. We hoped that returning the work to the participants, firstly in their photographs and secondly as the booklet, would inspire them to conduct their own research. The image in Figure 7.6, with its accompanying quote, provides an illustrative example featured in this booklet.

Figure 7.6   An example of an illustration taken from the booklet
'This is near Madurai. This is a very congested area; the buildings are very congested. And the life, the life of the people is very interesting – they will live very closely; they will mingle with each other very freely. So I like that, their life in this congested area influences me a lot.' (Male, Postgraduate)

This participant described the congestion in the city as environmentally challenging, yet culturally it is very significant to the everyday lived interactions of people, and he attributed this congestion to the global pressure of increased population in towns and cities. Many of the participants felt that it had become increasingly important for them to secure well-respected and well-paid careers within the city of Madurai in order to support their local communities to tackle this environmental challenge.

Data obtained from participatory tools such as Photovoice are the product of a non-traditional approach that is still testing barriers. How far one goes to analyse a photo remains a key question, and one that can be challenging to traditional approaches in research. However, continued exploration and use of such tools will ensure that it does not become an innovation too far for publication. Nonetheless, Photovoice gave us a rich insight into the significance of place for the participants and enabled them to reflect on how their locality influenced their aspirations. We utilised the essential elements of the approach without focusing on community action; instead we personalised this as a challenge to participants to consider their own future actions and aspirations. We believe the use of the methodology and our interaction with the participants gave them the opportunity to engage in a different way to that which they had experienced previously. At the same time our research allowed for an investigation into applying the tool in a different way to how it had been originally 'designed' to be used. The narrative and photographic elements of the data could then be examined and collated into specific analytic themes, ranging from gender and class to economics, politics and environment. While participants may 'struggle with the challenge of how to photograph non-tangible items or issues. [...] photography presents opportunities for creativity by lending itself to a certain depth of critical reflection' (Castleden et al., 2008 1402). The students embraced this creative process in two ways: first, through an engagement in the research process by utilising unfamiliar, innovative and non-traditional methods of enquiry, and second, as an opportunity to express their own personal narrative through discussing the influence of place on their aspirations. Finally, Photovoice left opportunities for both the facilitators and the participants to explore in the future.

Discussion

This chapter has critically investigated the practicalities of applying a participatory methodological framework in research with young people in an international setting, and has examined the capacity of this innovative method to investigate youth aspirations in Madurai, South India. As illustrated, Photovoice is a significant tool in youth research; it has the advantage of being highly adaptable and suitable to a range of settings. Yet it is not without its limitations, particularly in terms of the technology needed and its availability; for example, expectations of photographic technology will differ in each setting, and our own limited technology was a source of amusement that had the advantage of engaging the students into conversation with us about the potential of such equipment.

Green and Kloos (2009: 476) note that, 'Photovoice takes 'data' collected by individual participants and submits (or introduces) it to a process of group meaning-making. Thus, epistemologically, the Photovoice method is grounded in a participatory process of collaborative knowledge construction'. This group meaning-making is crucial to the success of this approach; our participants revelled in the opportunity to share their images, discuss shared experiences of the particular place photographed and offer an insightful examination of its relationship to their aspirations. The images often stimulated discussion among participants beyond the specific image under scrutiny. For example, we engaged in a lengthy discussion with participants about the ever-expanding IT industry within their city, which was a source of tension and contradiction in terms of the relationship between place and aspirations. Some participants aspired to a high-salary career in the highly respected IT sector (an aspiration shared by their parents); however, as noted above, participants were particularly vociferous regarding the physical encroachment of the associated burgeoning buildings required to house this industry on the city outskirts. In particular, they were very concerned about the loss of traditionally agricultural land to these developments, and unsure whether the decline in farming was *as a result of* or had *led to* the monopolisation of the IT industry. Indeed, the omission of any images of these large developments reflected participants' unwillingness to accept them as 'part of' their locality; facilitators of Photovoice must also consider what has *not* been photographed and be prepared to question omissions.

Photovoice enabled participants to be powerful actors in the research process as they generated and interpreted data about their own lived experiences and aspirations. In using photography, the 'participants distance themselves somewhat from embodied experience, taking on the role of contemplative 'quasi-outsider', which in turn invites deeper reflection and more meaningful interpretation' (Dennis et al., 2009). This deep reflection is indicative of the innovative approach of Photovoice upon which its validity in research with young people rests. To illustrate, see Figure 7.7, where a female participant uses an image of an 'ant home' (although it is difficult to see in the photograph) as her own analogy for the inhabitants of India. She explains that, while they live very closely, in congested areas like the 'ant home', they are each unique; however, she concedes that despite this, she feels most of her fellow compatriots are not ready to live outside their 'place', which is India, in spite of any aspiration to do so. In this case, the use of photography invited reflection and interpretation, leading to significant conceptualisations for participants.

Understanding of place began as a physical representation, taking pictures of their local environment, buildings, spaces, community issues and so on, but the focus group offered an important opportunity to then discuss the role they played in influencing aspirations. Another participant shared a similar concern for aspirations not yet realised in their locality, discussing her image (Figure 7.8) of a nearby tower block built over a decade ago, which remains uninhabited.

Figure 7.7   Example of how Photovoice elicits reflection and interpretation
'And this one is ant home. I saw this; this home I feel [is] like India. You know, so many people they live like that. They are having unique personality and unique thinking; unique ... but they are not ready to live outside of India.' (Female, Postgraduate)

She used this image as a physical representation of her aspiration in childhood to be 'big' in terms of her career as an adult; yet also represents the precariousness of this aspiration in discussing the subsequent failure of the building in its purpose, explaining that her community is not yet ready to live in this way, despite the homelessness apparent on the city streets.

In reflecting upon the researcher–researched relationship and the influence of gender and culture upon this, it is noted that both of us were young, white females operating within a patriarchal society. At 27 and 31, both unmarried and travelling without male counterparts, we were considered to be old and an oddity in their culture, which lent us a friendliness from our participants as we were a source of intrigue. They also asked questions of us about our culture and our position within it, which enabled a more equal researcher–researched relationship based on openness and reciprocity.

While we recognise and have discussed the limitations of Photovoice as a research approach, including its reliance on hi-tech and expensive equipment, and the need for intensive facilitation, we have sought to

Figure 7.8 Example of a physical representation of childhood aspirations
'When I was 7 years old, the time this building was built [...] I often told my father, I want to be [...] just like this building. So whenever I want to go [out], I go to this building, but no one using this building. They're not ready to live [in] this building because they are afraid to live here [...]. So many people are living on the [pavements] but this building is not useful for them.' (Female, Postgraduate)

illustrate the relative success of this flexible method in meaningfully engaging young participants to examine the relationship between place and aspirations. In undertaking a Photovoice research project, our aim was not to inform policy but to engage and inform participants, leading them to self-reflection and exposing them to the potentials of non-traditional research methods.

Suggestions for further reading

Related methodological literature

• Banks, M. (2001) *Visual Methods in Social Research* (London: Sage).

Banks provides a guide to the use and benefits of visual images in the field of qualitative research.

• Prosser, J. (ed.) (1998) *Image-based Research: A Sourcebook for Qualitative Researchers* (London: Routledge Falmer).

This collection provides an in-depth discussion of image-based approaches to qualitative research including examples of application in the field.

- Stanczak, G. C. (ed.) (2007) *Visual Research Methods: Image, Society and Representation,* London: Sage.

This book presents a theoretical and conceptual exploration of visual research methodology.

Examples of related youth research
- Thompson, P. (ed.) (2008) *Doing Visual Research with Children and Young People,* London: Routledge.

This collection addresses the use of images in research with stories from the field, noting the dilemmas and challenges the researchers faced.

- Wright, C. V., Darko, N., Standen, P. J. and Patel, T. G. (2010) 'Visual Research Methods: Using Cameras to Empower Socially Excluded Black Youth', *Sociology,* 44 (3), 541–58.

Wright et al. explore the use of participatory photography as a means of empowering young people.

8
Using Video in a Participatory, Multi-Method Project on Young People's Everyday Lives in Rural East Germany: A Critical Reflection

Nadine Schaefer

Introduction

Visual methods are increasingly used in participatory youth research, an approach which itself is becoming more and more popular in the social sciences (Rowe and Frewer, 2004). They are seen as a valuable tool to facilitate and acknowledge young people's agency by engaging them more actively in the research process (Allen, 2008; Thomson, 2008; Morrow, 2001; Murray, 2009; Hillman et al., 2008). Youth researchers thus have started using a wide range of visually oriented and task-centered methods such as drawings and mental maps (Blades et al., 1998; Harden et al., 2000; Hörschelmann and Schäfer, 2005), photo- or video projects (Young and Barrett, 2001; McIntyre, 2003; Holliday, 2007), diary keeping (Punch, 2001; Latham, 2003), guided walks (Ross et al., 2009; Pink, 2007a), film-elicitation interviews (Murray, 2009) and particular forms of participatory methods like participatory diagramming (Kesby, 2000; Pain and Francis, 2003). The underlying assumption is that visual methods enable young people to express themselves more fully, allowing for aesthetic, emotional and intellectual responses which provide different insights into their everyday lives than those generated by more traditional methods (James et al., 1998; Morrow, 2001; Thomson, 2008; Murray, 2009). It is further argued that visual methods help to create a less intimidating atmosphere and lessen hierarchical relationships within the research context (Punch, 2001; Bagnoli, 2004). Visual methods are thus seen as a way to increase young people's competencies and to empower them through the research process (Allen 2008; Sime, 2008). They offer an opportunity to incorporate 'all ages and both genders into a research process without discriminating between those with different abilities, confidence levels and educational attainments' (Young and Barrett, 2001: 151) and allow young people to take more control over the research process.

In this chapter I focus on one visual method in particular: the use of videoing/filming in youth research. Drawing on findings from my own doctoral research on developing a participatory research project with young people aged 14–16 years on their everyday lives (Schäfer, 2007; Schäfer, 2008; Schäfer and Yarwood, 2008), this chapter aims to contribute to the discussion on the value of visual methods in participatory youth research. Videoing was not the main method used but represented just one of the methods employed in a multi-method, participatory research project.

To gain an insight into the opportunities, limitations and challenges of using video in youth research I will focus on the young people's motives for taking part in the study. I will show that it attracted some young people. However, not all young people shared this fascination and interest in visual methods. Furthermore, I will reflect on the young people's rationales of deciding for or against using video as a research method in their own research projects. On the one hand videoing provided a valuable tool to capture research processes, to enable critical reflection, to facilitate alternative ways of expression for research participants and to facilitate young people's participation in methodological decisions. I argue, however, that visual methods should not be understood as specific to researching this group. Rather, in participatory research it is important to develop a research design, which allows methodological flexibility, so that young people's everyday contexts and their needs can be taken into account. One way of doing this could be to explore the advantages and limitations of different methods with young people, in order to decide with them which are most appropriate to capture their everyday lives.

The use of video/filming in youth research

Video and filming are increasingly used by social scientists as a way to create better understandings and representations of (young) people's experiences. Pink (2007a, 2007b, 2009), for example, has used multisensory video tours, which she describes as 'walking with video'. Such tours enable the researcher to record research participants during their walks and to capture their sensory experiences. Similar to this, but specifically used in research with young people, Ross and colleagues (as described in Chapter 3 and in Ross et al., 2009) conducted guided walks with young people in their local environments. In their project *(Extra)ordinary Lives*, which focused on the experiences of young people in public care (see also Russell, 2007), workshops on film- and music-making, as well as on photography, were provided by professionals to enable participants to be engaged in methodological decisions and in choosing the methods which were most appropriate for them. Their findings demonstrate that using visual and innovative methods can provide deeper insights into young people's lives and facilitate participatory research. Murray (2009) has further argued that the advantage of using film in youth research is to capture young people's mobilities in contemporary society and thus to take the increasing visualisation of people's everyday lives into account. In her work on young people's negotiation of risk on their journey to school, Murray has shown that young people interact very differently with the video camera, using different styles of filming. Such styles provide insights into young people's varying relationships with their journey and their mobile spaces, as well as how they contextualise time and space. Murray has also highlighted advantages of filming such as capturing sequences which can facilitate critical reflection among participants and which enable the researcher to explore non-verbal communication (see also Russell 2007).

The interest in the use of this particular visual and mobile method in youth research is based on the understanding that young people's lives in contemporary Western societies are increasingly characterised by the use of information and communication technologies and a growing importance of the visual. Visual methods such as videoing reflect this development of increased visualisation and can either build on young people's familiarisation with media technologies or help young people develop important visual literacy- and multi-media skills (Sime, 2008). Videoing might also offer an alternative means of expression for research participants. It may allow young people to 'use their whole bodies and material environments and communicate as such about the multisensoriality of their experiences through these performances' (Pink, 2009: 106). Visual methods thus have the potential of involving in the research process those who are traditionally hard to reach and/or who have reading or writing difficulties (Young and Barrett, 2001; Heath et al., 2009; Murray, 2009). Prosser and Loxley (2007) have stressed this aspect as one of the key differences in relation to more traditional research methods as it is 'a different way of knowing and telling which is more inclusive than the privileged world of number and word-based research' (63). Visual methods are therefore increasingly seen as valuable tools to understand issues of diversity and to provide deeper insights into the complexity of (young) people's everyday lives. They are seen as being particularly appropriate in the context of applied research and have made a particularly important contribution in the field of inclusive education (Prosser and Loxley, 2007; Murray, 2009). It is also argued that they are 'more fun' for young people and might get young people interested in getting involved in research (West, 1999; Young and Barrett, 2001). In this chapter I will reflect on the ways in which video was used in a participatory research project and how young people made sense and use of this tool.

Researching young people's lives in rural East Germany

The following discussion draws on my doctoral work exploring the everyday and imagined future lives of young people in rural post-socialist Germany (Schäfer 2007, 2008, 2010). The research followed a qualitative, multi-method participatory research design. It involved 67 young people (36 female and 31 male students) aged 14 to 16 years who were contacted through five different schools in a rural region in Mecklenburg-Vorpommern, one of the five 'new federal states' that formerly belonged to the German Democratic Republic. This region has been classed as an EU 1 region (Bundesamt für Bauwesen und Raumordnung 2000), which means that it belongs to one of the poorest and structurally weakest regions in Europe. The socio-economic disadvantages that young people have to face include high levels of unemployment, poorly developed infrastructure and drastically decreasing birth rates since unification. Such circumstances have implications for young people's everyday lives, as they have led, for example, to school closures, the closing down of youth services and facilities, and so on (see Statistisches Landesamt Mecklenburg-Vorpommern, 2003, 2005). Out-migration of young people in particular, is seen as a consequence of these changes, a trend which is likely to continue and which is one of the main challenges this region has to face (Fischer and Kück, 2004; Kröhnert, van Olst and Klingholz, 2004). Previous research has further highlighted that young people growing up in rural post-socialist Germany represent one of the groups most severely affected by the dramatic socio-economic, political and cultural changes since the unification of the two German states in 1990 (McAuley, 1995; Brake and Büchner, 1996; Kollmorgen, 2003).

While these structural changes and disadvantages have been put on the political agenda in Germany, there is still a lack of qualitative research focusing on the actual experiences of young people who are growing up in these regions (Dienel and Gerloff, 2003). My Ph.D. research aimed to address this gap by focusing on young people's own understanding of possible risks and opportunities regarding their everyday and future lives. It further aimed to develop deeper insights into the ways in which young people live with, respond to or even challenge perceived disadvantages.

To gain insights into the everyday lives of these young people, a qualitative, participatory research approach was chosen which aimed to encourage and increase participants' involvement in methodological choices over time. To achieve this, a range of methods was employed which offered different opportunities and worked with different levels of young people's participation. These included the use of more traditional research methods such as focus-group discussions (3–5 focus group discussions were conducted with each group depending on the interest and motivation of participants). Further, research training was provided to all participants at the beginning of the project so that they were able to develop their own research on topics that were relevant to them. The training further encouraged young people to become co-researchers and to develop and lead, for example, focus group discussions and one-to-one interviews with their peers and to design their own research projects (see also Schäfer and Yarwood, 2008). Finally, a range of visual methods, including the drawing of mental maps and collages, photo elicitation and videoing was used at different stages of the research process. Videoing was used, for example, to record the focus group discussions once participants had given their consent to be filmed. This created an audio back up of the interview in case the digital audio recorder stopped working. It helped to secure data generation and it provided additional insights into participants' behaviour and body language which aided the analysis of power relations among young people (see Schäfer and Yarwood, 2008). In addition, young people were introduced to the method of videoing and had the option to choose this method for conducting their own research.

The use of video in the project was inspired by the practice of participatory videoing (PV). PV has been used in the UK in community arts movements since the 1970s and has increasingly been adapted in, for example, social work and participatory education projects (Shaw and Robertson, 1997). PV is not exclusive to youth research. It is generally defined as 'a set of techniques to involve a group or community in shaping and creating their own film' (Lunch and Lunch, 2006: 10) and can provide an exciting way to involve young people in research. Participatory video projects often start with the training of participants in all aspects of video making and in handing over the camera to the participants. It aims to facilitate participation and communication, to support individual and/or group development and can lead to participants' empowerment. This is why my training session at the beginning of the project placed a strong emphasis on introducing participants to the video equipment and on encouraging them to use videoing during the course of the project and/or for their own research projects.

Videoing: A way to get more young people interested in research?

As noted earlier, it is often argued that visual and/or innovative methods are more fun and more interesting for young people and that they lead to an increased interest in participating in a research project (Murray, 2009). When asking my participants about their *initial motivation* for taking part in the research they generally seemed to support this understanding as a high number of young people identified their interest in using the technical equipment (video and photo camera in particular) as one of the main reasons for participating in the research (see also Schäfer and Yarwood, 2008). Throughout the research project, filming became a very popular tool of engagement and reflection. Participants often used breaks and times before or after our sessions to film themselves. Filming their own lives reminded them of things they had seen on TV – such as Big Brother. They found it fascinating to create their own little clips, to film themselves, to create short documentaries, or to adopt the 'extension of gaze' (Murray, 2009), which meant that they would keep the video camera running while being engaged in typical activities. Participants often stayed longer after our meetings to look back at their footage, to discuss and reflect on what they had been filming.

Towards the end of the project participants often expressed how much they had enjoyed using the video:

> Sven (m, 16): It was great that we were allowed to try out the camera and to play around with it. I don't have my own video camera so the project allowed me to learn a bit more about how to use it and stuff. And we had lots of fun trying it out.

Using a video camera seemed particularly attractive as most young people had a photo camera at home but only a few owned a video camera:

> Marie (f, 16): I have a photo camera but videoing is very different. We did some interview sessions with it and it was good fun. We also used

it to comment on specific topics or what we liked or disliked about the research. It was a bit like Big Brother – you could tell the camera whatever you wanted and then watch it afterwards again and again.

However, a closer analysis of participants' motivation to get involved with the research at the initial stage revealed that the use of filming represented a stronger motivation for male than for female participants. This indicates firstly that young people's motivation to participate in research can vary and might not be solely depended on the research design and/or the use of visual methods. It seems to support findings by Hill (2006) who has argued that children's and young people's interest in research depends on their perception of a number of issues such as their interest in the subject, the matter of the research, whether participation can be seen as personal education, therapy or empowerment, and their comfort with the research design (see also Schäfer and Yarwood, 2008).

That more male than female participants referred to using the technology as a key motivation to take part in the research secondly indicates that gender might have an impact on young people's perception of the attractiveness of specific research designs and methods. This observation is in line with findings by Holloway and Valentine (2000) who showed that children's gendered identities have an impact on their confidence in and use of information and communication technologies. However, the authors also identified ways in which girls, for example, contested regulative codes of gender and practiced agency by developing strategies to overcome issues such as lack of confidence. Research projects might have the potential to create a 'participatory arena' (see also Kesby, 2005), which facilitates such re-negotiations. One way of addressing possible power imbalances among young people could be to provide training in such methods to equalise and strengthen young people's confidence in using them (see also next section and Thomson, 2008). This is why I had planned a training session for all participants at the beginning of the project and enabled young people to make use of the video equipment throughout the research process to build up their confidence over time.

However, a few girls revealed that they had been unsure about participating in the project *at all* because of the use of videoing and the training in qualitative and visual methods. Fifteen-year-old Anna, for example, only agreed to come to the initial research training after I had promised that she would not need to stand in front of the camera if she did not want to. I had to reassure her that the training was absolutely voluntary and, although the training was about learning qualitative research methods and possibilities for young people to get actively involved in the research, it did not oblige her at all to take on the role of an interviewer or to make use of filming or any other visual method.

For me, the concerns raised by a few of the young people in this research project relating to the use of visual methods raises wider issues of inclusion, equality and participation in youth research. It reminds us to carefully reflect on the implications of such methodological decisions and to consider how they might affect young people's willingness and interest to take part. I thus caution against the understanding that a specific method or a specific type of method – such as visual methods – are understood as necessarily the most appropriate for researching young people, as they do not always account for young people's experiences, interests and abilities.

Research training

Training young people in research skills is often regarded as a way to minimise the power imbalance between young people and researchers, to get a deeper insight into young people's life worlds and to 'empower' them through the development of new skills of negotiation and awareness (see Barry, 1996). Thomson (2008) has thus argued that '[i]f researchers involve children and young people in visual research, they must now consider what they have to do in order to teach them about the equipment and its capacities and limitations' (12–13). I have critically discussed the challenges and complex issues related to training young people as researchers elsewhere (see Schäfer and Yarwood, 2008). Here, however, I want to focus on the way video was used in training participants in qualitative research methods and how participants reflected on this method.

I offered research training for those who expressed interest in participating in the project (n=67, total of 9 groups). The training sessions lasted 2½ hours and were divided into two main parts: first, a theoretical introduction to qualitative research methods was given to offer participants an overview of the different kinds of interview techniques. It included discussions on, for example, the way interviews should be structured, what kind of ethical aspects needed to be considered and how interview questions can be formulated. This then led to the second and more practical part of the session in which the technical equipment was introduced (such as laptop, digital voice recorder, digital photo- and video camera, tripod, external microphone). Participants then had time to try out these instruments themselves. The aim was that everyone in the group would feel confident and comfortable in using this technical equipment.

It became apparent that the boys were often eager to see which equipment I had brought and to try it out immediately. Some of them demonstrated great confidence in using the photo- and video-camera as well as the laptop. Female participants, however, were often more reserved, waited until the boys had finished exploring the camera, and stayed in groups with other girls to support each other when exploring the equipment. To address possible gender differences I had designed some tasks so that boys and girls had to explore the equipment together, taking on different roles in turns and providing enough time for individuals to get to know the equipment (see also Schäfer and Yarwood, 2008).

Anna, who had expressed her concerns about using visual methods, was very quiet and shy at the beginning of the training session, even though she knew everybody in the group, which consisted of eight of her classmates. It was difficult to motivate her to try out the equipment and I did not want to push her to take on a role related to filming. During the session her classmate Robert (16) tried to encourage her to be part of the interviewing exercise. He highlighted that the task to film their own interviewing attempts would help Anna to develop her communication skills:

> Robert (m, 16): I think this is pretty good training for future job interviews. I think we should start as early as possible to train for this, don't you think? And here we get pretty good feedback for it.

As participants in this group were in the process of applying for apprenticeships, this argument to take part in the filming and interviewing exercise seemed to persuade Anna. The video recording shows a very shy girl who gives only very short answers. Her body language reveals that she feels uncomfortable as she avoids eye contact with the interviewer and/or the camera, she seems nervous as she is moving restlessly on her chair and she immediately leaves the scene the moment the interviewer thanks her for the interview.

The research design aimed to increase young people's participation with time, allowing the young people to decide for themselves at which level they wanted to be involved. Anna seemed to have needed this time as she decided two months into the project that she wanted to be involved in the group's video project. In addition, the involvement with visual methods needed to 'make sense' with regard to her own abilities and needs (in this case as a preparation for possible future job interviews). Anna ended up doing the main work for this project on young people's everyday lives in her home town, for which she interviewed – in front of the camera – several adults and other peers on different topics. She had become much more confident during the research process and in the film she comes across as a very confident girl who speaks freely and interviews peers and adults in a highly vivid manner. At the end of the project Anna told me how much she had enjoyed becoming an interviewer and presenting issues in which she was interested in front of the camera.

> Anna (f, 15): I absolutely love standing in front of the camera and interviewing people. I would have never thought that I would enjoy it so much.

For Anna, the research project seemed to have provided a safe space to develop communication and presentation skills which these young people considered as crucial for finding a job and thus for their own future lives. Anna was much more open and engaged in the project towards the end and it seemed that her self-confidence grew over time. With regard to Anna, I feel that the project achieved what it was aiming for: to give young people a voice and to empower them to be heard. On the other hand, however, this incident also raises the question about how many young people did not come forward and decided not to participate in the research precisely because of the use of visual methods such as videoing.

Anna's case demonstrates that we have to reflect very carefully upon how we define key categories such as 'participation' and 'young people's involvement' and how we come to methodological decisions. It highlights that young people are a highly diverse group and that participation should not be thought of as being inherent to the use of specific methods. Further, young people's interest and confidence in getting involved might vary immensely and impact on their initial motivation to take part in the research. In addition, it can change during the course of the research project. The research design thus needs to account for the multiple forms of engagement and participation which means that participatory research is often less predictable than more traditional research. Referring to their own participatory research with young people in public care, Holland et al. (2008) argue that this is one of the risks of such an approach, as the 'voluntary nature of all aspects of the project also meant that young people could attend, yet withhold, or later withdraw permission for any data relating to them to be used in the analysis' (14). This openness and flexibility of the research design, however, represents one of the key aspects of participatory research. It is our responsibility as researchers to make sure that young people can make informed decisions whether they want to take part in the research or not. In this context the training of young people can represent one way of supporting informed decision-making. We have to keep in mind, however, that '[v]isual research should be seen as only one methodological technique among many to be employed by social researchers, more appropriate in some contexts, less so in others' (Banks, 2009:4).

Young people's rationales for using or deciding not to use videoing as a research method

In the second part of the research, participants were given the opportunity to develop their own research projects. These projects were seen as supplementary to the data collected from the focus-group discussions and provided deeper insights into young people's understanding, experience and perception of their everyday lives. At the same time these projects represent a possible way of acknowledging young people's agency, enabling them to develop further skills and giving them a voice.

I provided the technical equipment and financial support for transport, covered the costs to develop photographs, provided material for collages, helped with organisational tasks (for example, with editing software), and gave advice whenever needed. It was hoped to reach the highest level of participation at this stage of the research project (see Hart, 1997) and to enable young people to reflect on and address issues that were important to them. The most important aspect was, however, that participants could *choose* what they wanted to do, even if this meant that the project would not lead to particular forms of action or engagement with the local community or local gatekeepers.

Young people often saw visual methods as an interesting and appropriate way of engaging with research. Seven of the nine groups wanted to develop their own research project on a topic of their choice (with the remaining two groups wanting to carry on meeting for focus group discussions rather than developing a new project of their own). The projects which the seven groups developed on their own initiative varied immensely with regard to research topics and design, but all made use of visual methods such as drawing, photography or filming which highlights the popularity of visual methods among young people.

Nonetheless, only one group chose to use a video method in their project, a group of eight 16-year olds (4 girls and 4 boys) who wanted to produce a short film on their own lives. The starting point for their interest in using video was their fascination with capturing their own lives and being able to give other young people an insight into their everyday experiences, the place they were living in and the issues that concerned them. The group wanted the movie to capture three main aspects: first, they wanted to cover their personal hobbies, places they liked, where they met with friends and so on. Second, they wanted to interview adults who worked with young people in the area, such as the sport-trainer, the head of the fire brigade, and the dance-club manager. Participants felt that these adults could contribute to the movie by discussing what was available to young people in the area. Third, participants wanted to include a self-conducted focus group on their imagined futures, and things they were excited or worried about. Once the storyboard was developed the group decided who would film which scenes so they shared the work equally between them. It also allowed us to quickly identify when they needed the video camera and for how long. Furthermore, practical and ethical issues were discussed such as whether it was appropriate to film in their favourite discotheque or not (for a comprehensive discussion on ethical issues in visual research see Wiles et al., 2008; Dicks and Hurdley, 2009; Wiles et al., 2010a).

The filming was completed within a week and we had organised three further sessions to start the editing process. However, even though we had touched on editing issues in the training session it seemed that participants had not anticipated that it was still quite a lot of work to put the final film together. From the idea to incorporate background music, images of the town in between scenes and so on they quickly opted for the simplest way to edit the scenes. There was also still some work to do after the third editing session but participants seemed to feel that they had done the most important work (the filming) and they were happy for me to finish the editing process. 'Can't you finish off the editing? You know what we want the film to look like' (Markus m, 16). We had a long discussion about the editing process and I highlighted that it allows a great deal of manipulation and misrepresentation and that they should therefore be part of that process. However, it was summer time and participants did not want to spend more time on the project and trusted me in finishing it off. To still make sure that the film represented young people's voices as best as possible we agreed very clearly on the order and length of the scenes and I then edited the film in accordance with what we had discussed. This highlights the need to consider other commitments and interests, which young people might have and which might collide with committing to a high level of participation in research, a theme also discussed in Chapter 6.

Young people were very proud of the movie that we had produced and watched it again and again. They could not wait to show it to friends and family and were very keen to have the video included in the exhibition of the research project. They regarded the film as a major achievement and something that had captured their everyday lives for them – to look at in future – and for others:

> Sven (m, 16): It was amazing to look at the video and to see all of us in there. It is pretty cool to show this to our own children one day and to remember what we were like when we were young.

Although nearly all of the other groups had at one point discussed the option to make a small video project they subsequently decided against using video. One group of 16 year olds, for example, decided to document local apprenticeship and job opportunities. Their first idea was to take the video camera in order to walk through the town and film shops and to interview employers and employees about the type of jobs available and the possibility to be trained in that profession. The rationale for this project was to find out more about local opportunities, as participants felt there was an information gap on what they could do in the local area. They also wanted to inform other peers about such options. However, the group quickly decided against filming as they felt this might be too intrusive and that people might get scared if they turned up with a video camera. This group of young people thus decided instead to use photography to represent the different professions which they investigated, taking a picture of the shop or the person working in the shop if they agreed to be photographed, otherwise taking a picture of something which symbolised the kind of job or work they were investigating.

Within a week participants had identified 15 local businesses, had conducted interviews with someone working there and had taken a picture (see also Schäfer, 2007). They put these together for an exhibition, which they wanted to be shown in all the five schools that participated in the project. This example demonstrates young people's methodological sensitivity, stressing that even though specific visual methods – such as videoing – might be very appealing to young people they might consciously decide against using such methods for practical and ethical reasons.

Most of the self-chosen and self-conducted youth projects ended up employing photography. A group of teenagers with learning difficulties, for example, conducted a photography project. None of them had a camera at home. Some did not even own photographs of themselves. To be able to use a digital single-lens camera, to choose the right place where to take the picture and the best pose in which to position themselves in order to demonstrate what they wanted to be in the future represented a major achievement for them:

> Karl (m, 14): The best thing was that we were allowed to use everything [the technical equipment] and not to be shouted at not to break anything.

Although these young people enjoyed using the video camera during the focus group discussions and to film their peer-led interviews (see also Schäfer and Yarwood, 2008) they chose a project which could be finished in one afternoon. It does not mean that these young people would not have been able or did not have the skills to design and carry out their own film project. They rather decided to choose a method which allowed them to achieve more immediate results such as looking at the photographs on the laptop, choosing the one they felt represented them in the best possible way, and being able to own and display their own photograph. Some of them also connected a great sense of ownership with the idea of creating their own images and producing something individual rather than engaging in a group project.

The key rationale for favouring photography rather than videoing thus was related to young people's understanding that it was less time-consuming and less work-intensive than putting together a video. Furthermore, conducting a group video project also meant that a high level of group work and time management was required. Participants often highlighted, however, that they did not have the time to get engaged at such a high level, as they also had other commitments or hobbies. Others referred to difficulties in arranging additional meetings as they often lived in different villages to each other and there were only a few buses per day to the town where they went to school. Young people thus often felt that photo projects were more practical than film projects. Such practical issues need to be taken more seriously by youth researchers, as recent studies have highlighted that young people often only have limited time to take part in research projects (see for example Thomson, 2007; Holland et al., 2008; Schubotz, this book).

It was noted above that two out of the nine groups decided to carry on with traditional focus groups to discuss specific topics of interest in more depth, rather than using visual methods to express themselves. This reflects an observation made in previous research (Hörschelmann and Schäfer, 2007) where some young people had expressed that they preferred to 'just talk' rather than to engage in more task-oriented or visual methods. In the written feedback for this current study young people often highlighted how much they had enjoyed talking about their own lives and issues that were important to them:

> Markus (m, 16): It was great to have the time for once to talk with the others about issues which are important to us. Somehow we normally don't do that very often.
>
> Linn (f, 16): I somehow learned a lot about my classmates. It is weird, we know each other from childhood but very often we don't really talk about how we feel and what we are concerned about.

The potential for research to create a safe space for young people to discuss issues that concern them, to exchange ideas, interests, wishes and fears is thus valued highly by some young people. This challenges the understanding that traditional methods might not be appropriate in youth research and that innovative methods should be employed to keep youth participants interested. These findings rather encourage approaches, which combine more traditional and innovative methods and/or highly flexible research designs which explore methodological options with their research participants.

Discussion and conclusion

This chapter has discussed the value of videoing for researching young people's everyday lives. On the one hand I have argued that the use of visual methods – and of videoing in particular – motivated some young people to take part in the research, and for most participants repre-sented an interesting tool to at least try out. Young people often valued the use of filming as a way to increase their communication and repre-sentation skills, which were seen as crucial for succeeding, for example, in future job interviews. The length and level of involvement of all participants further indicates that the use of visual methods succeeded in keeping young people interested in the research. It could also be shown that young people demonstrated a high level of methodological sensitivity for choosing the most appropriate visual methods for their own research projects.

On the other hand, however, it became clear that young people's interest, their knowledge about and confidence in using visual methods varied immensely. Some gender issues became apparent with regard to young people's motivation for taking part in the research project and with regard to the research training at the beginning of the project. The provision of the training for all participants as well as the flexible research design aimed to address such differences and allowed a renegotiation of unequal power relations among participants over the course of the project. It indicates that the research design and the way in which visual methods are used can support the aim to create a more inclusive and participatory arena.

Anna's case demonstrated, however, that a minority of young people might not be attracted by visual methods, putting a question mark over the understanding that visual methods are generally more inclusive than traditional research methods and highlighting the value that traditional methods still have in youth research. I have argued here that a mixed method approach might bridge new and old approaches to youth research and allow researchers to negotiate the most appropriate methods in the context of each research project.

Even though many youth researchers increasingly argue that visual methods can provide unique insights into young people's everyday lives, the call for specific methods in youth research has been criticised. Alderson (1995), for example, has warned that an 'over-emphasis' on young people's 'otherness' and 'need of protection' can 'result in children being treated as passive objects, rather than as active moral agents on their own right' (ibid.: 68). It runs the risk of homogenising them as a social category. This, however, neglects the fact that some young people are more vulnerable than others and that some methodological decisions should be made with regard to young people's specific needs, interests and abilities, as well as with regard to the context they are living in. Valentine (1999) has thus argued that youth participation needs to be understood as a methodological approach that affects the entire project design (see also Alderson, 2000; Christensen and James, 2000; Pain and Francis, 2003; Kesby, 2005; Schäfer and Yarwood, 2009). Other social scientists have further highlighted that visual methods only capture *representations* rather than *reflections* and thus always need further verbal explanation (see Morrow, 2001; Murray, 2009; Pink, 2006; Rose, 2007). This is why researchers frequently combine some form of text-based data with visual images.

In agreement with these more critical voices, I stress the importance of an appropriate methodological framework rather than the use of youth-specific methods. I thus argue that the use of particular visual methods – such as videoing – do not, in themselves, guarantee high levels of participation. To avoid the risk of promoting a *tyranny of the method* (Cooke and Kothari, 2001) which disconnects research approaches and methods from the research context it is important to reflect more critically on the context within which visual methods are used, and to think carefully about ways in which they help facilitate young people's participation in and beyond the research context (see also Schäfer and Yarwood, 2008). Analysing young people's motives for using or not using specific visual methods provides an insight into young people's methodological sensitivity and might provide future youth research with valuable insights into young people's everyday lives.

Suggestions for further reading

Related methodological literature

• Lunch, N. and Lunch, C. (2006) *Insights into Participatory Video: A Handbook from the Field*, Insight, http://insightshare.org/resources/pv-handbook.

This handbook is a practical guide to setting up and running Participatory Video (PV) projects.

• Banks, M. (2009) *Using Visual Data in Qualitative Research* (The SAGE Qualitative Research Kit), London: Sage.

This book is a good introduction and provides a good overview of the general use of visual data in sociology and anthropology.

• Prosser, J. (1998) *Image-based Research: A Resource for Qualitative Researchers*, London: Routledge.

This book provides a good overview of key issues that need to be considered in image-based research.

• Thomson, P. (2008) *Doing Visual Research with Children and Young People*, London: Routledge.

This book discusses methodological, ethical and theoretical issues surrounding image-based research. It includes some chapters on the use of video in research with children and young people.

- Rose, G. (2007) *Visual Methodologies; An Introduction to the Interpretation of Visual Materials* (2nd Edition), London: Sage.

This book provides valuable insights into issues of visual data analysis

Examples of related youth research
- Murray, L. (2009) 'Looking at and Looking Back: Visualization in Mobile Research', *Qualitative Research*, 9 (4), 469–88.

In her work on young people's negotiation of risk on their way to school Murray used film elicitation interviews. Young people's footage acted as a focus for their group discussions.

- Pink, S. (2007a) 'Walking with Video', *Visual Studies*, 22, 240–52.

Sarah Pink discusses the method of walking with her participants and filming them to capture and better understand sensory experiences and to represent such experiences to a wider audience.

- Holliday, R. (2007) 'Performances, Confessions, and Identities: Using Video Diaries to Research Sexualities', in G. C. Stanczak (ed.) *Visual Research Methods: Image, Society and Representation*, London: Sage, 255–79.

In her research Holliday explores queer performances of identity and investigates the use of video diaries. She argues that video diaries provide deeper insights than audio taped interview and allow capturing the production of visual representations and the narrativisation of identities. Holliday also highlights the reflective potential of videoing.

9
Young People and Policy Research: Methodological Challenges in CYP-Led Research

Darren Sharpe

Introduction

This chapter outlines some of the methodological challenges that can arise in research led by children and young people. It does this through evaluating some critical moments relating to research projects designed and implemented by young people who were involved in the Young Researcher Network of the National Youth Agency during the late 2000s. Even as the work of young researchers helps to shed light on the social condition of their peers in British society, the major challenge for research of this kind is in achieving acceptance as a credible branch of the research community. Research by children and young people is often questioned, marginalised and devalued within policy and research communities because of misconceptions made about young people's evolving capacities and competencies to produce robust data that stands up to 'scientific' standards. Many people also work under the assumption that CYP-led research, by definition, needs to be young-person initiated, implemented and focused in its entirety. This chapter attempts to dispel some of these misconceptions and explores how they can be overcome through focusing on a broad range of research activities which need the involvement, consent or participation of young people in order for research legitimately to be considered 'CYP-led'.

Throughout this chapter, the term 'children and young-people-led research' is abbreviated to 'CYP-led research', and the term 'young researcher' is used to denote the different roles and responsibilities that CYP can take on in research projects. CYP-led research may be focused on issues specifically affecting younger generations or may be concerned with intergenerational issues; it may involve young people acting in a wide range of roles from peer researcher through to co-researcher; and may be led by children and young people or by adults working in collaboration with children and young people, or with young people acting as research commissioners. Critically, it is important not to become bogged down with labels but instead to focus on practice as the main indicator of CYP-led research.

The specific motivation or purpose behind support for CYP-led research among groups such as community youth workers or among specific policy and research communities is an interesting issue that can only be partially explored in this chapter. However, as a starting point we know that listening to what young people have to say is an integral part of the work of all of these groups. Directly involving young people in the research process is an extension of this part of the wider participation agenda, which is focused on fixing an imperfect child and youth sector. Wavering and doing nothing in this area fails young people in our commitment to ensuring that they have protection, are heard, have choices, are valued, have privacy, enjoy social inclusion and are not discriminated against. However, many public bodies and organisations are reluctant to spend their participatory budgets on CYP-led research, even though these budgets are designed to involve local people in making decisions on spending priorities, thereby bringing communities closer to decision making. They are perhaps uncertain, or maybe just not convinced of the value of research led by CYP. Yet, just as long as it is not tokenistic or for decoration, there are very few good reasons not to include children and young people in research. Economically, it requires capital investment but will help to make services for young people more cost-effective in the longer term. Politically, it is justified by the promotion of active citizenship and a subtle process of politicisation. Culturally, it echoes the evidence-based environment which, at least until fairly recently, had structured current thinking.

The current emphasis on CYP-led research is not new, but it has developed considerably in recent years, both in sheer volume and in the scope of its activities. It is a quiet movement, which has been challenging how service provision targeted at young people is being designed, delivered and evaluated. To date, the young people involved in the Young Researcher Network have built up their skills, increased their self-confidence and resilience, and have developed the ability to campaign and/or lobby behind an authentic and informed voice. CYP-led research has also added value to the quality of research 'on', 'for' and 'about' children and young people (see Kellett, 2005a, 2010; Delgado, 2006; Sharpe, 2009 and Boeck and Sharpe, 2009). Young researchers are then following in the tradition of past movements, such as those led by feminist and Afrocentric researchers, or researchers with disabilities, which have challenged the status quo of the academy and have broken free from traditional ways of doing research.

Background to the Young Researcher Network (YRN)

The Young Researcher Network is a project of the National Youth Agency (NYA). The NYA is the national expert and developmental organisation for supporting those who work with young people in England. It is a registered charity and aims to advance youth work in order to promote young people's personal and social development, and their voice, influence and place in society. The Young Researcher Network (YRN) was first established in 2007 and involves a network of organisations that support and encourage young people's active involvement in research in order to influence and shape youth policy and practice. Between 2008 and 2010 the YRN supported to completion over 25 research projects led by young people by providing a grants programme, research skills training, seminars, conferences, capacity building and more. During this period I worked as a Young People's Participation Development Officer for the NYA, working directly with the YRN. The idea of the network arose from the new requirement on local authorities to go beyond merely 'consulting' young people. The Local Government and Public Involvement in Health Act (2007) contains reference to the 'duty to involve', requiring that councils inform, consult and involve people in decisions on the design and delivery of local services. Impetus also came from the UN Convention on the Rights of the Child in the form of guidelines for the proper conduct of research involving children and young people (Beazley et al., 2009), as well as a plethora of other government Acts (see Chapters 1 and 6 for more on the drivers of the participatory movement in youth research more generally).

Prior to the development of the YRN very little was actually captured and shared about the work of young researchers in the UK relating to the challenges of doing applied social research (see too Brownlie, 2009). Throughout the UK, groups belonging to local and national charities, as well as those which are a part of local authorities, had been busy doing CYP-led research on a range of interconnected issues but to differing levels of quality, with varying degrees of impact, and largely in isolation from each other. The YRN linked emerging, established and advanced CYP-led research groups and produced a critical mass of young researchers. This was a crucial moment in the expansion of research led by young people in the UK.

The YRN was a product of its time, emerging during a period marked by an unprecedented growth in public spending on youth-led initiatives at the centre of government and a genuine commitment on behalf of public bodies to promote young people's active participation in local decision making. It may come as no surprise, then, that the involvement of CYP in research was largely borne out of practical considerations. The theoretical underpinnings of young people's involvement in research have not been the main driving force behind this movement. Instead, it has been the requirement to listen to users in the design, development and evaluation of services that has driven this agenda. This has been underpinned by a commitment to cost effectiveness, targeted intervention and compliance to evidence-based practice.

My abiding (albeit biased) view is that the NYA were trail blazers in establishing the YRN and helped to define the parameters of this emerging field. They proved to be one of the most innovative organisations in taking seriously the competency and capacity of young people to lead on research. That said and done, the supporters of CYP-led research have not always been best placed to advance methodological rigour. Despite being an avid proponent of CYP-led research, the NYA – like many other organisations working with young researchers – often wears a politicised straitjacket that hampers its ability wholeheartedly to embrace the academic enterprise at the centre of this endeavour. The difficulty arises when organisations working with children and young people are only interested in achieving short-term goals and are dismissive of conceptual, theoretical and methodological issues that lead to the production of high quality research. A commitment to research initiated and controlled by young people, underpinned by a principled politics of empowerment is admirable, but does not guarantee high quality research. 'Pure' CYP-led research – where young people develop the initial idea *and* decide how the project is to be carried out – is a high-risk strategy if the aim is to secure genuine and substantive change. Decision makers have to navigate a mass of research reports and official papers and need to be able to trust the information they have presented to them. They have the difficult task of judging the value of research findings against scheduled work programmes and budgets, in addition to having to negotiate the macro and micro politics of the policy process. The difficulty for decision makers is how to determine the trustworthiness and validity of CYP-led research and its findings if it does not follow the usual 'academic' standards, given the absence of any alternative criteria to those commonly used in the academic and policy research communities by which we might judge them (see Kellett, 2005b).

For this reason organisations supporting young people's involvement in research need to ensure that CYP-led methodologies are rigorous in design and implementation, in order to persuade decision makers not only of the need for change but how to create change.

A further empirical observation from the third sector is that young people's involvement in research is often viewed in terms of a crude and rigid dichotomy of active researchers versus passive research objects. Organisations and individuals can often become preoccupied with this issue, and are prone to talking themselves out of supporting the development of CYP-led research, perhaps forgetting all the positions that exist in between these two extremes. Young people's participation in research should be seen as existing on a continuum from adult-led and initiated at one extreme to young people-led and initiated at the other (see Box 9.1). What is borne out of the YRN experience is that the status of both young people and adults can change over time within the one CYP-led project. Therefore, methodologies involving young people need to be flexible and capable of addressing both different ways of working and different patterns of participation, at the same time allowing for ingenuity while still having moral integrity.

For instance, the idea behind the National Children's Bureau (NCB) research project on the media portrayal of young people (detailed later) was conceived by adults, developed by young research advisors and then conducted by a changing cast of young researchers. Young researchers slipped in and out of the study to continue with their education, with the support of two adult researchers who coordinated activities. Similarly, the UK Youth Voice Panel research, also on the media portrayal

Box 9.1 Typical response of young researcher to involvement in CYP-led research

What have you got out of doing this research?

'Lots of training and loads of new skills and [I] have learnt how to talk to more people. We didn't really talk to people much before, we were nervous talking to officials but when you know what you're talking about and know how to address people it gives you that confidence. Not only do we know what we're talking about, all the other young people in the area are saying this as well. More confident talking with new people because you've had training and that.'

Anthony, Young Researcher

of young people (again detailed later), came out of the annual campaign priorities established by the then outgoing Youth Voice Panel and taken up by the incoming Panel. The role of the adult advisor was crucial in managing the transition. In other cases, support workers have had to provide support in building self-confidence, coordinating special transport, and liaising with, and often working alongside parents and carers in order to secure the on-going involvement of young researchers in a non-tokenistic manner.

Based on my experience at the YRN, the actual practice of doing research has been of great value to young people in acquiring critical-thinking skills, getting their voices heard and providing concrete examples of active citizenship (see Delgado, 2006 and Box 9.1). To this end, CYP-led research has enabled them to delve deep into an issue and to interrogate what their peers as well as adults understand and think about the issue under investigation. This type of information is invaluable to policy and decision makers – as mentioned earlier – but only when it is done right. Research is one of the best tools to help accomplish positive outcomes for young people. However, the politics and processes of young people's involvement in research need to be understood for it to be effective.

Accessible and engaging methodological frameworks: The eco-system approach to CYP-led research

The YRN broke new ground with its context-bound *ecosystem approach* to guide the development and implementation of CYP-led research. I coined the term in 2009, although the central ideas stemmed from my work in participatory and user-led research in various contexts over the previous decade. It became clear to me that to ensure meaningful dialogue and exchange of ideas between all parties involved in CYP-led research, young researchers involved in the YRN needed to adopt a pragmatic position. This meant developing a balanced culture where CYP researchers were not only 'in the room' with decision makers from the outset but were also sufficiently trained to synthesise and share information with a view to building meaningful relationships with adult stakeholders. Thus, the ecosystem approach to CYP-led research is more of a model in doing research 'with' or 'by' young people than a methodology. It is a way to support young people to marshal evidence and establish a point of view, however insurmountable the challenges may appear.

Like all bio-diversity systems, each component of an eco-system – whether a town pond or a Council Chamber – is governed by its own set of rules and tensions, but while each component functions independently of each other they are all locked into an encompassing system and are interdependent for their survival. The same dynamic process also applies to CYP-led research. For example, the different household codes regulating curfews, family holidays and the observing of religious festivals such as Christmas or Ramadan impact on individual young researchers in a parallel manner to the way in which councillors, policy makers and chief executives work within their own sets of protocols, timeframes and reporting procedures. They welcome detailed information to support new youth initiatives or policy but this needs to fit into current policy or legislative frameworks. The ecosystem approach therefore straddles the public and private worlds of those involved in research, it places equal emphasis on process and outcome and values conversation, it knows how research is viewed and where it fits into an organisation, and addresses both the needs and ambitions of young people, while working together with the organisation they seek to influence.

Figure 9.1 illustrates the flow in communication and decision making experienced by members of the YRN when designing and developing policy research. The main audience for young researchers are commissioners, senior managers, policy officers and legislators. Therefore, they need an approach to help frame their thinking and measure their progression while acknowledging the different views of stakeholders. The eco-system approach takes into account the views of young people, parents, support workers and decision makers and values differences in opinion. The basic principles of the eco-system approach are not straightforward because young researchers' lives are not straightforward, neither are the ways youth participation groups work. Given that young researchers are the central research tool and stand at the centre of the process, the ecosystem approach does not overburden young people with structure and routine, in order to avoid further mythologising the research process and making it seem too much like hard work. Instead we try to make research fun and provide opportunities for creative and critical thinking, with checks and balances along the way, to ensure that young researchers arrive at recognisable standards in research. The approach therefore values and encourages *dynamism, utilitarianism* and *realism* in how CYP-led methodologies are designed and implemented, as the following examples demonstrate.

For instance, the Barnardo's Kirklees Khandaani Dhek Bhal Service research group, based in Kirklees, West Yorkshire, comprised five young researchers and three support workers and demonstrated real *dynamism*

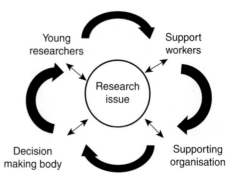

Figure 9.1   CYP-led ecosystem framework of influence

in how they went about building their research question. Over several intensive workshops and rewordings, the group arrived at a consensus and produced an answerable research question. The mission of the group was to turn the lens onto their own ethnic community and/or faith identity. They investigated the experience of living with a 'double identity' at home, at school and in their broader community so that the specific needs of South Asian young people could be better understood and therefore met by professionals. They were as critical of their home lives as they were of their schooling and other aspects of their lives. Another example is 'Investing In Children', based in Durham, which brought together an advanced group of young researchers with one support worker. Their work provides an exemplar of *utility* in research. Concerned for the health needs of young people in their district, they teamed up with their local Primary Care Trust (PCT) to tackle a recommendation from an earlier study, which they had been commissioned to undertake by the PCT. They were able to present their findings on the efficacy and cost effectiveness of health-liaison officers for young people in different health authorities from across the UK with the condition that the PCT would seriously consider adopting best practice. Lastly, an exemplar of *realism* in research is evidenced in the work of an emerging research group called 'Have Your Say', based in Newcastle-upon-Tyne. The group comprised of four young researchers, each with experience of public care, and two support workers (1.5 Full Time Equivalent [FTE]). Their mission was to examine the involvement of children and young people in the care-review process and to make practical recommendations to ensure reviews are more young-people friendly. Following the study the group was commissioned by the local authority to produce a DVD detailing their key findings so that all children and young people entering the care system in Newcastle would know their rights in a case review.

To summarise, the key characteristics of the eco-system approach are about joined-up research that does not take place in a vacuum. The approach walks a moral tightrope of pragmatism fused with applied social research. In other words, it is concerned with doing the right research that will produce a desired impact, as much as doing research right. It is driven by young people's own bottom-up perspectives of the world but with a strong emphasis on achieving a shared vision of change with adult collaborators. It could be true to say that the approach is more strategically positioned than many other research approaches and is clear on what it wants to achieve: research for change. It is more able than other research approaches to accommodate a variety of different research strategies (such as exploratory, descriptive or explanatory) to test theory or respond to tenders, but with its primary focus firmly on tangible, demonstrable and immediate change.

Negotiating CYP-led research methodologies

Overcoming the methodological challenges found in CYP-led research hinges on the possibility for young people to be supported, trained and efficiently resourced to undertake independent research. The YRN explicitly endorsed research that was CYP-centred. This meant demystifying research practices and research language, and negotiating research settings so that they were CYP-friendly. It is also important for the research methodology to negotiate effectively with the end users in order to ensure that they can work with the accumulated data and that the data adequately address a shared concern. This is not easy, but a necessary stage in the research process for the findings to stand a chance of making a real difference. This came as a surprise to some of the youth groups I have worked with. They only expected to speak with decision makers at the end of the research process but in CYP-led research the conversation starts at the outset. To reduce the possibility of unrealistic expectations creeping into the research process the YRN set itself up as a critical friend for each of the projects. We checked proposals to see if they spoke to any of the emerging childhood- and youth-policy directives and to check that projects were doable in terms of time and methodology. We also encouraged groups to consider the forces for and against their projects, the possible ways in which they could persuade cynics, and how to ensure impact was defined with end users, and provided practical assistance in the design of a dissemination strategy.

These checks and balances did not always work the way we antici-pated. For instance, a group of young researchers in a Midlands local authority aimed to survey young people's perceptions of the local bar-riers and drivers to accessing 'positive activities' (positive leisure-time activities). The group comprised three young people and two com-munity youth workers (1.5 FTE). Even though the research project was negotiated and championed by the Chief Executive of the City Council to inform the city's Myplace youth facility bid, the project did not suc-ceed in making an impact. The group did not successfully complete their research project because of slippage in decision making that negatively impacted on data collection. This was caused by poor communication due to regular staff absences and overstretched young researchers, all of which led to a situation where exact roles and responsibilities were unclear and little got done. My own experience suggests, then, that the support worker is an anchor to the research process and should be a physical presence, able to encourage creativity, imagination, curiosity, logic, rigour, reason and optimism among young researchers.

All things considered, fluid, flexible and organic research method-ologies have been the hallmark of YRN research. Even though CYP-led research strategies tend not to follow the usual rhythm and flow of professional research projects they often resemble the dynamism of grounded theory and action-based research. The methods adopted tend to give greater autonomy to the participants and provide a range of techniques and tools for the research group to utilise when needed. A prime example is 'After Wagon Time', a UK Youth Parliament research project comprising seven young researchers from Gypsy and Traveller backgrounds. The emerging research group adapted a photo-elicitation approach to produce an exhibition for Paultons Family Theme Park on contemporary Gypsy and Traveller cultures. Their mission was to produce research that would raise awareness of the ways Gypsies and Travellers live today. Due to the low literacy level of the group members, the researchers decided that any method involving a lot of reading, writing or reliance on the written word would not be appropriate. After a series of training sessions, the group decided to use photo elicitation as its primary data collection method: telling stories through pictures. The group agreed upon their qualitative approach, what type of pictures to take, and what range of questions to ask about them. Members of the group were given two cameras each in order to generate pictures of a personal nature and/or of importance to them, with the aim of capturing 'changes' in homes, furnishings, artefacts of life, family and community relationships etc. Photographs were combined with in-depth interviews. Notes were also kept and written reports of the stories captured.

As in this last example, much of the research in the YRN has been qualitative in orientation. This broad set of approaches has been thought to allow enough flexibility and scope for young people to feel truly involved in, or lead on projects. Where quantitative methods have been used, the sample population has not always been large enough to allow any higher-level statistical testing or generalisation to be made. This does not mean, however, that quantitative approaches should be avoided. On the contrary, young researchers should be trained in, or at the very least receive tasters of both qualitative and quantitative approaches in order to decide on the best approach to follow in any given research project. On this basis, two YRN partners have taken a quantitative turn. In the first example, young researchers involved in the aforementioned UK Youth Voice Panel designed a questionnaire aimed at young people aged 16–25 to find out their views on the representation of children and young people in the media, and to discover ways in which any misrepresentations could be rebalanced. They were able to gather the views and opinions of 588 young people from a target group of 1000 from across the UK. This success was achieved because they were able to utilise their online presence and their database of young people and networks.

The second example involves young researchers involved in 'v', an independent charity aiming to inspire a new generation of young volunteers. Through its 'vinspired' programme, *v* connects 16–25 year olds with volunteering opportunities throughout England. Members of '*v*20' – a group of 16–25 year olds who work right at the heart of *v*, helping to make decisions and consulting with *v* staff to keep the passions and interests of young people at the forefront of *v*'s work – were trained by the YRN to advise in the research commissioning process. The training emphasised, among other aspects, quantitative approaches in social research such as standardised data collection methods, patterns of causal relationships, hypothesis testing, and the importance of robustness in research findings.

Before going on to use or provide advice to others on quantitative and/or qualitative approaches, both of these groups of young researchers had the opportunity to consider their own roles and responsibilities in the research team. This was achieved through completion of an individual research skills audit and attending a workshop linking skills, attributes and knowledge sets to specific research tasks (see the YRN Research Training Toolkit: website details are provided at the end of this chapter). As a result, young researchers identified the research roles and responsibilities that interested them most and which, it was hoped, were likely to stretch them (Boeck and Sharpe, 2009). Based on my own experiences of providing support to the YRN, I would suggest that workers should be looking out for and encouraging a shift in consciousness as young people's exposure to research increases. Research can be unproductive if it is not properly supported. For example, I have observed how support workers sometimes struggle in moving smoothly between being a critical friend or an enabler and in spotting when to lead in order to overcome methodological hurdles. If we provide the right support, however, we will see more productive results. Young people will still feel confident that they have control over what they are doing, but with the added bonus that someone is there to help (see Box 9.2 below).

To summarise, the best outcome for CYP-led research is a butterfly effect that promotes understanding and educates those involved while bringing about positive outcomes, and which touches decision makers as well as other young people at the periphery. The ecosystem approach steers clear from any 'evangelical' or 'fundamentalist' belief that raises young people's rights above any other groups in society. Instead, it relies upon a pragmatic stance to bring about 'research for change', change that has been defined 'with' and 'by' young people along with change brokers and policy makers. CYP-led research must face the world front on and persuade cynics of its value.

Designing and implementing creative online methods

What deters many young people from doing research is that it often seems to be remote and is presented as being far too sophisticated

---

Box 9.2   Young researcher highlighting the balance between support and personal initiative

Were you totally in control of your project? Did you have support?

'We had support from the YRN and from the Local Participation Team in North Tyneside and they helped us get in touch with the young people because they had the contacts and supported us with the training. But it was our idea and mainly run by us'

(*Jason, Young Researcher*)

compared with the usual repertoire of activities that make up their daily lives. By designing research methodologies that start from young people's own perceptions of the world (Arches and Fleming, 2007) appropriate methods can more easily be identified and are more likely to be adhered to in the field. Not only will young people be more likely to feel ownership of the framework but also they will be more likely to remain part of the group for the life of the project. Thus, there is no riddle in how to select suitable research methods 'with' or 'for' young people. The trick is to identify methods that resonate with or can be easily transferred into their lives. For example, the YRN has, where appropriate, promoted and encouraged usage of new social media at each stage of the research process, allowing young researchers to share their problems, offer solutions, participate in real-time forums with policy and decision makers, gather data and, most importantly, disseminate key messages from their own research. These are tools that feature prominently in young people's lives and their inclusion stops research from being seen as dull. Without using such tools, it is often challenging to maintain the interest and focus of young people. To accomplish this end, research methods need to be creative and innovative (see OPM, 2010).

E-participation has also enabled young people otherwise disconnected by geography, mobility and time constraints to become meaningfully involved in research. However, not all young researchers have had access to the Internet or will have the competencies to feel able to blog and so forth. The belief that all young people are proficient computer users and have easy access to high speed broadband is not borne out in the experience of the YRN. Accordingly, our use of new social media was also underpinned by face-to-face contact. Neither does virtual networking work if it is 'cold'. It is easier to network face-to-face initially and maybe by text once people have established some sense of relationship before online platforms can really succeed. Even so, e-participation is not for everyone and the YRN has endeavoured to create the circumstances where the Internet is not the only means by which users can connect to a project. As many of the examples in this chapter highlight, we have not forgotten about using traditional research methods such as questionnaire surveys and interviews, but they are used with imagination and mixed with innovative methods. We have looked at the kind of activities and events attended by young people as a source of inspiration and interrogated such activities carefully, taking into consideration the aspects that could best be developed and/or integrated into an appropriate research framework.

Developing a reflective practice and nurturing sensitive young researchers

We were also clear that we needed to train young people to undertake research that fostered the values and principles of social pedagogy and/ or 'service learning', approaches steeped in the community education tradition (see Delgado, 2006). Service learning and social pedagogy have in common a multifaceted and incredibly flexible teaching and learning process. They are tailored to meet specific goals and community needs and to engage participants in meaningful and personally relevant ways. Thus, training in itself has been a means of empowerment at the YRN and has yielded insider knowledge that has enriched CYP-led research projects. However, common sense must prevail in order to develop and implement robust research methodologies. Therefore, young researchers require a negotiated research-skills training programme, covering topics such as:

- defining the topic or theme;
- specifying a research question;
- undertaking a literature review;
- selecting appropriate research methods;
- undertaking fieldwork; carrying out data analysis and interpretation;
- writing up; and
- dissemination.

Providing good research-skills training not only teaches young people how to stay safe but also how to take account of their decisions and actions in research. Good research-skills training makes a great effort to help young researchers express themselves naturally and honestly. How young researchers then translate these skills and newly acquired knowledge into ethical conduct is dependent upon how they are supported. A good example is the National Children's Bureau (NCB) young researcher group, which was mentioned earlier. NCB is the leading national charity that supports children, young people and families and those who work with them. The NCB young researchers group undertook a research project on 'the media portrayal of teenagers – impact and influences'. The aim was to ensure young people have a strong voice in all matters that affect their lives and to promote positive images of children and young people. First the group met to discuss all the ethical considerations of their research project. Each young person was given a project folder, which included a section on ethics. They looked at the YRN ethical framework (included in the YRN Research Training Toolkit) as well as NCB's ethics guidelines, and one member of the group attended the YRN ethics-training course (see Box 9.3).

The group discussed issues relating to informed consent, anonymity and confidentiality, including an exploration of the limits to confidentiality if a child protection issue arose. In relation to informed consent they decided to create an information leaflet. This explained who the team members were, what the research was about, why the research was happening and what would be involved if a young person decided to take part. It also made young people aware of their rights if they took part in the research, and explained that child protection concerns in relation to reducing harm would be classed as more important than keeping confidential any information that might be disclosed in the research process. All participants received an information leaflet covering these issues, and the ethical guidelines that the group was abiding by were reiterated at the start of the focus groups and interviews. To help with possible instances of disclosure or other unforeseen incidents, a project worker attended the focus group as a silent observer. All information was stored on the computer and password-protected. The support staff at NCB agreed a set time period for storing this information, after which it would be destroyed.

In generating robust data, then, young people need considerable support in developing sound ethical frameworks and protocols. CYP-led research needs to be made safe and to demonstrate rigour. From the outset ethical implications need to be taken seriously and also revisited at each stage in the enterprise. Young researchers need to consider whether it is justifiable to be asking other young people – or indeed adults – the kind of questions to which they seek answers. So bearing in mind that young people will not be seasoned researchers, they need a well-thought-through

Box 9.3   A young researcher's reflections on the training process

Did you learn any new skills?

'*YRN helped us to get training, interview skills training, analysis training, training for proposal writing, everything, questionnaire writing so we've got loads of new skills. We also did training on ethics and public speaking.*'

Daniel, Young Researcher

support system to be built up around them. This support system should, at the very least, provide support in relation to disclosures of potential harm, highlight clear exit points that do not equate to failure, and provide a system where expenses for fieldwork and the purchase of research materials can be quickly reimbursed or ideally paid up-front to mitigate any financial worries or concerns that might hamper young people's participation both as young researchers and as research participants (see Kellett, 2010: 66–7, Boeck and Sharpe, 2009: 15).

Conclusion

This chapter has demonstrated why and how young people can be involved in the research process and has considered some of the methodological challenges which their involvement presents. I feel that research standards are enhanced by the involvement of children and young people in the research process, and we can see how their involvement came to be increasingly valued by central and local government over the last decade or so. Undoubtedly, a power imbalance still exists between decision makers and young researchers. Decision makers have the power to structure the research field and the value system within which young people seek to get their voices heard. Even when research is done from the right standpoint and for the right reasons it will still counter arguments of inferiority due to the perceived inexperience of CYP, but this is true of much user-led research, not just that which is CYP-led. But with the power to marginalise voices also comes counter-power to decentralise voices. I have seen firsthand at the YRN how young researchers have fought to get their research message listened to. As a result, the YRN has been successful in helping to influence and shape youth policy and provision and in raising awareness on issues that matter to young people.

The reach and impact of the YRN has been demonstrated by its recognition both internationally and nationally. Internationally, we were able to assist the British Council in setting-up the Young Arab Think Tank, subsequently renamed the Young Arab Researchers Network. We also contributed to the development of the European Union 2020 E-Participation Directive for Young People. Nationally, the YRN, in conjunction with the Guardian newspaper, was given an award by *Children and Young People Now* magazine for the best positive press coverage of young people in 2010, awarded specifically for a special *Guardian Society* supplement which was co-researched and edited by the YRN.

During 2010–11 the YRN was sponsored by the Local Government Association to provide a new round of research funding for local authority youth participation groups interested in helping to shape and influence how local public budgets are spent. From the original cohort of funded YRN groups some have gone on to develop their work with young researchers. For example, Independent Academics Research Studies (IARS), a youth-led social policy think-tank that was set up in 2001 'to empower and give voice to young people so that they can influence policy and democratically engage in society as equal citizens' (www.iars.org.uk), provides accredited training for young researchers, while the NCB has extended the Young Research Advisors programme and works tirelessly to involve children and young people in health care policy and practice.

Locally, most of the YRN groups have met with local decision makers who have adopted recommendations that came out of their research. The YRN provided a coherent and innovative approach to supporting CYP-led research at a time when funding was available, to add value to emerging, established or advanced research groups. The future is now uncertain for many of the existing YRN partner organisations. The drawbridge has well and truly been closed for funding, which enables youth participation groups to marshal evidence to support or dispute a case or point of view on youth issues. The YRN, like many other youth participation initiatives, will need to take a different course to secure funding for policy research, and to combine this with seeking out new innovations in CYP-led research at home and abroad.

Suggestions for further reading

Related methodological literature
- National Youth Agency (2010) *The Young Researcher Network Research Training Toolkit*, available at: http://nya.org.uk/dynamic_files/yrn/ YRN Toolkit Dec 2010.pdf

This document provides an overview of the advice and guidance offered to groups of youth researchers involved in the Young Researcher Network. Other YRN training materials can be found at: http://www.nya. org.uk/integrated-youth-support-services/young-researcher-network

Examples of related youth research
Reports relating to some of the projects referred to in this chapter, as well as other examples, can be downloaded from here:
http://www.nya.org.uk/integrated-youth-support-services/young-researcher-network/yrn-research-reports

10
Youth Research in Web 2.0: A Case Study in Blog Analysis

Helene Snee

Introduction

New Internet technologies provide social researchers with an opportunity to conduct innovative studies in youthful spaces. Recent developments termed 'Web 2.0' offer a unique insight into the lives, tastes, preferences and interactions of young people. Social networking sites such as Facebook, for example, are hugely popular and part of everyday life. Recent Facebook statistics state that there are 400 million active users of the website, 50 per cent of whom log on in any given day (Facebook, 2010). This chapter draws upon a research project that examined the phenomenon of gap-year travel by utilising one such Web 2.0 development, the 'weblog' or 'blog', in order to explore young people's representations of their gap-year story in their travel blogs. The gap-year study highlights the benefits but also the challenges of conducting blog analysis. Benefits included the advantage of being able to access more gap-year stories than might be possible with 'offline' methods, and the ability to access textual accounts of experience that were spontaneous and naturalistic. Some of the challenges included dealing with lots of multimedia data, which raised the importance of considering what was central to the research questions; the question of whether traditional standards of validity are applicable to blog data, particularly with reference to authenticity and representativeness; two overlapping ethical questions: whether blogs are public or private data, and whether we deal with human subjects or authors when we conduct blog analysis; and the importance of matching research aims and objectives to the potential of online methodologies.

This chapter aims to prompt reflection upon these issues for those interested in the methodological potential of blogs (and other online resources) in social research. It begins with a brief introduction to the research project and the method undertaken to collect and analyse the blog data, and introduces the concept of Web 2.0 and blogs as data resources for the social sciences. The benefits of using blogs for research and the approach taken to analysing narratives in the gap-year project are discussed, along with some practical issues regarding the handling of large volumes of data and reflections on dealing with new forms of text. The validity of blog data is considered, due to the blurring of boundaries online and who might be captured in the research population. It then examines the ethics of conducting blog analysis and the decisions that were made in the course of the gap-year research. Some final considerations, including suggestions as to how researchers may take these issues forward, are offered in the concluding section.

The gap year project

Overseas gap years are becoming increasingly popular for young people who wish to take some time out before they embark on higher education. They often involve independently organised travel and they are built upon the tradition of young people 'backpacking' (Richards and Wilson, 2004). More and more gap years are now arranged through more formal 'structured' placements however, with a growing industry of gap-year-provider organisations co-ordinating accommodation, activities and volunteering or employment opportunities (Simpson, 2005). Gap years are promoted as an educational activity that could help young people gain valuable skills for employment, and therefore provide an insight into contemporary forms of cultural capital (Bourdieu, 1986). Heath (2007) suggests that not all gap years are viewed as having equal status, with the more expensive placements being seen to be the most beneficial. Furthermore, as these gap years invariably take place overseas, there are questions regarding the relationship of 'gappers' with the people and places they encounter (Simpson, 2004).

To explore these issues, the study drew upon Goffman's (1974) concept of framing, and its adoption by new social movement theorists (Benford and Snow, 2000), to examine the ways in which young people's stories were 'framed' by cultural resources, including values, shared meanings and narratives. Gap-year stories were accessed using the first-hand accounts of overseas gap years from young people's blogs.

Beer and Burrows (2007) suggest we can look at Web 2.0 content such as blogs as an archive of everyday life. Accessing the stories told by young gap-year travellers even ten years ago would have depended upon gaining access to either their correspondence back home, or their diaries. This, of course, presents certain ethical dilemmas, which will be explored in depth below. The term weblog was first used in 1997 to describe 'a webpage where a weblogger "logs" all the other webpages she [*sic*] finds interesting' (Blood, 2004). However, the 'rise of linkless blogging culture' (Wakeford and Cohen, 2008: 311) means the term has expanded to include online journals. Contemporary blogging conventions include

> regular and frequent updating, whether writing, photos or other content; the expectation of linking to other bloggers and online sources; a month-by-month archive; the capacity of feedback through comments to the blog; a particular style of writing which is often characterised as spontaneous and revelatory.
>
> (Wakeford and Cohen 2008: 308)

The blogs that formed the basis of the gap-year study can be categorised as 'travel blogs', which have parallels with the offline formats of travelogues and travel photo albums (Herring et al., 2004: 10). As such, they are less centred on providing links to other web pages, and are more concerned with providing a record and narrative of the author's gap-year experience.

Research design

The subjects of interest were the first-hand accounts of gap years by young people from the UK who spent their time out between school and university overseas. A theoretical sampling frame was built to capture the blogs that met these criteria. First of all, Internet searches were conducted using the phrase 'gap year' on two blog search engines: Google Blog Search and Technorati; and three blog platforms: Myspace, LiveJournal and the specialist travel journal site Globenotes. The 700 blogs that were collected and inspected during the search process were recorded, and included in the sample if the blog met the criteria for inclusion. These were: if it was clear that the author was from the UK and took their year out overseas; if it was clear that they had taken their gap year between school and university; and if they were of sufficient length to provide enough data (e.g. they did not consist of a solitary post). This process continued until a final sample of 39 blogs was reached. There were initially 40 blogs in the sample, but one was discarded when the author revealed that she did not fit the criteria, which highlights some of the quality problems with blog data that are discussed in more depth below. The sample was also checked to ensure that it was balanced in terms of gender and type of gap year (so that it did not contain gappers who had only undertaken structured placements, for example). Once the sample had been finalised, the blog posts were manually saved as text, and imported into Atlas.ti for coding. In addition to the blog data, all of the young people in the sample were contacted to ask if they would consent to an interview. Nine interviews were conducted, which provided valuable contextual information and enabled the themes identified in the blog analysis to be explored through personal interaction.

Being able to access young people's personal accounts of experience is a key advantage of blogs. However, as noted by O'Connor (2006), caution must be taken in using online methods, so that their potential is not overstated and the method used is appropriate to the research. In the case of the gap year study, blogs offered a number of benefits over more established qualitative methods such as interviewing.

Methodological issues

Benefits of using blogs

Mann and Stewart (2000) identify the following general advantages of conducting research online: extending access; cost and time savings; eliminating transcription bias and easier handling of data due to its presentation as the finished text; and more participant-friendly research, as thoughts are presented in an environment of their own choosing and using their own language (Mann and Stewart, 2000: 15–25). The practical advantages of blogs were particularly convincing for the gap-year study. The content generated was relatively easy to access, and in addition the sample could be extended to young people from a wide geographical area, including those who were still overseas during the initial sampling stage. Using blogs was therefore a way of accessing the gap year experiences of a greater number of gappers than relying on interviews alone.

This type of analysis, in which unsolicited blog posts are utilised as a form of documentary resource, would not be suitable for research with different aims and objectives, however. For example, if the gap year study had been specifically concerned with examining why young people undertook their time out in particular countries, then an analysis of pre-existing blogs would not have been appropriate, simply because it would not be possible to guarantee that the gappers would discuss this.

Blog analysis, therefore, should not be adopted for its own sake, it should reflect the theoretical grounding of the research. The stories told in the gap year blogs provided the participants' own official accounts of experience, and what they considered to be important to communicate to their audience. By conducting a blog analysis, it was possible to examine the frameworks of understanding employed by the participants and without intervention or prompting. Blogs thus enable researchers interested in narrative to access naturalistic and spontaneous accounts of everyday life, in which 'situated action [is] unadulterated by the scrutiny of the researcher' (Hookway, 2008: 95).

Analysing narratives using blogs

Narratives are defined by Hinchman and Hinchman (1997) as 'discourse[s] with a clear sequential order that connect events in a meaningful way for a definite audience and thus offer insights about the world and/or people's experiences of it' (cited in Elliott, 2005: 3). There are clear parallels between this definition of narratives as chronological, meaningful and social (Elliott 2005: 4) and the practice of blogging. The structure of blogs themselves are organised temporally; each post adds to a sequential account. They are, by definition, a chronological description of experience produced for an audience.

Other work that utilises blogs to investigate narratives has drawn similar conclusions regarding their value. For example, Karlsson (2006) examines the narratives of 'diasporic tourists': Asian Americans who present autobiographical accounts of their visits to their 'homelands' in Asia for a community 'back home' in the US. Hookway's (2008) research into everyday morality had to take into account the methodological problem of capturing moral narratives in everyday life, which he argues are not something that can be asked about directly but can be accessed through blogs (Hookway, 2008: 94).

Looking at how the participants communicated their experiences to an audience enabled a consideration of the unprompted narratives that frame the gap year. Although blog analysis was well matched to the research questions, it also presented a number of challenges.

Dealing with new forms of text

Blogs are multimedia texts, which presented some analytical challenges. Online researchers must handle Internet text and 'its inherent intertextuality, its lack of center [sic], its volume, its multimedianess, its international scope, its impermanence, and the resulting sense of authorship' (Mitra and Cohen, 1999: 199). A single page from the gap-year blogs could contain: a blog entry in text (which can be edited and reworded by the author), pictures, video clips, text or visual comments from readers and responses from the author, hyperlinks to other websites, advertisements from the host website and audio files. Some researchers have attempted to engage with the non-textual aspects of blogging. For example, Scheidt and Wright (2004) explore visual trends in blogs, such as the extent of customisation, and Badger (2004) examines the use of photography and illustration.

Moreover, blogs are dynamic. The interactive comments section, for example, is where meanings can be negotiated, questions asked of the author and representations validated or disputed. Blogs have a 'live' element that means that their content may change from one day to the next, or even from one audience to the next, given the capabilities of bloggers to restrict the access to some posts to particular users. While the gap year blogs were multimedia texts, the fact that not all of the blogs contained all of the same elements had to be considered. Therefore, a decision was made to focus only on the written content, including the comments sections, captured on a specific date and time. Furthermore, the analysis of the gap year blogs was concerned with the particular representations of the young people's gap-year experiences and the cultural resources they drew upon to frame their accounts, rather than examining the medium itself. Researchers may wish to consider if such multimedia elements are integral to their project and, if so, how to incorporate these into their analysis. There is also a need to balance the potential of blog data and what is methodologically interesting with pragmatic concerns. Consulting the literature on visual methodologies, for example, may be beneficial in such instances (see Heath et al., 2009: 116–31, for an overview of the use of visual methods in youth research).

Volume of data

Even focusing solely on the written text, however, raised some practical issues for the gap-year study. A large number of results were generated through the initial Internet searches, which included blogs that discussed gap years, but were not necessarily a young person's travel blog. Additional common problems when attempting to sample blogs include the collection of spam blogs, abandoned blogs, access-restricted blogs and non-traditional blogs (e.g. blogs that are hosted on social networking sites) (Li and Walejko, 2008: 282). All of these were encountered during the data collection process, but as the sample was constructed using theoretical sampling, rather than aiming for a probability sample, any 'problem' blogs were inconvenient but could be discarded.

Decisions also had to be made regarding how much of the blogs to include in the analysis, given that some extended before and after the gap year itself. This was necessary due to the sheer volume of data collected so that as little unrelated material as possible was analysed. Even so, the blogs in the final sample ranged in length from 5000 words to 118,000, with an average word count of 26,000. In total, the number of words collected was over 1 million. Some blogs contained over 150 individual blog posts. In order to manage the data, the blog pages were manually converted into text files. This was time-consuming but had a number of advantages over a more automated procedure. Firstly, going through each blog in this way helped to familiarise the researcher with each of the journals. Secondly, manually saving each page meant that it could be briefly examined and unwanted text deleted (e.g. navigation links). Finally, and perhaps most importantly, any multimedia objects could be seen in context and notes made in the text file where appropriate. This helped to mitigate the decision to focus on written text only. Tools are increasingly being developed to automatically capture blog data. For example, a prototype Blog Analysis Toolkit, a service of the University of Pittsburgh's Qualitative Data Analysis Program (https://surveyweb2.ucsur.pitt.edu/qblog/page_login.php), captures new blog posts in a format that can be imported into data analysis software, although it cannot retrieve those from the past.

Given the volume of data, the computer aided qualitative data analysis software (CAQDAS) Atlas.ti was employed to make data retrieval and management more systematic and efficient. While CAQDAS is a useful tool, it has been subject to some debate in the social sciences, particularly with respect to narrative analysis (Seale, 2000), and it is important to consider whether its adoption matches the theoretical grounding of the research. Narrative analysis takes descriptions of events as data, 'whose analysis produces stories (e.g. biographies, histories, case studies)' (Polkinghorne, 1995: 6). Using CAQDAS could fragment the flow and coherence of these narratives, and where analysis of individual narrative form is to the fore then CAQDAS may be less useful. However, the gap-year study was designed with reference to Polkinghorne's (1995) 'analysis of narratives', which examines data in the form of narrative accounts across a body of data to identify general themes and concepts (Polkinghorne 1995: 13). CAQDAS was a useful tool to collect and code the common elements identified in the stories told by the blogs and so in this case, CAQDAS was not inconsistent with the analytical framework.

Evaluating the quality of blog data

Blogs are a contemporary form of documentary resource, 'an artefact which has, as its central feature, inscribed text' (Scott, 1990: 5).

Interpreting documentary sources, according to Scott (1990), relies on assessing the quality of the evidence in terms of authenticity, credibility, representativeness and meaning (Scott, 1990: 6). However, it is not always applicable to apply such criteria to the assessment of Internet data sources.

A number of boundaries are blurred in the online environment: 'the computer stands between normal categories of alive/not alive, public/private, published/unpublished, writing/speech, interpersonal/mass communication and identified/anonymous' (Madge, 2006). These blurred boundaries problematise the issue of authenticity, given the potential for the Internet to allow individuals to experiment with the presentation of self online. From the outset, ethnographic work on Internet use has stressed how users can be liberated from their offline embodied selves and are able to experiment with their identities (e.g. Turkle, 1995). Therefore, an environment where anonymity and pseudo-anonymity are the norm necessarily has implications for conventional understandings of validity (Mann and Stewart, 2000: 208). Even if individuals are not deliberately misleading or playful, '[a]nonymity in text-based environments gives one more choice and control in the presentation of self, whether or not the presentation is perceived as intended' (Markham, 2005: 809). An alternative view is that the relative anonymity online means that people may in fact be more 'truthful', and that perhaps this notion of play is outdated (Hewson et al., 2003: 44). This has particular resonance with Web 2.0 and the documentation of everyday life online, although there have been some infamous cases of audiences being misled by fictional blogs (Rettberg, 2008: 121–6).

Hookway (2008) argues that the importance of whether a blog is 'authentic' or not is dependent on 'whether a researcher is looking at how blogs work to produce particular effects or whether they are looking at how blogs correspond with an "offline" reality' (Hookway, 2008: 97). Researchers may, in fact, be interested in this presentation of self, and some, for example, have utilised blogs to look at teenagers' identity work online (Bortree, 2005; Mazur and Kozarian, 2010). In the gap year study, the main concern was that it was focused on a particular type of year out. One blog initially included in the sample was discarded, as when contact was made with the author, it emerged that she was a lot older than assumed. Despite these concerns, the research was primarily based upon how young people told the story of their gap years and therefore what was important was the public presentation of experience, rather than some kind of offline 'truth'.

A strategy that was adopted in the gap-year study was to supplement the blog data with interviews. This enabled the participants' online representations to be placed in the context of how they articulated their experiences offline. The blog accounts were not particularly different to those given in the interviews, but combining the methods allowed a fuller picture to emerge. Concerns about the 'authenticity' of blogs should not be seen as a barrier to the use of these stories, they rather form a part of the considerations regarding whether it is an appropriate means of investigating the issues of interest.

Research population

A further consideration for the use of blogs in social research is the representativeness of the sample, and what sorts of conclusions can be drawn about wider trends. There is a 'digital divide' in Internet use, and certain groups are under-represented online (Dutton et al., 2009). The same groups would therefore be under-represented in Internet research, and furthermore, not all Internet users are bloggers. These concerns are seen by some as slightly outdated, and that representativeness in online research methods has become less of a problem as Internet use has increased in scope (Hewson et al., 2003: 26). However, Internet usage is still not uniform across all sectors of the population. Latest figures state that 30 per cent of Britons do not use the Internet on the basis of social, economic or physical barriers, or simply as a matter of choice (Dutton et al., 2009: 6)

In the gap-year study, it was important to recognise that young people who do not blog might have a different take on the gap-year experience, which had implications for the representation of less empowered groups. Even within a research population, variations in individual technical expertise and usage, and also literacy (Mann and Stewart, 2000: 189, 192), can affect the language, content and scope of blogs. The fact that the participants were bloggers thus restricted any generalisations about the wider gap-year population. This again raises the importance of considering whether the particular aims and objectives of research projects correspond with the potential of blog analysis. The accounts offered by the bloggers may not be representative of all gap year experiences, but what they did offer was an indication of how certain stories were told and the resources that were drawn upon to do this.

Both the practical advantages, and the potential to investigate naturalistic narratives, meant that blogs were a methodologically appropriate way of accessing the first-hand accounts of gap-year experiences. For those interested in blog analysis, the gap-year study highlights the practical challenges of handling large amounts of data and the need to consider whether authenticity and representativeness would be a key concern. Furthermore, the use of innovative methods such as blog analysis presents a number of relatively new ethical challenges, which are now considered.

Ethics

It must be stressed that it is important for blog analysis to be subject to the established ethical considerations that govern any research project. However, as Grinyer (2007:1) notes, the relatively novel online environment may pose dilemmas for researchers that may not be covered by existing ethical guidelines, although there is a growing awareness in research guidance of the potential ethical issues associated with online methods. For example, the ESRC's Research Ethics Framework (2010) has a number of references to the need for additional care in the online environment. A particularly useful document is the ethical guidelines of the Association of Internet Researchers (AoIR) (Ess and AoIR, 2002). The Internet as a medium is still relatively formative however, and new phenomena – such as blogs – are emerging (Eynon et al., 2008: 23), which means that guidelines can become dated relatively quickly. Moreover, the ethical standards for Internet research have been subject to some debate, centred on whether new ethical procedures are required or whether the fundamental principles of research ethics should remain unchanged. The ethical approach taken in the gap-year study, which is put forward by a number of internet scholars (Eynon et al., 2008; Bruckman, 2002) and which is reflected in the AoIR guidelines (Ess and AoIR, 2002), is that core ethical standards should be applied to Internet research, but that these need to be tailored to the specific research context.

The wealth of data that was available through conducting an analysis of the gap-year blogs had a price, in the form of some complicated ethical questions (Blank, 2008: 541). There were two key (overlapping) concerns: were these public or private accounts? And were subjects or authors being studied?

Blogs: Public or private?

A key issue in Internet research ethics is the 'blurred distinction between public and private domains' (Frankel and Siang, 1999: 2). Defining what is public and what is private has been a concern for Internet research for some time, but the nature of the Web 2.0 environment complicates this process further, as more and more personal information is volun-teered. The accessibility of blog postings may suggest that they are freely available in a public arena, yet it is debatable whether the availability of information on the Internet necessarily makes it public property. In addition, existing research has suggested that people may be more open online under a false or exaggerated expectation of privacy (Frankel and Siang, 1999: 6).

For youth studies in particular, the differences between a researcher's understanding of privacy and that of the young people being studied means that care needs to be taken. Empirical research suggests that there can be a lack of awareness about who can access blog postings. Viegas' (2005) study of bloggers who write about their working lives notes that some had lost their jobs due to misconceptions about their potential audience. A recent study of the content of teenage blog and social networking sites found that a 'considerable amount of personal information' is revealed (Huffaker, 2006: 6). The blogs sampled in the gap-year study were all freely available, and often contained the young person's full name, photographs of them and their friends, and their email address, alongside some intimate reflections. It was therefore important to consider the extent to which this information needed to be protected, even though it was available in a public domain. The responsibilities of researchers to protect privacy overlap with, and are informed by, a related concern: whether the bloggers can be considered as 'human subjects' or 'authors'.

Bloggers: Subjects or authors?

The AoIR guidelines pose this question in terms of what is being stud-ied: does the blog represent a 'person in space' or is it a text with a 'person as author'? (Ess and AoIR, 2002: 179). Viewing the producers of the gap-year blogs as 'people in space' would categorise them as human subjects, defined as 'a living individual about whom an investigator ... conducting research obtains data through intervention or interaction with the individual, or identifiable private information' (Frankel and Siang, 1999: 16). This requires close attention to the prevention of harm. One potentially harmful outcome of research is the risk of disclos-ing an individual's identity, and it is the responsibility of the researcher to employ preventative measures such as anonymity (SRA, 2003: 38–9). The difficulty with anonymising publicly available Internet data is that it is easily traced using a search engine.

Alternatively, if blog producers are treated as authors of public docu-ments then the ownership of this material must be considered. Bassett and O'Riordan (2002) argue that the Internet is a site for the 'cultural production of texts' (Bassett and O'Riordan, 2002: 235), and contest whether the human subjects model should apply to all Internet communications. Bloggers in particular may have chosen to deliberately publish in the public domain, so that rather than maintaining anonymity researchers should acknowledge the user's authorship. In such instances, Bassett and O'Riordan (2002) suggest that texts should be cited in the same way as traditional media (Bassett and O'Riordan, 2002: 244).

Conducting research using blogs, as with other online methods, requires researchers to carefully balance these issues. As noted by Hookway (2008), the choice for researchers who use blogs as primary data is whether to preserve the anonymity of participants or credit bloggers for work; there is a tension between acknowledging authorship and protecting identity (Hookway, 2008: 106). To resolve such dilemmas, the AoIR ethical guidelines suggest a setting-dependent approach to distinguishing between subjects and authors.

This also has implications for informed consent. If participants are authors of publicly available documents, then informed consent would not be necessary, but the nature of online content means that it is more complex to distinguish between published and non-published material (Bruckman, 2004: 103). The crux of the issue to determine if informed consent was necessary in the gap-year project thus centred upon the notion of private or public data.

Negotiating the public/private distinction

Frankel and Siang (1999) describe two possible perspectives to help delineate private boundaries online. A technological perspective assesses the privacy of data files on the Internet in terms of their accessibility, whereas a psychological perspective considers how the providers of the data may regard the information. Frankel and Siang (1999) suggest a combined approach to 'develop a technological understanding of the issue and then [expand] this understanding to include the psychological perspective of the participants' (Frankel and Siang, 1999: 11). This approach was adopted in the gap year project to evaluate the privacy of the young people's blogs.

In terms of technological privacy, the host sites enable 'secret' postings and have policies regarding the usage of data. According to the ethical guidelines of the AoIR, these blogs could be considered as a more technically public web page than, for example, conversations in a closed chatroom (Ess and AoIR, 2002: 5; 7). Whiteman (2007) suggests an awareness of unknown readers would indicate the perceived privacy of a venue. As noted above, there were indications of this from the interviews conducted. In the blogs themselves, there was also often an acknowledgement that the reader could be unknown. For example, the gapper would provide a short biography of themselves and an introduction to their trip.

The division between public and private in online spaces has to be considered as contextually dependent, and thus so must ethical decision-making. There was a strong case for considering the gap-year blogs to be in the public domain, as they were not only publicly accessible but also written for an audience that could be unknown. The blogs may be personal, but they are not private (Hookway, 2008: 105), and thus it was deemed that informed consent to analyse them was not required.

However, to view the participants as authors of public documents one must then deal with the issue of ownership of material and whether citation is appropriate. The distinction between subject and author is not so clear-cut in online spaces, especially as this imposes offline considerations of authorship and public content. For example, Reed (2005), in a study that explores the act of text production with reference to bloggers, states that the bloggers in his study are 'explicitly concerned with substituting texts for persons' (Reed 2005: 224). Moreover, the gap-year research was not specifically concerned with the participants as subjects per se; it was their representations of experience that were the objects of study.

It was necessary to bear in mind that younger people may be more open online (Huffaker, 2006), however, and as detailed above there were certain personal details provided on the blogs. They had chosen to make this available online, but not for the purposes of research. This meant it was important to consider the implications of directing readers to a young person's blog through citation. A reader could find out their name, information about their personal life, contact them (either via blog comments or directly) and see photos of their friends and family. Reproducing links to the blogs would expose them to the direct scrutiny of an unintended audience without their knowledge. The BSA advises 'err[ing] on the side of caution' (BSA, 2002: 5) with respect to Internet data, so links to the gap year websites were not provided, and personal details were disguised. The study therefore adopted 'moderate disguise' as suggested by Bruckman (2002). Verbatim quotations were used but names, pseudonyms and identifiable details changed. This approach was also adopted by Hookway's (2008) study of morality in everyday life, in which he also privileges the protection of his participants' identity over providing credit to them as authors (Hookway, 2008: 106).

A note about interviews and ethics

Textual extracts from blogs were not the only source of data for the gap-year study. Semi-structured interviews were conducted with a sub-set of the bloggers. During an interview, a researcher is interacting with an individual and obtaining information about them. In this context, therefore, the gappers I subsequently interviewed would be defined as human subjects, and it was necessary to obtain their informed consent to take part in the research. As this subset of the bloggers were clearly participating in the research as subjects rather than authors (by sharing their experiences 'offline'), it was seen to be appropriate to obtain their consent to use their online stories as well.

Conclusion

The discussion above has highlighted the importance of matching the potential of online methodologies to the central research concerns. The aim of the gap-year study was to examine how young people who under-take this activity frame and understand their experiences. A key finding was a tendency for the bloggers to use existing frameworks of understand-ing that were aligned with what gap years 'should' be about. While the study suggested that there was evidence of everyday reflection and agency in the young people's accounts, this was limited by these collective frame-works. The official version of the gap year suggested that young people make individual choices to pursue this worthwhile and beneficial activity. In contrast, the blog narratives demonstrated the often-habitual meanings that surrounded the practice and the importance of shared notions regard-ing value. Therefore, in addition to the practical advantages of blog analy-sis outlined above (such as extending access), an analysis of the narratives presented in the young people's gap-year blogs was an appropriate method of accessing how such stories were told. Hookway (2008) argues that blogs are a useful addition to the sociologist's toolkit in researching such mat-ters, as they 'help overcome issues of finding and accessing unsolicited personal diaries, while on the other hand, they are not "contaminated" by the predating interest of a researcher' (Hookway 2008: 96). Thus, blogs were able to demonstrate what the participants, without prompting, con-sidered to be important to communicate, which would not be possible via other forms of data collection. It is important to remember, however, that 'no data are untouched by the researcher's hands' (Silverman, 2007: 55).

This chapter has also discussed the methodological and ethical issues raised by the gap-year project, which those interested in blog research may benefit from considering. These are summarised below.

It was somewhat time-consuming to convert the data into text files so that it could be incorporated into data-analysis software. In addition, dealing with the multimedia elements of the blogs and the large volumes of data they generated posed some practical issues. A pragmatic approach was taken to focus on the text of the blogs only, although it is recognised that this did not capture all of the representations of the gap-year experience. Photographs in particular featured heavily on many of the blogs, although were not included in the analysis. Further research into the narratives presented in blogs may need to consider how to integrate the multimedia aspects into the analysis and may find it useful to consult the literature on visual methods.

The standard of authenticity in offline documentary sources was less relevant to the gap year research questions, as the research was driven by gaining an insight into participant accounts rather than 'accurate' presentations of experience. Issues of representativeness were also raised, given that the sample excluded gappers who did not blog about their experiences or take other forms of gap year, and so may have excluded alternative accounts. Again, it was not the intention of the study to draw any generalisations about the gap-year experience itself, but to explore how the stories of young people engaged in these sorts of activities can provide an insight into identity work and ideas about value. These measures of validity will be important in other research projects however, and their importance needs to be assessed if considering unsolicited blog research.

A particular concern for the gap-year study was defining whether the blogs were publicly available data, which was related to the status of the participants as subjects or authors. As the gap-year blogs were in the public domain, but relatively young people had produced them and disclosed personal information within them, there was a requirement for the 'moderate disguise' of the participants (Bruckman, 2002), which overrode concerns regarding their status as authors. The bloggers who were interviewed gave their informed consent for participation, given that they were more clearly defined as subjects. This supports the case for the importance of a contextual approach to ethics in Internet research, rather than blanket 'rules' (Ess and AoIR, 2002).

In addition to the use of unsolicited blogs as qualitative data, researchers may also wish to consider other means of using blogs in youth research. Looking for precedents of similar types of research questions can help in project design and in identifying potential methodological and ethical issues, and how to overcome these. Some alternative uses of blogs include: using solicited blogs alongside other forms of diaries (see

Moran-Ellis and Venn, 2007); conducting content analysis (see Herring et al., 2004); ethnographic participation in blogging cultures (see Hodkinson, 2007); using blogs as a research diary, or 'fieldnotes in public', and as a tool for reflexive writing (see Wakeford and Cohen, 2008). The case made throughout this chapter remains fundamental however: using blogs should reflect the theoretical grounding of the research, and existing ethical guidelines should apply, alongside sensitivity to context.

Suggestions for further reading

Related methodological literature

- Madge, C., O'Connor, H. and Shaw, R. (2006) *Exploring Online Research Methods in a Virtual Training Environment*, http://www. restore.ac.uk/orm/site/home.htm.

This research training resource for online methods includes useful bibliographies, summaries of key issues, self-study materials and case studies of the use of blogs.

- Eynon, R., Fry, J. and Schroeder, R. (2008) 'The Ethics of Internet Research', in N. Fielding, R. M. Lee and G. Blank (eds) *The SAGE Handbook of Online Research Methods* (London: SAGE), 23–41.

Eynon et al. provide an overview of ethical debates in online research.

- Heath, S., Brooks, R., Cleaver, E. and Ireland, E. (2009) 'Using the Internet for Youth Research', in *Researching Young People's Lives* (London: SAGE).

This chapter by Heath et al. considers the benefits and challenges of a variety of online methods for youth research.

- Rettberg, J. W. (2008) *Blogging* (Cambridge: Polity).

This is an accessible introduction to blogs in social and cultural context using insights from media and communication studies.

Examples of related youth research

- Bortree, D. (2005) 'Presentation of Self on the Web: An Ethnographic Study of Teenage Girls' Weblogs', *Education, Communication and Information*, 5 (1), 25–39.

Bortree utilises both blog analysis and online interviews in an examination of the ways in which teenagers use blogs to bridge their online and offline relationships.

- Hookway, N. (2008) '"Entering the Blogosphere": Some Strategies for Using Blogs in Social Research', *Qualitative Research*, 8 (1) 91–113.

This is a valuable methodological case study of how blogs can be utilised to access accounts of everyday life.

- Huffaker, D. and Calvert, S. (2005) 'Gender, Identity and Language use in Teenage Blogs', *Journal of Computer-Mediated Communication*, 10 (2), http://jcmc.indiana.edu/vol10/issue2/huffaker.html.

This article presents a content analysis of the language used by young people in their blogs to explore the use of blogs as a means of self-expression.

Acknowledgments

This work was supported by a studentship from the Economic and Social Research Council [award number PTA-031-2004-00276].

11

Public Profiles, Private Parties: Digital Ethnography, Ethics and Research in the Context of Web 2.0

Yvette Morey, Andrew Bengry-Howell and Christine Griffin

Introduction

This chapter explores some of the ethical challenges posed by digital ethnography as an innovative methodology for conducting online research. Digital ethnography shares many of the principles of traditional (offline) ethnography, including an ethnographic commitment to understanding participants' lives and experiences through observation and active participation (Hine, 2000). One of a number of virtual ethnographic approaches, digital ethnography can be distinguished from other approaches by its focus on the intersection of digital technologies with the Internet. Ease of access to a ready and rich body of data, and an active understanding of the meanings of everyday digital practices for research participants, are some of the key advantages of digital ethnography. However, as we will demonstrate, this convenience also acts as a disadvantage as it entails the negotiation of a number of complex ethical issues. While debates about the ethical aspects of conducting research online have taken place since the development of the first Internet browsers in the mid-90s (Naughton, 2000), a significant shift has occurred in the online practices of Internet users, and the ways in which the Internet itself has shaped these practices in the last decade. In particular, the advent of Web 2.0 has further muddied existing ethical concerns about overt and covert observation, blurred distinctions between the public and the private, complicated the question of informed consent and data protection, and thrown open questions about the authorship and ownership of data (Snee, 2008).

The chapter begins by providing a slightly fuller account of the issues described above in order to contextualise some of the key ethical challenges, and the advantages and disadvantages of digital ethnography in the context of Web 2.0. This account highlights tensions between existing ethical guidelines for research conducted online and the specific issues raised by Web 2.0. The discussion is situated by data from recent research which used a combination of traditional and digital ethnographic methods to explore how young people negotiate different forms of marketing, branding and 'managed consumption' in two significant youth leisure sites, namely: music festivals and free parties (illegal raves). We outline how the initial 'netnographic' (Kozinets, 2002b) analysis of festival and free-party web forums developed into a fuller consideration of the creation and sharing of digital content online, the significance of this for festival and free party-goers and the ethical issues raised thereby. We also discuss the use of social networking sites by free party networks and the nuanced nature of public and private (Lange, 2008) on these sites. Given that young people are the biggest users of Web 2.0 platforms such as social networking and media sharing sites we argue that it is important for researchers to establish a set of benchmark criteria for engaging with these platforms ethically. One suggestion is to look to the ways in which issues such as privacy, and attribution and redistribution of content, are already being dealt with in and across Web 2.0 platforms.

Ethics and the Internet

Concerns about ethical aspects of online research have been voiced since the earliest use of the Internet by the general populace in the mid-90s (Naughton, 2000). In 1996 the journal *The Information Society* published a special issue on online ethics entitled *The Ethics of Fair Practices for Collecting Social Sciences Data in Cyberspace* (Thomas, 1996). Contributions to this special issue identified a number of ethical issues which continue to inform guidelines about the ethical conduct of online research today. With respect to the social sciences a leading set of institutional guidelines for online research in the social sciences are those put in place by the British Psychological Society (BPS). The guidelines, *Conducting Research on the Internet: Guidelines for Ethical Practice in Psychological Research Online* (2007) identify a number of ethical issues all broadly related to the levels of 'identifiability' and 'observation' of research participants (BPS, 2007). In brief, the Society's main concerns are, firstly, with the verifiability of identity – how do we know whether the participants are who we think they are? Secondly, how do we assess what is public and what is private space online? A current ethical stipulation of the BPS is that 'unless consent has been sought, observation of public behaviour needs to take place only where people would "reasonably expect to be observed by strangers" (BPS, 2007: 3). This question therefore hinges on what participants' expectations of privacy online might be, so that postings to online forums or message boards cannot automatically be regarded as public activity. A third concern is with obtaining consent from participants when observing them online or collecting data from their online activity. Fourthly, participants should not be deceived as part of the research. The guidelines state that for qualitative online research deception is most likely to be related to researchers becoming members of chat rooms or discussion groups in order to 'lurk' and collect data. The final two concerns are with the preservation of participant anonymity (both on paper and online), and with the storage and ongoing use of participants' personal data which should only occur if they have consented to the use of this data. The BPS (2007) acknowledges that many decisions about ethics will depend on the research design being used, and that the constant and accelerating rate of change in computer mediated communication makes it impossible to anticipate all of the ethical issues that might occur. However, we argue that these guidelines fail to take into account the sea change in the practices of Internet users, and in the very nature of communication on the Internet itself. In the section below we outline some of the central features of this shift before going on to discuss some of the ethical challenges posed thereby.

Mediated lives: 'New' media, social media and Web 2.0

According to Murthy (2008: 849) 'day-to-day life is becoming increasingly technologically mediated'. For many people everyday reality is filtered through the use of a number of now-mundane devices such as mobile phones, mp3 players, digital cameras, and wireless laptops. Developments in technology have meant that these devices are increasingly integrated (for instance mobile phones can now function as phones, cameras, music players and Web browsers) and networked, thus making it easier for people to upload and share aspects of their lives online. Consequently, Puri (2007: 388) argues, the Internet is 'becoming a place where people live a part of their lives', while Negroponte (in Flew 2002: 12) states that 'Computing is not about computing anymore, it is about living'. This uploading and sharing of daily life – via status updates, tweets, photos, videos etc. – is enabled and radically expanded by the shift from a top-down, read-only Web to a fundamentally participatory and, above all, social Web. boyd (2009) states that the social web is enabled by a 'collection of software that [allows] individuals and communities to gather, communicate, share, and in some cases collaborate or play'. The notion of a set of software or online applications and platforms that are used socially is one of the defining characteristics of Web 2.0 – or what has been referred to as the second, *participatory* phase of the Internet (Anderson, 2007).

O'Reilly Media Inc., an American media conglomerate, first used the term Web 2.0 in 2004 to refer to a new set of online services and technologies that fulfilled a primarily social purpose (Beer and Burrows, 2007; Snee, 2008). Anderson (2007) characterises these services as working to 'facilitate a more socially connected Web where everyone is able to add to and edit the information space' (Anderson, 2007: 195). Examples of Web 2.0 platforms include blogging and micro-blogging sites (Twitter); Web forums and message boards; media-sharing sites (YouTube, Flickr); virtual reality sites (Second Life); social networking sites (Facebook, MySpace, Bebo); social bookmarking sites (Delicious); and mash-up sites (Google Earth). While the use of such platforms is not ubiquitous, several popular Web 2.0 sites account for a large percentage of all Internet traffic. Experian Hitwise collects data from Internet Service Providers in order to analyse national and global trends in Internet traffic and to calculate the market share of websites. Hitwise UK's list of the 20 most visited websites for the week ending 16 October 2010 ranked the social networking site Facebook second (just below Google) accounting for 7.53 per cent of all Internet traffic that week. The media sharing site YouTube ranked fourth, accounting for 2.24 per cent of traffic, while photo sharing site Flickr ranked eighth in the top ten entertainment websites for the same period. A brief look at Facebook's own user engagement statistics for October 2010 (http://www.facebook.com) reveals that the 500 million active users of the site share more than 30 million pieces of content (web links, news stories, blog posts, notes, photo albums, etc.) each month. Sites such as Facebook therefore enable a radical extension of the digital media we have at our fingertips, allowing this media to be shared, commented on, reproduced and remixed by a vast (and growing) audience.

Researching the social web

A number of disciplines are now starting to respond to the massive uptake of digital and social media and what is seen as a changing social fabric as a result of these (Beer and Burrows, 2007). The increased use of technology, and the increased amount of time spent online, has correspondingly brought about a number of changes in the ways in which everyday lives and stories can be ethnographically studied. The discipline of ethnography has seen the emergence of a number of distinct but related approaches to online research including hypermedia and multimodal ethnography (Mason and Dicks, 2001; Dicks, Soyinka and Coffey, 2006); cyberethnography (Teli, Pisanu and Hakken, 2007); netnography or Webnography (Kozinets, 2002b; Puri, 2007) and digital ethnography (Murthy, 2008). Digital ethnography can be distinguished from other virtual approaches by its focus on the intersection of everyday digital technologies with the Internet. Sharing the same principles as traditional, offline ethnography, digital ethnography upholds the ethnographic commitment to understand participant's lives and experiences through observation, engagement and participation (Hine, 2000). Consequently, Murthy (2008: 838) argues that 'as ethnography goes digital, its epistemological remit remains much the same ... telling social stories'. A key advantage of digital ethnography is, therefore, that through its engagement with new and digital media it not only provides researchers with access to rich, diverse and ready bodies of data, but also enables an exploration of the ways in which research participants make use of a variety of everyday digital technologies to construct and share meaningful experiences and identities online. However, it is this very convenience and access to the often-private aspects of participant's lives that poses the greatest challenge to researchers using this approach as it entails the negotiation of a number of complex ethical issues. However, Murthy (2008) states that while ethics will be one of the key areas by which social science's engagement with new and digital media technologies will be judged, professional bodies and methodological literatures remain ambiguous on their treatment of the subject.

Ethics and the social web

The ethos of the social web is informed by two significant cultural shifts: a radical erosion of the boundaries between the public and the private, and the move to active participation in, and creation of, online content. These, in turn, give rise to corresponding ethical dilemmas for researchers. Snee (2008: 3) states that 'personal lives are increasingly exposed in Web 2.0 applications as part of a broader cultural shift towards openness and changing notions of privacy'. Many Web 2.0 platforms involve the sharing of personal information as the basis of membership and belonging – for example, social networking and micro-blogging sites in which users update their profiles and post updates on what they are doing. In this regard profiles on social networking sites (and sometimes on other sites such as media sharing sites or Web forums) represent a considerable investment (in time, energy, creative and emotional labour) in that they require constant updating and fine-tuning in order to present a stable and desirable identity to online friends, acquaintances and, increasingly, strangers. Boyd (2009) and Lange (2008) argue that previously dichotomised versions of private and public – distinctions based on the hidden versus the open, or the individual versus the collective – are confounded by practices and expectations around the sharing of information on Internet sites. Nissenbaum (in Lange 2008) introduces the concept of contextual integrity to account for the expectations that people have about the collection and distribution of information in different contexts. However, Lange (2008: 364) extends this argument by arguing for the recognition of nuanced versions of public and private *within* particular contexts – she refers to such nuances as the 'fractalisation of the public and private'. Lange (2008: 364) argues that this fractalisation is evidenced by the way in which users of social networking sites employ the 'technical and social affordances' of such sites to manipulate and negotiate access to content on sites.

The second significant cultural shift is the shift towards user-generated content and active participation and collaboration in the production, recycling and remixing of online content (Anderson, 2007; Snee, 2008). Web 2.0 largely embraces the move towards Open Access content and Anderson (2007: 14) argues that this entails a change in the way in which data is viewed, which is increasingly as a resource that 'can be repurposed, reformatted and reused'. This change in perception and practice, Anderson (2007) argues, can be compared to the DIY ethos associated with Punk in which young people took control of the production and promotion of their own entertainment and content by forming bands and writing fanzines and so forth. Consequently, people now see themselves as the creators of, and experts on, the online representations of their experiences and identities and Anderson (2007: 15) argues that this poses a significant challenge to perceptions of 'who has the authority to "say" and "know"'.

The discussion above highlights some of the tensions between existing ethical guidelines for research conducted online and the kinds of ethical dilemmas introduced by Web 2.0. In summary, the shift towards making the private public suggests that identity online is currently less about experimentation, as suggested by Turkle (1995), for example, and more akin to Giddens' (1991) notion of identity as an ongoing and reflexive project. The frequent recycling and repurposing of data on Web 2.0 complicates ethical concerns about the verifiability of identity and data protection and skews these so that a new set of concerns is raised about how to negotiate authorship and ownership of content that could be used as data. We now go on to unpack some of the ethical challenges and dilemmas we faced in relation to accessing and using the (very different) online content of festival and free party participants in our research.

Researching festivals and free parties online

The research study forming the backdrop to this chapter, *Negotiating Managed Consumption: Young People, Branding and Social Identification Processes* (ESRC RES-061-25-0129), employed an innovative combination of qualitative methodologies to explore how young adults negotiated different forms of marketing, branding and 'managed consumption' in two youth leisure sites, namely, music festivals and free parties, and how this impacted on their social identities and networks. Music festivals were selected as examples of youth leisure events that are highly branded, with substantial levels of commercial involvement and relatively managed and regulated forms of consumption on offer. The last five years have seen a dramatic increase both in the number of music festivals – over 500 festivals took place in the UK in 2008 – as well as in the corporate branding of music festivals (Porter, 2006). Corporate festival organisers draw on the significance of festivals to British youth culture and the subcultural capital (Thornton, 1995) embodied in the notion of a festival as a 'free' space away from the dominant symbolic frameworks that structure everyday life to manufacture an 'authentic' experience and to construct the festival space as a cultural site in which participants' 'authentic' selves can be expressed (Lea, 2006; Purdue et al., 1997). The festival industry has a significant online presence with numerous commercially driven websites dedicated to the promotion and marketing of festivals, as well as websites and forums run by and for festival-goers.

Free Parties, by contrast, involve minimal commercial involvement in the form of sponsorship or branding, and have a history of dissent and opposition to the consumerist ethos of more 'mainstream' music-related leisure events. In the aftermath of the legislation against and criminalisation of free festivals (the Public Order Act, 1986) and raves (the Criminal Justice and Public Order Act 1994) recent years have seen something of a resurgence of unauthorised music events in the form of the British 'free party' scene (Morris, 2006; Lewis, 2006). Free parties are unregulated, illegal, outdoor parties or urban squat parties during which members of party crews set up mobile sound systems to play amplified repetitive beats such techno, hard house, drum and bass and psy-trance, usually over the course of a weekend (Riley, Griffin and Morey, 2010). There is an emphasis on dancing, hedonism and the use of recreational drugs (Riley, Morey and Griffin 2008). Traditionally the date, time and location of free parties has been a closely kept secret, with information passed on to trusted members of the network, or accessed via party lines (anonymous telephone numbers using recorded messages to impart information about directions to party locations) closer to the time of the event. While the non-commercial, illegal and secretive nature of free parties means that there is less of an online infrastructure around them, free parties and free party networks have a significant presence on the Internet, albeit one that is radically divided in relation to the use of Web 1.0 and Web 2.0 platforms.

The research design involved two stages – one for each case study. The first stage of each case study involved a netnographic analysis (Kozinets, 2002a) of various web forums to explore whether and how participants were talking about the commercial aspects of festivals and free parties, as well as to identify key discourses involved in the representation of these events online. However, it was during this first stage of the research that we realised the full significance of online representations and constructions of festival and free party experiences, which extended well beyond web forums and included the use of a number of Web 2.0 platforms including media sharing sites (Flickr, YouTube); virtual map sites (Google Earth); and social networking sites (Facebook, MySpace). In the section below we discuss the use of these platforms, focusing on the differing use of web forums by festival and free party-goers, as well as the move from web forums to social networking sites, and the implications thereof, for free party-goers.

Festivals online: A year-round experience

There are a number of well-used festival web forums where current and prospective festival-goers can communicate with each other by posting or commenting on a variety of threads (topics) ranging from talk about aspects of particular festivals (the line-up, tickets, anticipation, memories) to talk about the generic aspects of festivals (such as camping, and organising lifts). Festival forums can be read by anyone with access to the Internet. However registration and membership, by means of setting up a personal profile with a verified email address, is required in order to post or comment on a topic. Typically profiles require a username with the option of adding an avatar (a small representative graphic such as a picture or photo) and information about age, gender and location. Email addresses can be set to private (no email can be received from other members) or, if preferred, members can be emailed or messaged via 'click here to email me' or 'send me a message' icons. Members can also display email addresses and URLs for blogs or websites openly should they wish to. While most members' usernames are different from their actual name, our feeling is that such names are largely chosen to signal a certain affiliation or identification, or to make a personal statement to fellow forum members rather than as a means of disguising identity. We found that forum usernames were often consistent across a number of platforms, so that it was possible to read a member's posts on the forum, find and view their photos on Flickr, and find and watch their videos on YouTube.

Unlike other types of forums in which communication is primarily text-based, festival forums are replete with (embedded or linked) identifiable media such as photos and videos. These can be uploaded prior to an event, as part of the preparation for, and anticipation of, the festival; taken during the festival and uploaded from the site; or edited after the festival and shared with forum members (and anyone else who cares to see them). A familiar forum topic that is often revived in the run-up to festivals concerns the organisation of collective camp sites by forum members. The chosen camp site is identified and located through the use of a distinctive tent flag which is photographed and uploaded onto the forum for the benefit of other interested parties. In a similar vein many forum members create their own tent and stage flags and upload photographs of these to the forum prior to festivals. A remarkable and unanticipated use of the forums prior to festivals was the creation and sharing of festival site maps. This practice ranged from the adaptation and editing of official maps to reflect personal preferences (for example, maps pin-pointing the position of bars selling ale on-site), to the creation of entirely new types of maps (contour maps showing the best places to camp should it rain). An interesting example is the creation and sharing of the *Glastonbury Festival 2003 – Memory Map*, an interactive annotated satellite image of the 2003 festival site. By hovering a mouse over the different stages and areas depicted on the onscreen image a series of text boxes appear, each containing a comment by different festival-goers. The memory map can be seen as an example of a digital mash-up – a piece of digital media that combines different kinds of media (in this case text and image) in order to create a new work. The map, created by Luke Robinson (accessible via his Flickr profile at: http://www.flickr.com/photos/mortalcoil/9298831/) is also a prime example of the multiple layers of ownership and authorship that accompany digital content on Web 2.0. The use of Robinson's interactive image is governed by a set of licensing benchmarks known as the Creative Commons (CC, 2011). Stemming from the Open Content ethos of Web 2.0 Creative Commons licenses are a set of four flexible permissions for how digital and online content can be used by others. These permissions, which can be used singly or in conjunction with each other, range from the attribution of content at the most permissive side of the scale to stipulations that content must be attributed, that the user is similarly obliged to share their own content, and that the content can only be used for non-commercial purposes and in its present (verbatim) state at the least permissive side of the scale. Luke Robinson's memory map is governed by two Creative Commons permissions, constituting an Attribution-Noncommercial licence. However, while CC licensing aims to permit flexibility and negotiated consent – and Robinson was willing to waive the Noncommercial component of his chosen permissions for potential reproduction in this volume – the image is nevertheless a composite of other kinds of content (Google satellite imagery and text-based comments) deriving from different author-creators and, in some cases, subject to copyright. These kinds of complications serve to highlight the disjuncture between the fluidity of content on Web 2.0 and the all-rights-reserved paradigm of traditional copyright (see: http://creativecommons.org/licenses/).

Other commonplace examples of mash-ups are to be found on YouTube. Many festival goers edit together music, video, photos and text to create films of their festival experiences. Arguably the sharing of different kinds of media, both within and outside of festival forums, signals the importance of both the individual and collective experience of festivals. Festival forums and media sharing sites such as Flickr and YouTube enable a radical extension of festivals from events taking place in a field and lasting for a few days, to the year-round celebration, re-living, and anticipation of festivals online. Furthermore, this social construction of festivals online engenders a sense of the co-creation and co-ownership of the festival experience both on and offline, and outside of the domain of sponsors, organisers and, indeed, copyright holders.

Free Parties: From forums to social networks

In contrast to festival forums, communication on free party forums is largely text-based with an emphasis on containing and restricting the exchange of information to well-known and trusted forum members. We explored two established and well known free party forums, one of which has been active since 1997 and was set up in response to the banning of raves by the Criminal Justice Bill in 1994. As with festival forums, posts can be read by anyone but posting and commenting require registration and membership. Forum members have usernames and avatars, yet these are not generally consistent across platforms. There is a shared (and probably correct) consensus on free party forums that they are monitored by the police, hence extreme caution is exercised when it comes to posting information about the dates or locations of forthcoming free parties and party lines. Suspicion and often downright hostility are shown towards requests for, or sharing of, such information. For example, on one forum a 'sticky' (an important post or thread always kept at the top of the list of threads) originally posted in 2005 warns forum members to think before they type and a 'newbie' requesting information about local free parties is told, in no uncertain terms, that no-one is likely to share that information with him until he is known and trusted. Other requests for party line numbers are met with contempt and identified and disparaged as veiled attempts by the 'OB' (Old Bill, police) to gain information.

However, despite the continued, if dwindling, use of free party forums, the manner in which information about free parties is disseminated has also undergone some radical changes over the past six years, particularly with the advent of social networking sites such as MySpace and, in particular, Facebook. There is however a marked difference between group and individual free party profiles on Facebook, as well as a difference in the ways in which information is shared within such profiles. Many free party networks or sound systems have set up group (rather than individual) profiles on Facebook, and while requests to join some groups are vetted by group administrators, many can be joined by anyone with a Facebook account. Group pages often serve to promote the legal events and activities of free party networks on their profile page, while making use of the personal message system to send information about forthcoming illegal events to group members. After joining a number of these groups we received a message with information about the 2008 UK May Day Teknival (a big event on the free party calendar in which multiple sound systems from across the country come together over the May Day bank holiday) including a party line to ring for details about the location. While this information is, in some senses, shared privately – rather than broadcast publically – the relative ease of becoming a member, and the amount of information freely shared between all, including new and unfamiliar members, means that privacy is extremely permeable in such groups.

Individual Facebook profiles and accounts allow for a more complex restriction of information whereby a range of privacy settings may be tweaked to display different levels of personal or identifying information to different friends. The amount of identifiable information and media content shared on individual free party profiles varied from user to user. Some users displayed virtually no identifiable information about themselves on their profile pages, choosing to share information via personal messages to people on their friend lists; others shared a lot of identifiable information, including videos and photos as well as links to media on other websites. Interestingly we found that 'friending' practices with free party-goers on Facebook occurred differently to the ways in which these practices generally occur with other users. It has been argued (Lampe et al., 2006) that on the whole Facebook users generally search for or 'friend' existing friends and acquaintances. However, we found that many free party users had large numbers of friends and that many of these friends formed part of a larger network of free party-goers and enthusiasts. We made use of both an individual profile (that included information about the lead authors' research interests as well as a link to the project's website), as well as setting up a group page which stated its purpose as the collection of information about sound systems and linked back to the individual profile. We found that our group page was unsuccessful in terms of collecting information or recruiting participants. However, using the individual profile we found that we were able to 'friend' many other free party users and in this way we were able to access a wide range of information about events. The importance of being friends with a wider, visible (virtually anyway) and familiar network of free party people on Facebook was evidenced when one user challenged my friend request, asking who I was. I replied that we had a Facebook 'friend' (someone I was familiar with from previous research on the free party scene but did not know personally) in common, that I had seen this person's name on our mutual friend's 'friend list', and that I thought their name and avatar looked interesting. I also said that I was interested in the regional free party scene. Thereafter my request was accepted and I was encouraged to attend forthcoming parties. Arguably, trust on free party social network profiles is less about delineating the public and private – profiles are often a mix of both – and more about a perception of like-mindedness and the recognition of a similar or familiar friendship profile.

Concluding comments: An ethical commons?

Web 2.0 platforms provide digital ethnographers with a ready body of rich and diverse data. However existing ethical guidelines, which we argue do not adequately engage with the complexities of the Web 2.0 environment, make it difficult for researchers to make decisions about how to work with this data. Investment in the construction and mainte-nance of personal profiles render binaries such as overt and covert obser-vation somewhat redundant, along with questions about the verifiability of identity. Moreover, the fundamentally shared nature of content on Web 2.0 – so that once any text, photo, video or hyperlink is displayed online it becomes subject to being forwarded, downloaded, remixed or uploaded elsewhere – means that it becomes very difficult to ascertain whose consent is required for the use of data. The affordances and fea-tures of social networking sites allow users to manipulate privacy set-tings, yet the primarily social function of these sites means that they are nevertheless often very permeable and that information has a tendency to leak from them. In this regard, friending practices, including the increased exposure of personal and private information and sharing of content, significantly muddy a range of ethical issues around identifying what is public and what is private, obtaining informed consent, decep-tion and lurking. Expectations about privacy, about what is revealed and hidden and what is shared, differ significantly between users of differ-ent platforms, as well as between users of the same platforms, bearing out Lange's (2008) arguments about the fractalisation and extremely nuanced nature of public and private on Web 2.0 spaces.

Beer and Burrows (2007) argue that in order to react to the changing social fabric being wrought by Web 2.0, researchers will have to

> become part of the collaborative cultures of Web 2.0, we will need to build our own profiles, make some flickering friendships, expose our own choices, preferences and views, and make ethical decisions about what we reveal and the information we filter out of these communities and into our findings.

This will require an extensive revision of existing ethical guidelines so that they are able to engage with collaborative cultures. Furthermore, given that young people are the biggest users of Web 2.0 platforms such as social networking and media sharing sites we argue that it is important for researchers to establish a set of benchmark criteria for engaging with these platforms ethically. The ethos of bodies such as the Creative Commons and the Open Commons suggest that it is trust and transparency, rather than confidentiality that are valued in Web 2.0.

Suggestions for further reading

Related methodological literature

- Murthy, D. (2008) 'Digital Ethnography: An Examination of the Use of New Technologies for Social Research', *Sociology*, 42 (5), 837–55.

This paper provides a good discussion of digital ethnography as part of an overview of the use of new digital technologies for social research. The paper examines the use of four new technologies including: online questionnaires, digital video, social networking sites and blogs.

- Bober, M. (2004) 'Virtual Youth Research: An Exploration of Methodologies and Ethical Dilemmas from a British Perspective', in E.A. Buchanan (ed.) *Readings in Virtual Research Ethics: Issues and Controversies* (London: Information Science Publishing).

This chapter discusses some of the ethical challenges facing researchers studying young people's use of the Internet, situated in a British context. The chapter provides an overview of different methodologies for online research including participant observation and the construction of the author's own teenage website in order to perform a 'technobiography'.

Examples of related youth research

- The Digital Ethnography Working Project at Kansas State University

This project makes use of digital technology – particularly video – to explore the ways in which society and culture are effected by social media. Project leader Michael Wesch and his students have produced an inspiring series of videos on topics ranging from Web 2.0 (*Web 2.0 ... The Machine is Us/ing Us*) to YouTube (*An Anthropological Introduction to YouTube*) which can be found on the project's website (http://mediatedcultures.net/mediatedculture.htm).

- Ito, M., Horst, H., Bittanti, M., boyd, d., Herr-Stephenson, B., Lange, P., Pascoe, C.J., and Robinson, L. (2009) *Living and Learning with New Media Summary of Findings from the Digital Youth Project* (Massachusetts: MIT Press).

A report summarising the findings from a three-year ethnographic study into young people's participation in new media.

• boyd, D. (2008) 'Why Youth ♥ Social Network Sites: The Role of Networked Publics in Teenage Social Life', in D. Buckingham (ed.) *The John D. and Catherine T. MacArthur Foundation Series on Digital Media and Learning* (Cambridge, MA: The MIT Press).

This paper uses on and offline ethnographic methods to examine young people's use of social network sites and how this impacts on identity formation and peer sociality.

12
Positionality and Difference in Cross-Cultural Youth Research: Being 'Other' in the Former Soviet Union

Charlie Walker

Introduction

The Eastern European revolutions of 1989 and subsequent collapse of the Soviet Union in 1991 opened up new possibilities for comparative research in countries which had previously been all but closed off to Western academics. Youth research in particular has begun to flourish in the post-socialist period (Walker and Stephenson, 2010), as research- ers have been able to conduct ethnographic and qualitative fieldwork with young people whose lives had previously been viewed from afar. As in Western youth research, the adoption of such methodologies has provided a more nuanced and sympathetic understanding of different aspects of young people's lives – in particular youth cultural practice and transitions to adulthood – than that provided by the more main- stream, survey-based approaches, which continue to dominate in this part of the world. While being able to draw upon an existing set of methodological practices, however, ethnographic research with young people in Eastern Europe and the former Soviet Union poses a range of problems for the Western researcher, both in terms of the practical difficulties of navigating less familiar environments, institutions and languages, and in regard to the issues of power and positionality that invariably arise when researching 'across difference' (Heath et al., 2009). This chapter explores the ways in which such problems emerged in a series of case studies addressing the changing nature of transitions to adulthood among working-class youth in the former Soviet Union. The case studies – in Ul'yanovsk, Russia (2004), St Petersburg, Russia (2007), and Vilnius, Lithuania (2009) – produced more than 200 in-depth, bio- graphical interviews with young people training in vocational colleges, and have shed light on processes and patterns of social stratification in the areas of education, employment, housing and migration. The chapter explores the range of ethical and practical issues that were confronted during the course of conducting these case studies, including gaining access to sensitive educational institutions and workplaces, developing relationships with young people, and overcoming language barriers. It pays particular attention to the ways in which these issues were variously amplified and mitigated by the status of the researcher as a Western 'other', and the impact of this on the knowledge produced by research encounters.

Growing-up working-class in the former Soviet Union: Three case studies

> There's nothing to like about working there. They don't pay you, they pay you nothing, neither workers nor students training there. What's the point of staying at your workplace? It's just for people who've got nowhere to go, they just work for kopecks year after year.
>
> (Sergei, Metal worker, Ul'yanovsk)

In most Western societies, young people leaving school with few academic qualifications face very different prospects from those of their parents' generation. In the context of deindustrialisation and globalised, flexible labour markets, the traditional 'apprenticeships' followed by working-class youth (Cohen, 1997; Cohen and Ainley, 2000) have been all but replaced by transitions into hyphenated forms of service-sector employment and extended periods in education and training (Nayak, 2006; Walkerdine et al., 2001; MacDonald and Marsh, 2005; McDowell, 2003; Murad, 2002). My research has explored parallel developments in the former Soviet Union, where the unravelling of working-class transitions to adulthood has taken a somewhat different form, resulting not from the gradual economic shifts which have taken place in the West, but from the catastrophic collapse of a state-led economic system. While parts of the former socialist bloc have undergone significant economic restructuring and achieved a degree of stability in recent years, social and economic life in much of the former Soviet Union continues to be marked by the dislocations rendered by neo-liberal reform, such that new types of economic activity have been slow to develop, and declining forms of employment and training in many cases have not been replaced by anything new. For young people such as Sergei in the Russian city of Ul'yanovsk, options after school were not the McJobs of post-industrial cities in the West, but an impoverished form of the traditional school-to-factory transition, in which jobs were guaranteed, but wages, prospects and prestige were close to zero (see Figure 12.1).

Ul'yanovsk – a developed industrial region situated 500 miles south-east of Moscow – was the site of the first of three case studies I have undertaken on the changing nature of working-class youth transitions to adulthood in the former Soviet Union. The institutional focus of the study, conducted over an 8-month period in 2004–5, was the initial vocational education and training (IVET) system, which is the main post-15 educational route for young people from manual-worker backgrounds in Russia. The first aim of the study was to gauge how IVET colleges in the region were adapting to the collapse of the industrial and agricultural sectors and the subsequent impoverishment of the job opportunities they had traditionally relied upon for their graduates. The main thrust of the research, however, was to explore how young people experienced the transitions into 'poor work' offered by their colleges, and how they attempted to negotiate alternative transitions through emerging opportunities in further and higher education, newer but limited forms of work in the nascent service sector, and migration to other towns and regions. These themes were further explored in two additional case studies, first in St Petersburg in 2007, and then in

Figure 12.1 The mechanical factory, Ul'yanovsk. Photograph by Charlie Walker

Vilnius, Lithuania, in 2009. The se cities were chosen because both have significantly better-developed service and manufacturing sectors than Ul'yanovsk, and therefore allowed for comparisons to be made with the experiences of young people in more favourable economic conditions. In addition, Lithuania presented an opportunity to explore the ways in which the labour market and educational prospects of working-class youth in the former Soviet Union had been affected by accession to the European Union, not least with regard to migration prospects.

While concerned with the influence of different structural contexts on young people's transitions, the primary focus of all of these projects has nevertheless been on the active ways in which young people negotiate such contexts, and therefore, on young people's agency and subjectivities. In this respect, all three case studies have been able to take their methodological cues from recent studies of youth transitions in the West, which have increasingly moved away from the quantitative, structuralist approaches that dominated youth transitions research during the 1980s (Roberts, 1997). Recognising the growing complexity of transitions to adulthood, Western youth researchers have adopted a more holistic perspective, viewing transitions not as linear movements or 'trajectories' in social space, but as a series of interlinked transitional 'strands' across a number of life domains (Coles, 1995). This perspective has been realised by the use of a range of qualitative, ethnographic methods, not least the adoption of biographical, life history approaches (Heath and Cleaver, 2003; Henderson et al., 2007). Such approaches not only provide the flexibility for researchers to capture the breadth of young people's experiences beyond a narrow focus on school-to-work careers, but also allow them to look backwards into young people's late childhood and early teenage years, thereby glimpsing how the overall directions of transitions were originally established (Allatt, 1997; MacDonald et al., 2001: 11). In addition, biographical approaches allow the researcher to see how respondents' 'storying' of the past, as well as their projections of the future, are central to the ways in which they understand and negotiate the present (Hodkinson, 2005: 4). To supplement the 'longer view' provided by a biographical approach, I chose to interview two cohorts of young people in each of the three studies, including both final year students of IVET colleges and young people who had graduated from the same colleges in the past few years. While some forms of biographical research (the use of personal diaries, for example) encourage respondents to provide 'free' monologues, the present research was pursued predominantly through semi-structured interviews addressing transitions in education, work, housing and family, which were supplemented by other ethnographic material such as conversations in and around respondents' colleges and workplaces. In total, the case studies produced a body of interviews with over 200 young people across the 3 sites (95 in Ul'yanovsk, 65 in St Petersburg, and 60 in Vilnius).

The principal innovation of these studies does not, of course, lie in the use of semi-structured, biographical interviews, which, having been used and discussed widely in Western research, constitute a relatively 'mainstream' methodological approach compared with some of those described elsewhere in the book. Rather, it lies in the novelty of applying such methods, or any ethnographic methods for that matter, in this particular 'field'. The very possibility of employing genuinely ethnographic methods in Russia and Eastern Europe only emerged after the fall of communism, prior to which the political realities of the Cold War meant that sociologists, like historians and other academics, had very limited access to data, and even more limited opportunities for fieldwork. A study by Allen Kassof (1965) exploring the aims and effectiveness of Soviet youth policy is a case in point. Kassof's study charts the emergence of what he calls the 'superbureaucratisation of childhood' in the Soviet Union (1965: 74), through which every aspect of young people's lives came to be monitored and regulated in the name of constructing a 'new Soviet person'. While a solid exposition of the workings of Soviet youth policy, however, Kassof's study was less successful in gauging the way in which it was actually experienced, characteristically lacking access to the voices of young people themselves and relying instead on anecdotal evidence and conversations with émigrés to supplement official and media sources.

With the opening up of the field, however, a number of sociologists have taken the opportunity to conduct research in the region, both independently and through collaborations with domestic scholars. Somewhat curiously, although not entirely surprisingly, the body of work which has emerged from these endeavours roughly mirrors the quantitative–qualitative split – and its associated theoretical and epistemological divisions – which has traditionally characterised the sociology of youth in the West (Griffin, 1993). On the one hand, academics favouring survey methods have been able to take advantage of the largely quantitative social science tradition which had existed during the socialist period, when questionnaires measuring the proximity of young (and other) people's values to those endorsed by socialist ideology formed the dominant mode of enquiry. Although some survey-based work on youth in Eastern Europe has made a significant contribution to current debates (Roberts, 2009; Roberts and Pollock, 2009; Wallace and Kovatcheva, 1998; Glendinning et al., 2004; Tomanovic and Ignjatovic, 2006), as in the West, such methodologies have at times rested upon a somewhat 'problem-centred' approach (Tsentr sotsial'nogo prognozirovaniya, 2005, for example), in which young people are used as a barometer for a wide range of social ills. Indeed, this type of approach reached a nadir in the early post-socialist period, when the various dimensions of systemic collapse in the region were translated into an apparent 'loss of values' among young people, who, abandoned to the free play of market forces in a rudderless society, came to be portrayed as materialistic, apolitical and lacking a moral compass (Riordan et al., 1996; Williams et al., 2003). In stark contrast to such studies has been the body of qualitative, ethnographic work produced both by the qualitative sociologists and sociological research centres that have emerged within post-socialist states since 1991 (www. regioncentre.ru, http://youth.hse.spb.ru and www.cisr.ru in Russia, for example) and by visiting scholars from western Europe and the US conducting collaborative and independent research in the region. Again, as in the West, by drawing upon methodologies such as participant observation and in-depth interviewing, such research has turned the spotlight away from matters of structure and 'values' and instead has shifted attention towards the active ways in which young people negotiate such structures and the meanings they attach to their activities (Pilkington et al., 2002; Pyšňáková and Miles, 2010; Tereshchenko, 2010; Read, 2010; Walker, 2011).

While thus making a similar contribution to ethnographic youth research in Western sociology, however, the difficulties involved in conducting this type of research, both in preparation and in negotiating the 'field', are amplified for those working in different cultural contexts. Above and beyond the practical demands of cross-cultural research – learning a different language and gaining access to foreign institutions in an unfamiliar legal context – it is incumbent upon ethnographers of youth to gain a close appreciation of the ways in which the identities and strategies available to young people in different aspects of their lives are shaped by the particular cultures and histories of the places in which they are situated (Back, 1996; and Nayak, 2006, for instance). Gaining an understanding of those histories and cultures, then, requires much greater preparatory work for those investigating unfamiliar contexts. As well as achieving a close understanding of the particular contexts in which young people's lives are played out, ethnographers of youth are also required to achieve a degree of 'closeness' to their research subjects.

The extent to which it is possible to achieve this has, of course, been the subject of significant epistemological debate, with discussions regarding the insider–outsider status of researchers taking place across the social sciences (see Fay (1996) for an overview). Such discussions, centring on the ways in which social characteristics such as gender, ethnicity and age shape relations of power and degrees of empathy between researcher and researched, are especially pertinent to cross-cultural studies, where one aspect of difference – nationality – takes on an 'elephant in the room' quality. However, while adherents of 'standpoint epistemology' might question the validity of research conducted in cross-cultural contexts, as I will argue below, the difference between researcher and researched can provide a platform for intercultural understanding and communication. The remainder of the chapter will explore first of all the ways in which I prepared myself for cross-cultural research, and secondly, how my status as an outsider affected the ways I accessed research subjects, the subjectivities I took with me into the field, and the nature of the relations that emerged between my respondents and me.

Preparing for the field

My interest in Russia and Eastern Europe dates back to my undergraduate studies in history, but was more comprehensively developed during the course of a Masters degree in Russian and East European Studies at the University of Birmingham. Like other 'area studies' postgraduate programmes, this degree was multidisciplinary, and drew upon up-to-date research exploring the various social, economic and political changes taking place in post-socialist states across the region. I was thus introduced to a range of themes – 'virtual economies' and the spread of 'hidden unemployment', the development of 'survival strategies' (street trading, self-provisioning) in the face of economic dislocation, and an increasing dependence on family and kinship in the context of a shrinking economy and welfare state – which allowed me to develop a broad understanding of key developments in post-communism. When I began my doctoral research, however, it was necessary to develop a closer understanding of the particular region I had chosen as the location of my case study. To some extent, this choice was based on the fact that there were strong connections in place between my home university and a major university in Ul'yanovsk, which, as will be explored below, provided crucial support. At the same time, however, as a heavily industrialised but de-industrialising region, Ul'yanovsk was an ideal location in which to explore what was happening to working-class youth in post-Soviet

Russia. Before embarking on fieldwork, then, I gathered as much information as I could find on social and economic developments in this part of Russia, including both statistical and scholarly sources and newspaper articles from the Western and post-Soviet press.

One theme emerging from this preparatory work which would later become central to the research itself was Ul'yanovsk's demographic history, which was characterised by major rural–urban migration relatively late in the twentieth century and heavy in-migration from other regions of the former Soviet Union as late as the 1980s. Both of these migratory patterns, which reflected periodic industrialisation drives in the region, had a strong echo in the transitions of the young people in the case study. Given the impoverishment of prospects in Ul'yanovsk's industrial sector, many young people in urban areas were keen to move away from the region altogether, while respondents in rural areas largely planned to move to the city, and it was predominantly through relatives living elsewhere that they planned to do so. Few, if any, respondents were planning to make the housing transitions necessary to facilitate migration through the underdeveloped and largely inaccessible private rental sector, but due to the migratory patterns of recent decades, many had opportunities to negotiate these transitions through extended family living elsewhere. Thus, plans for migration among my respondents appeared to reflect both the wider shift towards greater familial interdependency in post-socialist states in the context of a slowly developing market, and the pronounced nature of Soviet migratory patterns in this particular region (Walker, 2010).

Both on a general level and in particular cases, then, an appreciation of the particular cultural and historical setting one enters provides a framework through which to think about one's findings. At the same time, however, cross-cultural research, like research in one's 'home' country, throws up a great many surprises, for which it can be difficult, if not impossible, to prepare oneself. Such surprises are particularly likely to emerge in cross-cultural research because of the preconceptions and subjectivities we inevitably carry with us into the field (Willis, 1997: 247), and which sometimes cause us to 'misrecognise' social actors and phenomena as being more familiar than they really are. In the Ul'yanovsk case study, I had expected the dominant theme of the project to be the youth labour market, on the basis that I was addressing transitions to adulthood among a group of young people who, in contexts such as the UK, have historically been glad to leave compulsory education at the earliest opportunity. This appeared to be in keeping with the reputation of IVET colleges in Russia as an educational destination for school 'dropouts'. In the event, however, the overwhelming majority of my respondents in Ul'yanovsk, and later in St Petersburg and Vilnius, were thinking primarily about present and future transitions into further and higher education, and any labour market transitions they were pursuing were largely viewed as secondary to their plans in the educational sphere. Thus, a primary task of the research in Ul'yanovsk then became to understand how young people who had left the mainstream academic school system at the age of 15 had somehow 're-engaged' with education and were planning to continue their studies for up to 4 more years. To do this, I began exploring the literature on young people's learner identities and learning careers and making connections with the respondents' more positive experiences of education after leaving general schools, as well as their increasingly pragmatic view of educational qualifications in a difficult labour market. Thus, the 'read-do-write' model often prescribed for doctoral research (Crang and Cook 2007:203) can be even more difficult to uphold when conducting research in cross-cultural contexts.

One aspect of cross-cultural research about which one can be more certain is the need to be able to speak the language, or one of the languages, of one's country of interest. By and large, language proficiency is an entrance requirement of language-based area-studies (LBAS) doctoral programmes, whether in Russian and East European Studies, Latin American Studies, or Chinese Studies, and intensive language training tends to be a central component of Masters degree programmes in these subjects. Of course, for more senior sociologists conducting large-scale international projects, it is more often the case that co-researchers (usually native speakers of the countries in which the research is taking place) are the ones 'at the coalface'. However, those in the earlier stages of their careers, and especially Ph.D. students, are unlikely to possess the resources necessary to employ research assistants, interpreters and translators for long periods, and would probably struggle to direct a successful piece of ethnographic research without the experience of having conducted one themselves. In my case, I undertook two years of intensive language training, first as a Master's degree student and then during the first year of my Ph.D., followed by a three-month overseas institution visit (split between Moscow and Ul'yanovsk) to conduct pilot research and further develop my language skills. While continuing to make mistakes (although people were too polite to point this out), I became fluent enough to be able to arrange, conduct and analyse my interviews with young people and expert informants alike, not only in Russia, but also in Lithuania, where many young people, and working-class youth in particular, continue to speak Russian (see below). While language proficiency was thus a practical necessity, I would also argue, certainly in my case, that knowledge of a language brings to a research project far more than linguistic competency. There are countless examples across each of my case studies in which the nuances of young people's narratives could easily have been lost had they been read in translation. My male respondents' use of the word *patsani* ('lads') to refer to their friendship groups, for example, was part of a class cultural form that indicated a sense of allegiance to a particular group and locality, and in turn, pointed to the ways in which young people's perceptions of opportunity were shaped. As will be explored below, speaking to young people in their own language also had important implications for the relations of power between researcher and researched.

Negotiating access

In order to make comparisons between different groupings (particularly by gender and locality) all of my case studies have required the participation of relatively large (for qualitative research) numbers of respondents, such that gaining young people's involvement has always been a central concern. In St Petersburg and Vilnius, I was able to recruit a small number of young service sector workers by approaching them directly in their workplaces (hairdressers, restaurants etc). However, the overwhelming majority of the young people in all of my case studies have been either final year students or recent graduates of specific vocational colleges. Therefore, as in most youth research with an institutional dimension (Heath et al., 2007), the possibility of conducting these case studies has been heavily reliant on the goodwill and cooperation of gatekeepers such as college directors, teachers and a range of employers. By and large these gatekeepers have been approached in the first instance as respondents, and after having conducted an expert interview about their college or business, have been asked for their assistance in arranging interviews with young people.

As in the case of any researcher in the world who conducts fieldwork, the success of my requests for assistance from educational professionals and employers has depended either on the level of interest I am able to generate in the individuals I encounter, or simply on how busy they are. At the same time, however, of consistent importance in these encounters, irrespective of the outcome, has been the fact that I am from a Western country. Although ultimately gatekeepers are under no obligation to provide any assistance and therefore hold the 'power' in these situations, it became increasingly obvious that my being from a powerful Western nation meant that I carried a certain amount of cultural capital when meeting gatekeepers, and that this would often open doors. Levi-Strauss, reflecting on his anthropological research in Brazil, notes a similar feeling: 'not only does a journey transport us over enormous distances, it also causes us to move a few degrees up or down in the social scale' (1989: 105). In my case, the kudos attached to being a Westerner, particularly in a provincial region such as Ul'yanovsk, pushed me several degrees up the social scale, such that many gatekeepers went out of their way to help me. College directors and their staff willingly participated in interviews, allowed me to conduct interviews with their students and graduates in the college, were instrumental in arranging many of those interviews, and even provided me with meals and drove me home at the end of the day.

Precisely why I was offered so much assistance was never stated explicitly, but it was apparent at times that there may have been an expectation among college staff that some form of collaboration or exchange may materialise in the future. Given that I was in no position to offer such an exchange, I was careful not to encourage these assumptions, although I could not stop them from being made in the first place. Nevertheless, it is incumbent upon Western social scientists conducting research in countries outside of the global 'core' to find ways of evening up what at times can feel like an exploitative relationship. As Sidaway (1992) argues, overseas fieldwork has a tendency to produce a one-sidedness – with Western scholars 'mining' for data and leaving nothing behind – that is not entirely dissimilar to colonialism. To redress this, it is important at least to be open about the aims of one's research and whom it is funded by, not to ride roughshod over the laws of the country one is visiting (obtaining the correct visa, for example), and to share one's results, something which I achieved by publishing in a professional journal read by vocational education practitioners (Walker, 2005). In addition, I reciprocated interviews about IVET in Russia by discussing at length the nature of vocational education and training in the UK. Also, while the motives of some gatekeepers may have been formed around the powerful institutions I was perceived to represent, others had a more personal interest simply in meeting and becoming acquainted with a British academic. In such cases, exchanges drifted from vocational education into areas such as football, politics and family, usually involving the drinking of vodka if the director in question was a man. There was even a case in which I was granted access to conduct interviews with staff at a factory in St Petersburg because of the manager's wish to subvert what s/he perceived to be increasingly anti-British sentiment from the Russian government at the time (in the wake of the Litvinenko affair, when the British government's demand for the extradition of a murder suspect was refused).

For similar reasons, being a Westerner sometimes hindered rather than helped in my attempts to gain access. In Russia I was turned away from a number of colleges whose directors treated me with a great deal of suspicion, which could have reflected either the deteriorating international relations noted above, an ongoing suspicion of foreigners inherited from the Soviet era, or a general suspicion of outsiders, given the threat of closure that so many IVET colleges were facing at the time. More generally, and reflecting the lack of a tradition of independent research in Russia, or at least the periodic subversion of that tradition, it was sometimes very difficult to explain who was funding my research (the Economic and Social Research Council, and therefore, in the last analysis, the British government) and what they planned to do with it. Similarly, some employers were very reluctant to grant access to talk to their employees, possibly reflecting the ambiguous legal position of their business, or of the terms on which their employees were hired. In such cases it was necessary to respect the fears of gatekeepers, whether they were employees of state institutions or representatives of private companies. In some cases, however, I felt justified in adopting a more assertive approach. On one occasion, having already conducted a number of interviews in a college that was attached to an armaments factory in Ul'yanovsk, I was told that I could not take any further interviews without the express permission of the regional educational administration. It is in such situations that institutional connections in the country in which one is conducting fieldwork can prove vital. My colleagues at Ul'yanovsk State University drafted a letter to the University Dean, who in turn wrote to the Head of the educational administration, and finally the latter wrote a letter informing the director of the factory that my research was not concerned with whatever it was that the factory was producing. Relations with gatekeepers in Vilnius were somewhat less intense; rather than an exotic outsider who should either be embraced or shunned, I was seen as a European 'colleague', and my presence seemed to be welcomed more soberly, possibly as further evidence of Lithuania's European integration.

Negotiating difference

While my nationality played a role in negotiating access to institutions and enlisting the support of gatekeepers, it has been in interviews with young people themselves that being from a Western country has played the most significant role, and that I have most clearly been researching 'across difference'. In this respect, my research is of significance for recent debates regarding the ways in which a researcher's social characteristics shape both the conduct and the outcomes of their research, and related calls for greater reflexivity with regard to issues of power and positionality. Whether or not researcher and researched share the same gender, ethnicity, or social class, for example, has been seen to have an important impact on the practicalities of fieldwork, affecting, for instance, a researcher's ability to establish a rapport with their respondents (Padfield and Proctor, 1996). In addition, such aspects of 'sameness' and 'difference' may have epistemological as well as practical implications, shaping the extent to which a researcher is able to comprehend the experiences of subjects who may be 'other' to them, and therefore, to produce 'valid' data (Fay, 1996). Indeed, the trend towards peer-led research discussed in other chapters in this volume suggests that youth research poses particular problems in this regard, as the tendency for youth researchers to be older than their subjects further complicates relations between them by introducing an age divide (Heath et al., 2009: 39). In my own research, however, while age, gender and class have all played some role in defining the 'social relations of fieldwork', it has been my nationality, or more broadly, my perceived Western-ness, that has consistently been most salient in research encounters with young people.

If being a Westerner could at times provide me with privileged access to expert interviewees, the fact that I was a visitor from the UK almost always seemed to have a positive influence on whether or not young people would volunteer for interviews. While there are likely to be a number of reasons for young people to participate in research projects (getting out of lessons, for example, if they are still in an educational institution), the chance to meet a foreign visitor appeared in my case to provide an extra incentive, such that in some colleges more young people volunteered than I could include in the research. While difficult to measure, on one occasion this dynamic was made explicit, when a female graduate who had been reluctant to meet me quickly changed her mind after I told her that I would soon have to travel back to the UK (not the Baltic states, as she had assumed from my accent). This general fascination with meeting a westerner was indicative of the historic one-dimensionality of the relationship between Russia and 'the West' (Pilkington et al., 2002), and added to the already unequal relations of power at the heart of the research process. In particular, my own, heightened sense of mobility in conducting fieldwork in distant countries seemed to draw greater attention to the *im*mobility of young people who, especially in Ul'yanovsk, may never have left their town or village. Thus, as in interviews with college directors, I was constantly aware of the greater institutional, financial and cultural resources I possessed, not only to construct a whole series of fieldwork encounters, but also to leave them once I had 'extracted' the necessary data (Gray, 2003: 75–6; Coles, 1997: 82–3) (see Figure 12.2).

While in some ways nationality threatened to exacerbate the power imbalances between researcher and researched, however, ultimately it was my 'outsider' status that provided the means with which to mitigate them. In particular, the very fact of my presence, of my interest in Russia and Eastern Europe, and of my speaking Russian, appeared to run counter to the normally uni-directional relationship with the West. Respondents clearly perceived me as an outsider, but

Figure 12.2 Charlie Walker with a respondent in Ul'yanovsk. Photograph: Albina Garifzyanova

one who was actively interested in them, their country, their town, and their college, and the very novelty of this appeared to facilitate the establishment of a rapport between us. In addition, my outsider status acted not only to mitigate, but also to reverse the researcher–researched relationship, as I encouraged respondents to feel free to ask me questions about anything they wished, not only about the research project, but about life in the UK, about my life, about my views of Russia and Eastern Europe; whatever, if anything, interested them. Thus, informal conversations about football, the price of mobile phones, British cars [*sic*], pubs, the difference between the Scottish and the English, how hard it was to learn Russian, whether I was sure I was not actually from the Baltic states (a question never posed in Lithuania), why Britain was at war in Iraq and later Afghanistan, why I chose to be a sociologist, all went on for some time both before and after 'formal' interviews. Treating the research encounter as a form of cultural exchange took a somewhat different tone in Lithuania, where many respondents had already visited the UK, and were able to use first-hand knowledge of British cities to project a more 'cosmopolitan' identity than their Russian counterparts. In addition, the linguistic competencies of Lithuanian respondents – who were often not only fluent in Lithuanian, Polish and Russian, but also possessed a good level of English – put my own language skills into stark perspective, and imbued them with a higher degree of cultural capital in this respect than I could ever hope to achieve. At the same time, conducting interviews in Russian with young people who use Lithuanian in formal contexts (at college for example) but, due to the tendency for working-class youth in Lithuania to be of mixed backgrounds, speak Russian or Polish among family and friends, further helped to establish rapport.

As well as acting as a bridge rather than a barrier to communication, my otherness as a Westerner was also instrumental in mitigating other aspects of difference. Social class, for example, is less discernible when taken out of its national context, and any perception of me as affluent would have had more to do with my nationality than my social location. Similarly, being other in national terms removes some of the constraints associated with age difference. For all three of these case studies I have been at the top end of what I consider the youth age bracket (28 in Ul'yanovsk, 31 in St. Petersburg and 33 in Vilnius), and therefore noticeably older than the majority of my respondents. However, as a non-native, I have been able to bypass certain cultural norms associated with language – which stipulate that my respondents would normally use the formal *vy* rather than the informal *ty* when addressing me – without looking like I was 'trying too hard'. Wearing youthful clothing is similarly likely to be seen as more acceptable by young people when the older person in question is non-native. By contrast, gender difference stood out as an aspect of the social relations of research which was not mitigated by otherness in national terms, although it was *refracted* through it. That is, interviews with young female respondents took place within a wider cultural framework which has positioned Western men and young women in the former Soviet Union in a highly commoditised relationship, as depicted in both Soviet and Western cinema (*Interdevochka* (Todorovsky, 1989); *Lilja 4-ever* (Moodysson, 2002)) and indicated by innumerable international dating websites. Therefore, my questions regarding prospective family transitions with current or future partners may have appeared loaded or intrusive. Gender sameness, on the other hand, was facilitated by my national otherness, as young men were adept at using cultural difference as a vehicle for conversations about typically male practices and subjects (beer and cigarette preferences, purchasing one's first car, and so on).

In practical terms, then, my cultural otherness has more often facilitated rather than hindered relations with respondents, most notably by allowing research encounters to be treated as a form of cultural exchange. In a similar way, the principal epistemological implication of researching across difference has been to open up, rather than close off, spaces for communication with respondents. In particular, respondents' perceptions of me as an outsider have led them in many cases to form their responses through a kind of 'relational' reflexivity, whereby their narratives of self have been formulated in the context of what they perceive to be wider social norms for the benefit of their interlocutor. For example, a respondents' intention to use extended family to negotiate the housing transitions necessary for migration would be framed as 'normal', thus not only indicating the particularities of an individual case, but also pointing to a broader cultural form which I had begun to recognise. Similarly, a respondent's description of the acquisition of higher education as 'necessary nowadays in Russia' pointed not simply to their individual aspirations, but to a wider development that required further investigation. In this way, my experiences of researching across difference echo those of Carter, who finds that, *pace* the arguments of 'standpoint' epistemology, 'it is the gap in experience between interviewer and interviewee that creates a space for respondents to describe and tease out meanings and assumptions that may otherwise remain unspoken' (2004: 348).

Conclusion

Debates about sameness and difference in social research have largely revolved around within-society characteristics, most notably gender, ethnicity, age, sexuality and disability (Heath et al., 2009). As this chapter has shown, conducting research in different cultural contexts adds a further dimension to the already complex relations researchers have to deal with in the field, both in terms of the practicalities of conducting research and the nature of the data one produces. As in any research across difference, while it is not possible to dissolve these complexities, it is incumbent upon cross-cultural youth researchers to reflect upon and, where possible, mitigate the wider sets of (unequal) social relations in which research encounters take place. In this chapter I have attempted to show how, when approached as a form of 'cultural exchange', cross-cultural research can actually transform difference into a vehicle for discussion, thus facilitating both the establishment of rapport with respondents and their own reflections on their lives.

While proponents of 'standpoint epistemology' may point to the perceived limitations of researching across difference, I would hope that the findings of the three case studies described above testify to the value of cross-cultural research, not only in and of itself, but also, for the contribution it is able to make to wider debates within the social sciences. In my case, these studies have contributed to current debates regarding processes of individualisation and detraditionalisation in late modernity, and the ways in which these processes have impacted upon the lives of young people with different social characteristics and in different cultural and national contexts (Brannen et al., 2002). As I have argued elsewhere (2011), the experiences of working-class youth in post-Soviet states, particularly their 'embeddedness' in resources of family and kinship, indicate the limited reach of processes of detraditionalisation identified among young people in Western societies. At the same time, the changing subjective dimensions of social inequality among my respondents, characterised not by a class–cultural identity, but by an increasingly individualised attribution of failure, point to the ways in which neo-liberal forms of governance may have similar effects wherever they take root (MacDonald and Marsh, 2005; Murad, 2002).

These findings, I would hope, point to the particular value of cross-cultural research for Western social science in general. As Sidaway argues in reflecting on 'Third World' research by geographers: 'Research in/of "other" cultures and societies ... at its best ... offers a counter to universalistic and ethnocentric views. It is the enemy of parochialism ... research in ... the (contemporary) periphery of the world system may pose challenges to frameworks and assumptions developed in the core' (1992: 406). Indeed, it was a piece of cross-cultural youth research – Margaret Mead's *Coming of Age in Western Samoa* (1973) – that arguably provided a starting point for the sociology of youth as we know it. Observing the experiences of adolescent girls growing up in a Samoan village, Mead exposed the apparently 'scientific' definition of adolescence as a period of 'storm and stress' as a cultural construct specific to a particular time and place (mid-twentieth century North America). Thus, whatever might be the difficulties of researching across difference, it is a worthwhile endeavour.

Suggestions for further reading

Related methodological literature
• Pilkington, H. (1994) *Russia's Youth and its Culture: A Nation's Constructors and Constructed* (London: Routledge), pp. 144–55.

This chapter of Pilkington's monograph on Russian youth culture contains a sensitive treatment of some of the aspects of difference explored here.

• Hollands, R. (2003) 'Double Exposure: Exploring the Social and Political Relations of Ethnographic Youth Research', in Andy Bennett, Mark Cieslik and Steven Miles (eds) Researching Youth (Basingstoke: Palgrave Macmillan), pp.157–69.

Hollands, a Canadian, is one of the few authors undertaking youth research in the UK to have addressed nationality as an aspect of 'difference' in his research.

• Sidaway, J. D. (1992) 'In Other Worlds: On the Politics of Research by 'First World' Geographers in the 'Third World', *Area*, vol. 24 (4) (Dec. 1992), pp. 403–8.

This article explores some of the ethical dilemmas researchers face in conducting fieldwork overseas, with a particular focus on power imbalances between Western researchers and their non-Western colleagues.

Examples of related youth research
• MacDonald, R. and Marsh, J. (2005) *Disconnected Youth?: Growing up in Britain's Poor Neighbourhoods* (Basingstoke: Palgrave.Macmillan).

MacDonald and Marsh focus on the lives of 'socially excluded' youth in the UK, but many of their insights into processes of social stratification and the experiential dimensions of social inequality apply on a broader scale to my respondents in Russia.

- Roberts, K. (2009) *Youth in Transition: Eastern Europe and the West* (Basingstoke: Palgrave Macmillan).

Ken Roberts' book contains findings from qualitative and quantitative research in a range of post-Soviet countries (Armenia, Georgia and Ukraine, for example) exploring the changing nature of transitions to adulthood among young people from a variety of backgrounds.

- Walker, C. (2011) *Learning to Labour in Post-Soviet Russia: Vocational Youth in Transition* (London: Routledge).

This monograph contains a complete exposition of the findings of my first piece of research in Ul'yanovsk.

13
Double Reflexivity: The Politics of Friendship, Fieldwork and Representation within Ethnographic Studies of Young People

Shane Blackman and Gemma Commane

Introduction

This chapter is a joint production focused on the politics of fieldwork and the representation of young people in ethnography. The paper brings together the Ph.D. supervisor and the doctoral student, focused on three thematic issues derived from their separate fieldwork: risk, friendship and integrity. We look across the different research sites and select examples as part of a joint research imaginary where we have identified a commonality of experience and understanding (Marcus, 1998). Moving beyond the uniqueness of the ethnographic experience we want to share how research friendship enabled us to integrate the research subjects into our lives in an attempt to obtain authentic voices. In a theoretical sense, we have tried to achieve this through reflexivity in fieldwork, which takes into consideration the feeling of the research subjects as we seek to represent them in the text. We came to an understanding that there were two defining moments of reflexivity, one in fieldwork and one in representation. Although ethnography demands that fieldwork, analysis and writing all occur simultaneously, we want to draw attention to the fact that the ethnographer, when writing-up, returns to the field through the research imaginary, and encounters what we call the double reflexivity.

Background: Two Ph.D. studies: Blackman and Commane

Shane: My Ph.D. was completed in 1990, at the Institute of Education, University of London and later published as *Youth: Positions and*

Oppositions – Style, Sexuality and Schooling (Blackman, 1995). The research was an ethnographic study of young people within Marshlands Comprehensive School in the South of England. The sample consisted of over 120 girls and boys aged 15–17, including four major groups: mod boys, new wave girls, boffin boys and boffin girls. When I undertook the study I was 22. All the young people were studying for a large number of examinations. There was one other group I studied called the 'criminal boys' who were largely non-attendees at school.

The ethnographic fieldwork entailed sharing the experiences of these various groups both inside and outside the school in leisure and family spaces over a period of two years. In this chapter I will specifically focus on fieldwork relationships with the criminal boys, mod boys and the new wave girls. Throughout the fieldwork with the new wave girls we conducted our relationship through an awareness of play and physical contact such as walking arm in arm. I went to their parties, gigs and dances, slept overnight at their parents' houses and attended girl-only gatherings. Fieldwork relations were similarly emotionally and physically intensive with the mod boys. Fieldwork with the criminal boys was thorough at first but slowly waned as the police and courts removed them from the area. The wider context to the research sought to explore the relationships between subculture, social class, intellectual ability, sexuality and patriarchy in young people's lives.

Gemma: My Ph.D. research, which I completed in 2011, is an ethnographic study on the range of femininities within BDSM (bondage, discipline, sadism and masochism), fetish and performance art cultures, with a specific focus on burlesque. The rise and popularity of burlesque in mainstream culture has opened up more opportunities for young women to express their femininities away from the domestic sphere. The inclusion of these identities in club sites populated by a range of ages meant that the conditions of these environments needed to be experienced, regarding the impact on young women's sense of gender, sexuality and identification. The age profile of my sample was between 18 and 40, but primarily focused on young women. The data sets and samples consisted of two case studies, five ethnographic discussions, six gatekeepers, 20 core participants, over 109 performances seen and over 600 conversations noted in the field. The research was conducted in club environments where diverse youth subcultures were found. These included burlesque and performance artists, pole dancers, BDSMers and the kinky, Goths, Industrial Goths, modern primitives and other clubbers. The research was conducted within club spaces, at private parties and friendship groups in and around these leisure experiences. Going into venues and helping out being a stage hand with one performer also transformed leisure spaces into work spaces, showing how performers had to negotiate the club space and the punters after performances. The focal point of the research was the ways in which young women negotiated their femininity and sexuality within these spaces and through specific styles of performance and dress. For anonymity, participants in the ethnographic examples will be identified by their gender (Mr, Miss, Ms) and individuated by a letter. The application of these titles gives participants agency, status and authority.

Ethnographic examples and thick description

In this chapter we focus on field relationships, as these are the key to understanding the ethnographic method and the importance of friendship as a force which moulds social status, meaning and understanding during fieldwork and write-up (Coffey 1999). The purpose of the ethnographic examples is not to promote an authorial sense of a finished product. What we will try to do is give the reader an insight into the emotional dynamics of fieldwork friendship and the complexities of writing-up. These examples are designed to support Geertz' (1973: 23) argument that 'ethnographic findings are not privileged, just particular'. For Geertz (1973: 16), 'Ethnography is thick description' in the sense that it is 'very densely textured facts to support broad assertions about the role of culture' (28). Double reflexivity enables the researcher to demonstrate commitment in fieldwork and write-up. At the same time, Geertz lays special emphasis on 'imagination' in ethnography. He (1973: 18) argues 'a good interpretation of anything ... takes us into the heart of that of which it is the interpretation'. The social awareness created by 'doing ethnography' engages with the 'humanity' of the original fieldwork interactions and how we as authors present 'subjects' out of context in the study of their everyday life. These examples try to evoke the life of the ethnographer with the researched and show how fieldwork and interpretation are delicately in balance but liable to fall apart as we strive to grasp culture in action. For us the priority is not on the ethnographer but what the ethnographer experiences, creates and discovers with the participants. Our position is that through dialogue with the research subjects we can show interactivity and visibility in the production of the text as researcher and researched participate together to create an understanding (Hammersley and Atkinson, 1995). The aim is to present a flavour of how reflexivity was negotiated in action between the researcher and the researched. Although we are demonstrating that the data is prepared rather than discovered, we want to energise the reader to bring them in to the situation of data collection to engage their reflexivity where meaning in fieldwork and analysis is created, sustained and understood. Rather than hide the analytical constructions of textual production, we want the reader to be with us at the moment of intimacy and risk, not to affirm the author's intentions but allow what Roland Barthes (1977: 148) described as the 'birth of the reader'.

Risk within fieldwork

As ethnographic research is often based within field sites where non-normative identities and behaviours may be present, there is always a risk. Within youth research, Hunter S. Thompson's (1966: 283) participant observation with Hell's Angels is the archetypal example of danger, leading to a 'fractured skull' and an 'exploded groin'. Risk not only covers the personal safety of the researcher as they negotiate the lives, identities and spaces of the researched; but also what the participants say or do when being observed. This risk is increased and still present when writing up field notes and applying examples within critique, highlighting a precaution governing how to re-present participants without incriminating them, revealing their identity or allowing misreading to take place. As Robert Carins (1994: 6) maintains, in relation to young people's lives it is vital to understand risk in order to recognise the social dynamics present in the exchanges in field research. Contemporary ethnography deals with the 'messiness of everyday life': whether it is love, loss or hatred, these are the same experiences Malinowski encountered nearly a hundred years ago.

Risk: Criminal boys: The knife

Within the first few days of fieldwork at Marshlands school I was introduced to the so-called 'criminal boys'. They were not very interested in me, but I was keen to speak with them. Further contact happened sooner than I thought. The eight boys often came in late or were sent out from lessons and found me in the school open areas writing up notes. This unplanned contact brought me into a close relationship with them. At other times they deliberately came to see me, even returning to school to break their skiving. We played cards; they talked of 'close situations' with school, parents and police. Some joked about being removed from the area for their criminal activities, which included 'joy riding,' violent behaviour, petty theft from houses and churches and selling stolen property. Conversations with the boys were not based on lists of questions. We just spoke or rather they tended to speak to me. After a couple of weeks they began asking questions about how to best dispose of stolen property. In school they had a powerful reputation based on both rumour and reality. The criminal boys were aware of their label but were ambivalent about it; some saw it as evoking danger, while others thought it reinforced their stigma and lack of a future. After a month of fieldwork, the boys all came into school and found me and asked for a talk. Ken and Ray were boasting about a fight and were celebrating their masculinity. Then Lee pulled out a long knife from his jacket and gestured to the two boys. 'Next time we'll get them with this'. He continued to play with the item and threw it in the air, catching the knife by the handle. He wiped the blade up and down his arm. I felt at risk. As Winlow et al. (2001: 11) note in relation to ethnographic research, 'it is not feasible to side-step forms of behaviour that one would normally avoid at all cost'. The boys had never brought any weapons into school before and today no teachers knew they were at school. I was concerned about the knife and I made an effort to move the conversation on. Although I did not realise it at the time, this was to be the last meeting with all the criminal boys together. The following weeks saw them moved to secure units in other parts of the county. I was concerned for my safety although I felt that the weeks of close meetings had brought a solid base of empathy. Being privileged to share guilty knowledge about their criminal activities did perhaps give a false sense of solidarity although, as I was aware of their insecurities, I still felt incredibly uncertain when Lee talked about his violent past and demonstrated his dexterity with the knife. In another sense this event could be seen, from their position, as signing off from fieldwork. I think they were more aware than I was, of the transient nature of our encounters, and perhaps I misunderstood the nature of my risk. They knew I held knowledge of their deviance and their forced removal was unrelated to me. Only in the write-up did I realise that this display was probably a comradely signature of their departure.

Risk: Mr P

During the ethnography I met Mr P, a middle-aged man, at Scarlet, a BDSM, fetish performance art club, where he seemed to know the management and was popular with clubbers and performers alike. We had conversations about the performances, art and life. Mr P accompanied me and other research participants to a variety of clubs, making him appear trusted. However after a while Mr P's behaviour became suspect, highlighting the risks to my personal safety. On several occasions, while watching BDSM scenes, such as whipping, in the dungeon with participants and other clubbers, he suggested I try it myself with someone I trusted, insisting that if I was writing about it then I should really do it, like a rite of passage which insiders within any social space may use to distinguish themselves from 'tourists' (Pitts, 2003; Anderson 2009). This was something which none of my other participants asked because they respected my 'vanilla' (non-kink) identity and, since there were a variety of young people there for many reasons, BDSM was not something participants mainly focused upon, nor was it the main factor in which solidarity was communicated. On several occasions Mr P seemed to get frustrated when I ignored his suggestions and his growing insistence, alongside constant attempts to buy me drinks, further highlighted the specific risks in this exchange.

Other participants voiced their concerns about his intentions and I found out that he had been the same with other young women in the club and that they now ignored him. Seeing how he behaved with other young women and how he got them to agree to do play sessions, even after they told me that they were not keen, made me feel that if I had met him by myself, I might either have been raped or never have been seen again. I felt that he had been trying to groom me into complying with what he wanted, making me feel naive, all of which illustrated the great risks female researchers may encounter in conducting ethnographic fieldwork, expressed by Eva Moreno through being raped by a male participant in the field; an experience which, she maintains, 'differs from anything that our male colleagues have to contend with' (Moreno 1995: 248). However, this is the only time I felt that this could possibly happen, even in environments where sexual expression was overt and a variety of sexual activities were happening. Although field research had dangers, danger cannot always be applied automatically to youth subcultures because there are specific measures and etiquettes within the sites which structure behaviour. Thus, risk cannot always be applied to describe a specific social group or what is 'expected' of their behaviour, rather it should be applied within specific situations, as and when the researcher is negotiating the field. Subsequently risk has to be continually re-negotiated because risk can apply anywhere and to anyone, even beyond the field site.

Friendship within fieldwork

In field research the friendships built over time show how trust, respect and a sense of togetherness is vital to how the field is understood and then conceptualised. In youth research the relationship between 'Doc' and William Foote Whyte (1943) in *Street Corner Society* is seen as a defining moment of contemporary reflexivity between researcher and the researched. More recently, Brian Wilson (2006) and Rachel Colosi (2010) developed research friendships within their respective communities to understand the social world participants occupy and its constraints. If the researcher's identity as 'researcher' fades over time and they become an accepted part of the group studied, this shows how successful the approach has been and how both the researched and the researcher become one. The sacrifices participants make to be part of a researcher's work and to be part of their life is something that must never be forgotten or disrespected. Understanding the dynamics of friendships shows how vital it is to negotiate consent through trusting and always respecting the decisions made about what can be included in the write-up. Significantly, understanding friendship allows critique to shine a positive light onto the moral codes and achievements of groups, which is often absent from understandings of young people's culture.

Friendship: Mod boys – the fight

It was about two months into the fieldwork with the mod boys. On Friday night I had been with them on a pub-crawl in the village. It was Keef's 16th birthday, and that night three of the boys and I slept over at the house of one of their parents. It had been a restless night as a consequence of consuming too much alcohol. In the crisp morning we walked to the bus stop to take the journey into Folkestone to spend the day shopping. In the town the boys visited innumerable clothes and music shops and we had lunch in the 'mod cafe'. The young mods conformed to Hebdige's (1975: 89) interpretation of 'high-speed interactions' to consume style. Gradually during the afternoon the mod group grew from four to ten and, on arrival at the skating rink, to 15 as some met their girlfriends. At the rink the mods were tentative on their skates. I noticed that there were a group of eight rockers who were good skaters quickly manoeuvring in and out of teenagers and children. The precariously balanced mods felt vulnerable, especially after Header (one of the mods) was ran into and punched when he was on the ground. The mod boys were galvanised and ready for action. They talked like crazy and then one of the mod boys phoned his father. I could certainly anticipate what was going to happen as the mods gathered round the exit. One of the mods, Hat, asked me 'Are you with us?' I said that I was with them in case anyone might get hurt. But secretly I was wondering if they might help me out if *I* got hurt. All of a sudden I did not want to be doing fieldwork. I was powerless to stop the impending fight. There was a signal that Header's father had arrived; the rockers were already outside the rink. The mod boys and girlfriends all slowly moved off. Just before I went outside I suddenly remembered to collect my cassette recorder from the caretaker at the cloakroom.

I stepped outside and within a second the fight began. The mod boys and rocker youths fought head on. All fighting participants were lashing out with fists and feet. The embattled youths swayed to and fro delivering punches and shouting, almost in slow motion. Header's father stood at the back of the mod group, apparently playing no great role. The two fighting forces separated. The rockers had been pushed to the floor and were symbolically and physically beaten. Threatening gestures and heavy insults were traded between both forces. The two groups moved back to reveal the injuries of blood splotches, broken teeth and ripped clothes. The mods moved away from the seafront and went into a large department store, to the top floor for a coffee, and entered into a narrative. They were shaking, even agitated, and so was I. After 15 minutes, everyone moved off to the bus station and home. Two hours later in the early evening, I arrived with the original group of mod boys at a party given by a sixth form girl. They sat round a large oval table in the dining room and I recorded their retelling of the fight. In ethnography friendship can move beyond the field through shared experience and equal participation. Two years on I went on holiday with the mod boys to the Isle of Wight and then began to write for their DiY mod fanzine: *The Undecideds*.

Friendship: Ms T

In field research all manner of friendships develop and this is especially the case when conducting participant observation. Ms T, a young queer burlesquer, became both a case study participant and a friend, showing how identification and inclusion in a social group is developed through emotional rituals. For over a year and a half I accompanied Ms T to venues, and hung out with her in other spaces where we talked, ate and drank together. This case illustrates how essential it is to become a part of the social world of the researched during field research, because becoming close friends allows the researcher to negotiate constraints. Mirroring the dynamics of Colosi's (2010) work in a lapdancing community, a rapport with Ms T was built and our conversations were not always fixed within the 'field' but about family life, the people we fancied and the clothes we had bought recently. Consequently the scope of the field has to develop and expand beyond the physical location of the study, to include the dynamics of social relationships. What this achieves is a constant narrative throughout the research process, detailing any re-negotiations and issues which affect these dynamics and, subsequently, the outcomes of research.

As Ms T's identity had to be protected it was important to continually re-address consent and apply reflexivity, acknowledging that not all that she said would be 'on record'. Although consent was initially negotiated through descriptions of her performances and almost full use of the transcript, these had to be renegotiated when writing up as her circumstances changed dramatically. It was necessary and ethical to suggest becoming anonymous, writing performances in theme-styled areas to decrease identification and only to use the quotes within the chapter after her final consent. The consequence of friendships means that participants can feel obliged to continue working within the initial parameters of negotiation and consent, yet it is vital that they are always aware of their rights, which includes their right to change or retract their consent completely. Ms T was always aware of this and chose to be written about anonymously, even though she knew that identification was only substantially decreased by this strategy and not totally eradicated. What renegotiation suggested was that I had constantly to apply care, as it was my responsibility to respect her choices as a participant and respect her decisions as a friend. Although friendship is a potential source of tension, renegotiating consent and continually reaffirming the participants ownership of their words allows participants to decide for themselves what they permit the researcher to use. The sacrifice participants make is high risk, showing how important it is to write the field and experiences in context with a careful consideration of the effects a participant's involvement with the research may have on their lives.

Integrity between the researcher and the researched

Commitment through the emotional bonds between the researcher and participants can be negotiated to form a communal integrity based on social and emotional relations and rituals. The end product of integrity is rich data. For example, Howard Becker's (1951) study on jazz musicians, Paul Willis' (1978) work on hippies and Rosemary Pringle's (1988) ethnography of secretaries each demonstrate a concern to put forward an authentic voice of the research subjects where recognition and emotion combine (Ribbens and Edwards, 1998). There are limits to dialogue or participatory research with young people; as Les Back (2007: 17) argues, 'It is the task of sociological writing to bring to life the people we work with and listen to'. However, integrity does not just cover what the research participants think, but how academics from the disciplines the researcher is from may respond to what is read. This can be the case if a researcher finds themselves in a compromising situation with members of the opposite sex due to heteronormative gender assumptions, even if the exchanges are part of the friendship dynamic between the researcher and participants. This highlights the tensions held between hiding the ethnography and concealing your identity in the field (Blackman, 2007: 700). However, integrity is a two way process, thus any inconsistency in ethnography will show an imbalance of power both in the fieldwork and write-up.

Integrity: New wave girls

The telling of these fieldwork stories is to evoke the ease, enjoyment and everyday context of shared time spent with the girls on their territory. Throughout the fieldwork and afterwards our relations were chaste, yet there was a high degree of flirtatiousness, physicality, sexual innuendo and playfulness which was a feature of the girl's openness towards me and my equally open expression towards them. Unlike anthropology (Warren, 1988; Kulick and Willson, 1995), sociology has only recently begun to be open about the erotic nature of fieldwork, where flirtation and play form part of exchange-based relationships. Anthony Gunter (2010: 48), Les Back (1996: 25) and Nayak and Kehily (2008: 11) have all raised issues about the sexualised nature of fieldwork and how as a male researcher one should respond to and write-up one's research subjects. My first meeting with the new wave girls was when I was invited to a cafe when they were skiving. This invitation helped to consolidate my early relations with them. Sharing moments of 'guilty knowledge' was an integral feature of our experience, as it helped to develop our friendship. These tests of trust never really stopped, but as we moved from one parent's house to another, from the girls bedrooms, to all-night girl gatherings, I was allowed to be part of a space which is usually off-limits to male researchers and who consequently experience exclusion (Blackman 1998: 209; O'Brien 2009).

During the second month of the study, one Friday afternoon, without any specific plan, I left school with some of the girls and ended up back at Cathy's mum's house. Cathy, Debbie and I sat with her mum, chatted, had coffee, saw the trailers on TV for that night's film and had a couple of snacks. By early evening, Cathy and Debbie set off to walk to the pub, *The Jolly Boatman*, where Debbie worked behind the bar. Debbie did a short shift while Cathy and I talked and listened to the jukebox, noting our favourite tunes. At the end of her shift, I bought Debbie and Cathy a drink. Afterwards we walked along the coast road to Debbie's parents' bungalow, arriving back at around 11.30. We spent time talking with her dad, before we went to Debbie's bedroom where she played some music, the girls read my field diary and then Debbie showed me to my bedroom. I started to undress, but then both girls came into my room wearing their nightshirts. Cathy said: 'I'm wearing the knickers; Debbie is not, so you can see her lovely bottom'. We talked and laughed for sometime, Debbie let me use her toothbrush and they secretly smoked a cigarette with the window open. Then we went back into Debbie's bedroom, where the walls were covered with the girls' pictures, poems and drawings. I started to fall asleep, so I made my way to my bedroom. In the morning the girls crashed into my room. Debbie found some ice cubes and rubbed them on my chest and leg as Cathy jumped about on the bed and talked about what we were going to do today. Then we all got dressed and went into the kitchen. Here Cathy made me some toast and Debbie got ready for her Saturday morning shift at the pub. When she left, Cathy, Debbie's mum and I talked and read the morning newspapers while drinking tea, as Deb's mum also did some ironing. It was great fun and gossip! At 11 in the morning Cathy and I walked arm in arm and arrived back at her mum's house, then shortly afterwards it was decided to walk over and see Sioux at her place. From there the fieldwork continued.

This section shows that I was permitted access to the new wave girls' bedrooms. My presence in this personal and private space usually occurred with one or up to five of the girls and took the form described by Lincoln and Hodkinson (2008: 40) of drinking, smoking, chatting, listening to music and having fun. From the fieldwork diary account it is possible to see the degree of contact that I had with the girls' mothers in their parent's house and the type of space we shared and the conversations had at the level of the everyday. Being able to comfortably talk and share food with the girls and their mothers brought increased trust between the new wave girls and myself. The parents got used to me being with their daughters as an ordinary event. My purpose during fieldwork was to respond positively to the girls and if that included acknowledging their sexual desirability this would occur but this did not lead to me taking advantage of the situation. As fieldwork proceeded I was able to engage with them in various ways, ranging from someone they could turn to for support and to personally confide in, to someone they could tease but still walk arm in arm with and kiss goodbye: they were able to joke and flirt knowing that they would be safe. I was able to empathise with the girls, whether this was talking personally with them about 'losing your virginity' or helping them counter aggressive forms of sexism from males.

The research relationship sought to be beneficial to participants. Our close relationship enabled stories to emerge and as the fieldwork proceeded I became part of some of their stories. This resulted in disclosing parts of my own life to the research participants and we worked together on an exchange basis. Sharlene Swartz (2011: 55) states 'expressing my values encouraged rather than limited young people's frankness with me'. It was clear to the girls that by arriving and leaving school together and going out to their leisure spaces, I shared my life with them. This description puts a priority on how male ethnographers respond in intimate contexts. I have tried to show that male researchers can experience emotion and 'acceptance' with female participants on the basis of intimacy, not exploitation. One key factor of the research relationship was deliberately not to ask questions at certain times and make a conscious effort to play the role of the listener. The point of being an ethnographer is to learn. Les Back (2007: 8) notes 'the listener's commitment to hearing places us on the side of the story from the outset'. Through listening to the girls I demonstrated my personal commitment. Following Pat Sikes' (2006: 114) assertion 'that honesty in writing is important' both Gemma and I showed our writing at different stages of production to our research participants. Our aim has been to make our fieldwork, analysis and write-up more accessible, founded on our belief in moving beyond the *hidden ethnography* in sociological writing.

Integrity: The submissives, the mistress and Mr H

At a BDSM community event I met Mr D, a man in his thirties, and we hit it off straight away. I told him about my research and he invited me to a monthly event, where he would arrange for some female submissives to talk about their experiences. As I entered this space one young and two middle-aged women with whom Mr D had arranged meetings welcomed me warmly. We developed a bond during the interviews in the beer garden as stories of intimacies flowed. During the last interview, a young man, Mr H, walked by and I heard him asking two of the participants who I was. After the last interview ended he asked me if I wanted to interview him and I said no. He shouted loudly, that I 'must be a feminist' because I wasn't interested in him. As my participants led me into the social event in the pub, I could feel that my presence was unwelcome to Mr H. Throughout the night he tried to embarrass me, but the women I had interviewed knocked these comments back and told him to leave me alone. This showed that the empathy I had with their experiences made a good impression, creating a feeling of togetherness (Anderson, 2009). They asked if I wanted to be on their quiz team, showing unity beyond the interview and demonstrating that the group who had accepted me as their friend did not share Mr H's views. However, his intimidation increased throughout the night, and as the event drew to a close, I wished I would never see him again.

After this encounter I saw Mr H at the Skin Two Expo in 2009. This filled me with dread, even though the other members of the social group he was with liked me. His mistress and other people we jointly knew were excited to see me. However, he first commented on my outfit, saying that I wore the same skirt last time he saw me, and after he made a few more negative comments his mistress told him to behave. This did not, however, stop Mr H breaking free from the group and talking with a well-known Dominatrix on the London fetish scene. I saw him point at me and insinuate that I was an outsider. I became frightened because I knew that he would try and get someone to be on his side. However, the Dominatrix paid no attention to him and carried on the conversation they were having before his outburst. What this demonstrates is that the relationships built between participants and the researcher can, through solidarity, overcome threats within the field.

Critically merging the new reflexivity and research friendship

A key argument we want to advance and develop is related to Bourdieu's (1992) emphasis on reflexive sociology in qualitative research, where the sociologist is aware of their own cultural habitus as a source of influence over how research subjects are observed and written. Applying Bourdieu's idea we argue that there are two key defining reflexive moments in sociological ethnography: firstly, fieldwork; and secondly, write-up: we call this the 'double reflexivity' of research friendship. Research friendships are a better term than research relationships as it maintains consistency and context. Fieldwork is where reflexivity in a practical sense begins, because researchers are engaged in negotiation and entry into the field. This necessitates close communication with human subjects as the ethnographer makes decisions in action and manages expectations within field relations.

Also, we argue that reflexivity is centrally part of how the sociologist writes and re-presents the researched. In the construction of the textual representation the sociologist can apply rhetorical devices to craft a seamless web of interpretation. But as Clifford Geertz (1973) has identified, where a thin description is apparent, no matter how many literary devices are employed, these cannot breathe life into absent lived experience. In the write-up ethnographers are immersed with their research subjects, who surround them, and may even appear to be leaning over their chair as they write. When the ethnographer is writing the researched and structuring their cultural and social world into a text it is a political and ethical action. As Anthony Gunter (2010: 44) demonstrates when speaking about his research subjects: 'I felt that in most cases they did not fully understand. As far as the young people were concerned they were helping out Anthony to write a book about us, the youth of Manor'. During the write-up the researcher is once again living an emotional life with the research subjects. Through reflexivity, conscious awareness keeps the sociologist focused on the practical everyday life of the researched. They come to life and engage in dialogue as the researcher formulates ideas and works the ethnographic imagination to write a sensitive and informed ethnography (Atkinson, 1990).

The new reflexivity has enabled qualitative research to put forward more realistic fieldwork accounts in response to the critical arrival of postmodern ethnography in the 1980s, which was understood as creating a 'crisis of representation' (John Brewer, 2000: 44). The postmodern position on ethnography put forward by Clifford and Marcus (1986) maintained that we should not *represent* the world, but rather should *evoke* it. The strength of the post-modern ethnographic contribution is to centre upon 'fiction' not as falsehood, but as a revelation into authorial construction of partial narratives, which offer momentary glimpses into the lives of people. We assert that a weakness of the *crisis of representation* argument that ethnographic accounts impose unity on research subjects is not borne out in our studies because both during fieldwork and textual construction we struggled with a fragile connectivity where research subjects constantly required human reparation. Through fieldwork intimacies our approach of taking on many different roles and statuses towards research subjects was characterised by friendship on the basis of gathering joint memories. When the research subjects told stories the ethnographer was part of the telling, or sometimes participants cited the field diary or interviews as a source of legitimacy.

In youth research Karenaz Moore (2003: 152) has described how 'my own youth became crucial' in establishing the fieldwork friendship. Also for Malbon (1999: 32) age and familiarity gave access to fieldwork sites as 'his job'. In our studies we also consider that the age of the researcher does facilitate openness towards intimate data otherwise not accessible. This is specifically the case when dressing like participants, giving more access to developing friendship dynamics within spaces where a mixture of ages and youth cultures converge, highlighting that familiarity, style and solidarity become inversed, and producing openness through the researcher applying their own background. A similar insider perspective is put forward by Paul Hodkinson (2002: 1), who notes that as he gets into a car: 'we are five Goths on our way to spend a weekend'. Blending in with the young research subjects is also a crucial part of Phil Jackson's study on sensualities (2004: 174), where friendships among his clubbers from the different scenes were 'grounded in a virtually shared body as each member possessed the embodied memory of all the passionate, wild, wonderful times they'd shared together'. Cotterill (1992: 599), however, argues that there is a major issue concerning the blurring between research friendship and non-research friendship. Rachel Colosi (2010: 7) already had strong friendship connections in her ethnographic study on lap dancing as she had worked at the club for nearly 2 years. She states: 'I was able to generate such rich data only accessible to those actively engaged in the culture being studied'.

Ultimately, where does research friendship lead? Robert Hollands (2003: 165) raises the issue of whether an ethnographer does in fact ever leave the field. He states: 'With one trainee in particular, I developed a close personal friendship which still continues today'. We too have remained in contact with our respective research subjects, resulting in the integration of them into our friendship networks. In contrast, Ruth Emond (2003: 108) understands social proximity as possibly causing 'hindrance' because some youth researchers 'believe they are still young and have to therefore make little effort to be the stranger'. While these studies speak about the advantages of insider status they also highlight the problems of undertaking research on peers where researcher authority can be questioned or research subjects may feel threatened to conform to researcher-generated expectation (Davis, 1999). A significant weakness in the youth studies literature on ethnographic reflexivity is an over-preoccupation with contemporary reflexivity shown by little reference to the sociological history of biographical methods in social research (Merrill and West 2009). There is an occasional reference to Whyte's (1943) classic study of *Street Corner Society*, such as by Cieslik (2003: 3) and McDonald and Marsh (2005: 68), and sometimes a reference to the Chicago School of Sociology (Hodkinson, 2005: 131). However, these references are largely for the purpose of legitimacy. What is absent is any detail of the origin or relevance of early sociological studies of young people employing ethnographic tools and reflexive methodologies (Heath et al., 2009; Blackman, 2010).

The new reflexivity has enabled sociology not only to be aware of prejudices and subjective influence over the construction of the researched. Awareness of how the researcher engages with the research subjects to produce a text has to be accounted for through the sensitivity of the research relationship, understood as the emotional context. This does not mean we want to deny the presence of the ethnographer, nor do we want to inoculate the reader so that they are seduced by the data before the analysis. For Liz Frost (2003: 129) and Robert Hollands (2003: 162) there is no such thing as a neutral role in ethnographic fieldwork with young people, as issues of social structure such as ethnicity, social class, gender or age come into play and shape the responses of both the researcher and the researched. The ethnographic examples in the chapter demonstrate how power relations are enacted in practice and we want to allow the reader to see the multiple ways participation and exchanges are worked within the research setting. The intention has been to allow the data to be read and assessed by the reader alongside the author's interpretation, in terms of suggestion and feasibility.

Solidarity between the supervisor and the researcher

Gemma: It was vital to be supervised by an ethnographic specialist when I conducted research on young women in clubscapes associated with sexual expression, danger and resistance. The solidarity and integrity demonstrated by Shane Blackman's work ethic and experience in the study of youth cultures and young women allowed me to refine my own ethnography with confidence and empathy towards participants. Care and responsibility were central throughout the research, allowing reflexivity and renegotiation of consent to display the ethical approach to research participants. Both of our research areas join through the acknowledgment of the importance of challenging *hidden ethnography* inherent in sociology regarding the gender of the researcher and their thoughts and feelings produced through friendships made in the field, especially in youth research. For each field site Shane always knew where I was, at what times, and I would notify him via email to say I was back safe. The trust and openness shared allowed the scope of research to expand without constraints being imposed on me. The only constraints I felt were from the wider community concerning my gender and wellbeing, and these only served to replicate heterosexist attitudes towards women in research. This imposition compromises the agency of the participants and hinders the development of ethnography and how it can be understood, specifically as contexts are ignored. Therefore it is vital to challenge tensions and opposition created by reactions to ethnographic research, in particular when critiquing data, the gender of the researcher and the discipline they are from.

Shane: When supervising Gemma I operated a holistic strategy whereby three interwoven features – rapport, openness and trust – were always at the centre of our interaction during fieldwork and writing-up. This enabled me to assess and monitor the quality of the ethnographic study and through the supervision we both became aware of the intimate relationship of *double reflexivity* as we tried to stay true to the original feelings encountered rather than become distanced. For us the ethnographic experience should be based on the principle that this method makes us human like our research subjects. The positive and creative dynamic of our supervisory interactions we feel were partly related to what Sharlene Swartz (2011: 63) calls the near taboo issue that the research participants 'enjoyed being involved': they experienced pleasure, interest and learning from their participation, as we both did.

Conclusion

Each of the ethnographic examples has meaning through fieldwork friendship, which takes a reflexive stand on the basis of cooperative and collaborative participation. Here the researcher and the researched are seen in active dialogue, sustaining and renewing relationships on the edge of emotion and play through commitment. The concept of double reflexivity as an idea operates as a check on the researcher, preventing them from drifting back into being a 'transcendental other' because the same degree of intensity of fieldwork mood is experienced again through the social conditions of the write-up. The ethnographic examples point towards complex realities and identities and the diverse forms of ethnographic data collected enable the researcher to put forward a creative and crafted account where the researched have a voice. For us double reflexivity shows that the researcher and the researched are engaged in mutual dialogue to understand meaning. Behind the ethnographic examples is the idea that we are relying on the research subjects' voices to put forward Geertz' theory of thick description, so indexicality or empathetic co-constructions of narrative development are at the centre of the telling and re-telling of stories (Robinson, 2010). Through participatory and exchange-based interactions the shared experience is woven into the social life of the research method.

Suggested further reading

Related methodological literature

- Colosi, R. (2010) *Dirty Dancing? An Ethnography of Lap-Dancing* (Devon: Willan).

This study puts forward new and critical thinking regarding qualitative research in a sensitive area, which has previously had little coverage.

- Back, L. (2007) *The Art of Listening* (Oxford: Berg).

This book is a valuable contribution to understanding contemporary cultural issues alongside theoretical and practical guidance for qualitative researchers.

- Kulick, D. and Willson, M. (eds) *Taboo: Sex, Identity and Erotic Subjectivity in Anthropological Fieldwork* (London: Routledge).

This critical and sensitive collection advances our understanding of the intimate relationships between the researcher and the researched.

Examples of related youth research

- MacDonald, R., Shildrick, T. and Blackman, S. (eds) (2010) *Young People, Class and Place* (London: Routledge).

This collection of new youth research studies interrogates broader processes of social change through new theoretical approaches.

- Aldridge, J. Measham, F. and Williams, L. (2011) *Illegal Leisure Revisited: Changing Patterns of Alcohol and Drug Use in Adolescents and Young Adults* (London: Routledge).

This revised empirical and theoretical study of young people and intoxication contains insight, breadth and a critical social policy stance.

- Nayak, A. and Kehily, M. J. (2008) *Gender, Youth and Culture* (London: Palgrave Macmillan).

An innovative empirical and theoretical study on young people's gender identities, focused on new cultural developments encountered by youth.

• Pitts, V. (2003) *In the Flesh: The Cultural Politics of Body Modification* (New York: Palgrave Macmillan).

This insightful qualitative study on contemporary issues of the body and subculture combines new thinking with textual methods on the social structure and sexuality.

14
Conclusion
Sue Heath and Charlie Walker

Giving this book the title of *Innovations in Youth Research* always had the potential to make us hostages to fortune. We admit that it has been with some trepidation that we have used this title, as making claims to innovation is inevitably a rather perilous business (Travers, 2009; Taylor and Coffey, 2008). What might be innovative to one person, or within one particular field of study, might well be old hat to another person or within another field of enquiry. For this reason we have chosen to conceive of innovation for the purposes of this book in terms of research methods and approaches that have not yet filtered through to the mainstream within youth research, if by 'mainstream' we mean *a dominant tendency*. So the specific methods written about in this book are, for the most part, not completely new (although the contexts in which they are applied might be), but neither, for the most part, are they yet widespread. Many of these methods are, though becoming increasingly popular within youth studies, particularly among younger generations of researchers, and in our view deserve a wider audience. This is particularly so in relation to the growing popularity of visual, online and mobile methods, approaches which have featured in many chapters in this book. Importantly, they testify to a current wave of methodological creativity within the field of youth research, partly a response to the possibilities afforded by new technologies, as well as to the growing popularity of participatory and mixed methods approaches which have encouraged researchers to think more imaginatively about issues of research design.

Perhaps surprisingly, as it is by no means a new approach, this collection has also included several examples of ethnographic research. Charlie Walker ended Chapter 12 by providing a healthy reminder of the ethnographic roots of youth research, citing Margaret Mead's iconic anthropological study of *Coming of Age in Western Samoa*, which was first published in 1928. Mead's work and the classic sociological studies of the Chicago School, such as Thrasher's *The Gang* (1927) and Foote Whyte's *Street Corner Society* (1943) all set the stage for a strong ethnographic tradition at the heart of youth research, which continues to this day. It is largely because of this link between ethnography and the origins of youth research that we chose to include some examples of contemporary ethnographic research in this book. Ethnographic methods of enquiry may be very well established yet, as our examples have demonstrated, the approach is constantly evolving in new contexts, whether in relation to forms of digital ethnography (Chapter 11), ethnography in cross-cultural contexts (Chapter 12), or ethnography conducted in the shadow of postmodern critiques of representation and legitimation (Chapter 13). Even the most established of methods do not stand still, but adapt in response to new empirical contexts and theoretical currents.

What we have sought to do in this book, then, is to showcase some recent examples of youth research which have used a wide range of imaginative methods of enquiry: not necessarily the only examples of their kind, but certainly *good* examples. Our aim – and that of our contributors – has not been to argue that these methods are somehow better than more widely adopted methods, nor has it been to suggest that all youth research should necessarily incorporate methods of these kinds. Rather, we encouraged our contributors to open up the debate about methodological innovation by highlighting both the strengths of particular methods and approaches alongside some of the methodological and epistemological challenges which inevitably arise in using them. It should be apparent by this point that these are rarely new challenges, but more often than not are familiar challenges in new guises: but no less challenging for that.

In the introduction to this book we highlighted four broad themes which we felt cut across the collection as a whole. These were: the pervasive influence of participatory approaches to youth research; the centrality of ethical considerations; the increasingly common use of mixed methods approaches in youth research; and the importance of reflexivity in relation to the social relations of fieldwork. We identified a number of common threads in relation to these themes and readers will no doubt have drawn out many others of their own under these four broad headings. In this final chapter we seek to pull out two new cross-cutting themes and to revisit one of our original themes. The two new themes relate to the extent to which certain methods might legitimately be considered to be particularly appropriate to youth research, and to the potential for innovative methods to capture the complexity of young people's lives. The theme we revisit is that of the 'new ortho-doxy' of mixed methods research. We close the book with a few final reflections on future innovations in youth research.

Youth-friendly methods?

This book is premised on an assumption that the methods used by our contributors have been particularly appropriate to the specific contexts of *youth* research. That is not to suggest that these methods could not be used in other contexts, but to assert that researchers might find them particularly useful in researching the lives of younger people. It is important to acknowledge, then, that a significant driver of much recent methodological innovation in the context of youth research has been a desire to develop and use so-called youth-friendly methods. Yet it is worth pausing for a moment and considering whether certain meth-ods are indeed inherently more 'youth-friendly' than others. Online methods, including those described in this book, are often assumed to have an intrinsic appeal to young people, a group deemed to enjoy high levels of engagement with web-based technologies and to have a general savviness in virtual environments. This point was emphasised by Darren Sharpe in Chapter 9, where he argued that web-based tech-nologies 'are tools that feature prominently in young people's lives and their inclusion stops research being seen as dull. Without using such tools, it is often challenging to maintain the interest and focus of young people.' Visual methods are similarly presumed to have a particular appeal to young people by virtue of assumptions concerning their visual literacy and their familiarity with technologies for producing visual images. Yet our assumptions about what constitutes a 'youth-friendly method' may not always be accurate. In Chapter 8, Nadine Schaefer highlighted how some of the young people involved in her research on the everyday lives of young people from the former East Germany were reluctant to use video-based methods, preferring instead to use other, less time-consuming and technically demanding methods such as still photography and interviewing. Sometimes a researcher's choice of methods may even be a source of some amusement to participants. In Chapter 7 Amanda Brown and Suzanne Powell noted the amused disdain with which some of their South Indian research participants viewed the disposable cameras which they proposed to use in their research on space and place. Some of their participants even resorted to using their own digital cameras or the cameras on their mobile phones rather than having to use the low-tech equipment provided by the researchers!

Implicit within exhortations to use 'youth-friendly' methods is a view that more conventional research methods are unhelpfully adult-orientated, possibly requiring skills and levels of confidence that may be beyond many young people. However, the inherent danger of this assumption is that the widespread conceptualisation of young people's interests and competencies as existing *in opposition to* those of adults is – albeit inadvertently – reinforced, which rather undermines the emancipatory ethos of much participatory research. 'Youth-friendly' methods, especially those based on creative approaches such as pho-tography, film, drawing or collage, do nonetheless bring into sharp focus the question of individual competencies in relation to different methods (regardless of age) and how this might impact on the task of analysis. Again in Chapter 8, for example, Schaefer reported how one young woman was initially extremely nervous about the prospect of involvement in film-making, despite receiving training in the method, although she eventually ended up embracing the method with confi-dence. Nonetheless, it would be unwise to assume that young people are universally confident in using supposedly 'youth-friendly' meth-ods. This is by no means an issue unique to participant-produced visual data – anyone experienced in qualitative interviewing will, for exam-ple, be familiar with contrasting levels of articulacy among research participants – but it is perhaps more readily apparent in relation to some forms of data than others. In the same way that some people are better than others at telling stories about their lives, so some people are simply better at – or maybe more enthusiastic about – utilising creative methods than others. The various examples of participant-produced mental maps included in Richard Green and Anne White's chapter (Figures 4.1 to 4.4) and of self-portraits included in Anna Bagnoli's chapter (Figures 5.2 to 5.6) demonstrate this point very well. Anticipating this issue in relation to their use of mental maps, Green and White note that 'it was stressed from the very beginning that this was not an art exercise, and that we were not expecting perfect draw-ings; rather the interest was in the 'content' and not the 'beauty' of the maps'. Nonetheless, variable artistic ability or engagement may inadvertently affect our view of the content, such that researchers may 'read off' more from a well crafted mental map or collage than they might from one produced by someone lacking artistic talent or motiva-tion. A degree of caution is, therefore, wise when approaching the task of interpretation and analysis.

Methods for capturing the complexity of young people's lives

We noted in Chapter 1 that one of the important catalysts for methodological innovation and experimentation has been a desire to hone the methods used by youth researchers for capturing the complexities of young people's lives. This has been driven by a concern that more established methods are not always best suited to exploring some aspects of everyday life, particularly those relating to relatively new or rediscovered areas of enquiry. The growing popularity of mobile and visual methods of enquiry has, for example, been linked by some of our contributors to the rising contemporary interest in young people's geographies and questions of identity, space and place, with these methods deemed particularly well suited to exploring such themes. Mainstream methods such as observation and interviewing have, up to a point, been very useful in researching space and place, yet alternative methods may be needed 'to reach the parts that other methods cannot reach'. White and Green's use of mental maps in their research on young people's attachment to place (Chapter 4), for example, was underpinned by their view that 'the method is particularly revealing for understanding the subjective relationships (for example, perceptions, attitudes, and experiences) that people have towards the objective spatial world(s) they inhabit and which shape their behaviour.' Similarly, inspired by the 'new mobilities paradigm', Nicola Ross and colleagues (Chapter 3) used mobile methods – walking interviews and in-car interactions – as part of their research into the 'place-making practices' of young people in public care. They point out that 'in these mobile research encounters motion and commotion were used to productive effect, as the shared journeys, perceived and experienced, generated assemblages of connections, understandings, closeness, distance and diversions.' The implication of such comments is that other methods might have been less revealing of young people's relationships to space and place and the ways in which they impact upon their lives, which seems to be born out in the detailed examples provided in each of these chapters. Ross and her colleagues would no doubt agree with Fincham et al.'s (2010: 10) assessment that 'the realisation that there is something different in social relations constituted in motion, that data generated on the move is somehow distinct in character or studies that recognise that motion is of central importance to understanding certain aspects of the social world is gathering pace.'

Similarly, Nicola Allett's account in Chapter 2 of her use of music elicitation with Extreme Metal fans suggests that the methods she used were extremely effective in accessing affective aspects of fandom.

By inviting her research participants to listen to examples of Extreme Metal music in the research setting, she was able directly to tap into some of the emotions experienced by fans as they engage with the music which they love. Allett acknowledges that 'an auditory encounter is never the same, even when we listen to a familiar piece of music', and in that sense music elicitation 'creates a particular moment for the respondent(s) and researcher to share the music encounter'. Presumably this 'particular moment' will consist as much of memories of past listenings as of immediate 'in the moment' responses to the music. Nonetheless, it is difficult to imagine being able to access the rich, emotion-laden responses that Allett's method achieved through discussions of Extreme Metal music purely in the abstract. Allett's example demonstrates the potential strength of elicitation techniques more generally, not just music elicitation: through direct contact with a particular medium – whether a photograph, a piece of art, a newspaper article, a piece of music – research participants are transported to a different emotional space. In our view, though, Allett's specific use of music as an elicitation technique does have particular resonance for youth researchers, given the centrality of music to so many aspects of most young people's lives. It is a rarely used method which has great potential for wider adoption in a broad range of contexts, and Allett's work should be considered as pioneering.

Hybrid and crossover methodologies

It is striking that the different methods used across this collection have rarely been used in isolation. Instead, methods as diverse as mental mapping, walking interviews, music elicitation, self-portraits, surveys, digital ethnography and blog analysis have been included as part of a palette of complementary methods, with the strengths of one method complementing the strengths of others. It is also significant that few of these examples have involved the utilisation of these different methods *instead of* interview-based methods, but have rather used them *alongside* qualitative interviews and/or focus groups, with various creative methods often used as forms of interview elicitation. This highlights the ongoing importance of qualitative interview techniques within youth research, a set of methods which arguably remain at the heart of much work within this field of study. In the wake of frequent reminders in recent years of the limitations of the interviewing method, this may seem to some observers to be a rather old-fashioned perspective. Yet qualitative interviewing has by no means stood still in recent years and has itself been subject to innovation and development, not least in relation to the growing use of narrative and biographical approaches (see e.g., Henderson et al., 2007), and the incorporation of various elicitation techniques to enhance the interview encounter. Importantly, by combining interviews with other creative methods researchers are able to move beyond the limitations of a single method research design.

We noted in Chapter 1 that the adoption of mixed methods research designs has become something of a 'new orthodoxy' in the social sciences, as much the case within youth research as in other fields of enquiry, especially those fields which often have an applied edge to their research agendas. 'Mixed methods research' is a term which has been used to cover a multitude of different approaches, from the combination of methods drawn from both quantitative *and* qualitative traditions (for some, the definitive form of mixed methods approach) through to approaches using a combination of *only* qualitative or *only* quantitative methods. There is also much debate within mixed methods circles about the appropriate balance between the particular elements of a mixed methods design and the implications of this for the analysis and interpretation of findings. Tashakorri and Teddlie (2002) provide a very thorough overview of the complexity of much of this debate. Their book also highlights how, for some, mixed methods has come to represent a new paradigm in its own right, while for others methodological pragmatism has become the order of the day. Nonetheless, mixed methods research often adds up to no more than the sum of the different parts involved, with each method tending to retain its distinctiveness, rather than the combination of methods creating something new in the mixing.

In response to this, we suggest the terms 'hybridity' and 'crossover' as alternative metaphors to the *mixing* of methods, as the more usual label of 'mixed methods' does not, in our view, do full justice to the process of creative blending that we have witnessed in many of the examples included in this book. Metaphors are undoubtedly important within methodological debates, as they have the power either to open up or to close down the terms of debate. In our view, hybridity and crossover are metaphors which have the potential to open up the terms of what has become a rather turgid and arcane technical debate in recent years. We share Law's contention that methodological creativity should cultivate 'the capacity to think six impossible things before breakfast. And as part of this, it is about creating metaphors and images for what is impossible or barely possible, unthinkable or almost unthinkable' (Law, 2004: 6). Our alternative metaphors of hybridity and crossover strive to do this. They are terms which try to capture the sense in which distinct methods used in creative combinations can sometimes become much more than the sum of their parts, and can even become something entirely new. We do not propose these metaphors as replacements for the mixed methods metaphor, but view them as heuristic devices which have the potential to extend the terms of the debate, as well as to provide useful descriptors for (combinations of) methods of data generation and/or analysis which do not necessarily fit neatly into the established language of mixed methods. It strikes us that much that is creative and innovative in contemporary youth research is grounded in the imaginative use of hybrid and crossover approaches to method: these metaphors are therefore worth pushing to their limits in order to consider the possibilities that might thus be opened up for researchers.

Concluding thoughts

This collection has, of necessity, been selective in terms of its coverage. We have not, for example, had space to include examples of other equally important developments, such as qualitative longitudinal research, an approach which has strong links to youth research (Henderson et al., 2007; McLeod and Thomson, 2009) or to include examples of the latest developments in computer-assisted survey interviewing (Conrad and Scober, 2007). Neither have we had room to cover exciting developments in methods reliant on qualitative Geographical Information Systems (GIS) (Cope and Elwood, 2009), nor to review advances in multimodal and hypermedia ethnography (Dicks et al., 2005). And it is undoubtedly the case that if a book like this is published in ten years' time it is likely to include all manner of as yet unimagined methods for researching young people's lives, particularly as Web 2.0 technologies continue to evolve and develop at a rapid pace. However, we think it is equally likely that tried and tested methods that currently lie at the heart of much youth research – surveys, qualitative interviewing, participant observation – will continue to be important methods of enquiry, albeit more widely complemented by the use of imaginative approaches to researching young people's lives such as those included in this collection. Innovation is important, and there is much to celebrate in this regard within contemporary youth research, but we do not envisage – nor desire – a world where these more well-established methods are rendered redundant. Whether the sorts of innovative methods which we have showcased in this collection have by then achieved the status of mainstream methods, as in a dominant tendency, remains to be seen.

References

Adam, B. (1990) *Time & Social Theory* (Cambridge: Polity Press).

Adam, B. (1995) *Timewatch: The Social Analysis of Time* (Cambridge: Polity Press).

Alderson, P. (1995) *Listening to Children: Children, Ethics and Social Research* (Essex: Barnardos).

Alderson, P. (2000) 'Children as Researchers: The Effects of Participation Rights on Research Methodology', in P. Christensen and A. James (eds) *Research with Children: Perspectives and Practices* (London: Routledge Falmer), 241–57.

Aldridge, J. Measham, F. and Williams, L. (2011) *Illegal Leisure Revisited: Changing Patterns of Alcohol and Drug Use in Adolescents and Young Adults* (London: Routledge).

Allatt, P. (1997) 'Conceptualising Youth: Transitions, Risk and the Public and the Private', in J. Bynner, L. Chisholm and A. Furlong (eds) *Youth, Citizenship and Social Change in a European Context* (Aldershot: Ashgate), 89–102.

Allen, L. (2008) 'Young People's "Agency" in Sexuality Research Using Visual Methods', *Journal of Youth Studies*, 11 (6), 565–77.

Anderson, B. (2004) 'Recorded Music and Practices of Remembering', *Social and Cultural Geography*, 5 (1), 3–20.

Anderson, B. (2005) 'Practices of Judgement and Domestic Geographies of Affect', *Social and Cultural Geography*, 6 (5): 645–58.

Anderson, P. (2007) '"All that Glisters is Not Gold" – Web 2.0 and the Librarian', *Journal of Librarianship and Information Science*, 39 (4), 195–98.

Anderson, T. (2009) *Rave Culture* (Philadelphia: Temple University Press).

Arches, J and Fleming, J. (2007) '"Building Our Own Monument": A Social Action Group Revisited', *Practice*, 19 (1) 33–45.

ARK (2003–09) *Young Life and Times Survey, 2003–09* ARK, www.ark.ac.uk/ylt/

Atkinson, P. (1990) *The Ethnographic Imagination* (London: Routledge).

Atkinson, P. (2009) 'Ethics and Ethnography', *Contemporary Social Science: Journal of the Academy of Social Sciences*, 4 (1), 17–30.

Aubeeluck, A. and Buchanan, H. (2006) 'Capturing the Huntington's Disease Spousal Career Experience: A Preliminary Investigation using "Photovoice" Method', *Dementia: The International Journal of Social Research and Practice*, 5, 95–116.

Back, L. (1996) *New Ethnicities and Urban Culture: Racisms and Multiculture in Young Lives* (London: UCL Press).

Back, L. (2007) *The Art of Listening* (Oxford: Berg).

Badger, M. (2004) 'Visual Blogs', in L. J. Gurak, S. Antonijevic, L. Johnson, C. Ratliff, and J. Reyman (eds) *Into the Blogosphere: Rhetoric, Community, and Culture of Weblogs*, http://blog.lib.umn.edu/blogosphere/women_and_children.html, date accessed 27 May 2010.

Bagnoli, A. (2001) *Narratives of Identity and Migration: An Autobiographical Study on Young People in England and Italy*, Unpublished Ph.D. Thesis, University of Cambridge.

Bagnoli, A. (2004) 'Researching Identities with Multi-method Autobiographies', *Sociological Research Online*, 9 (2), http://www.socresonline.org.uk/9/2/bagnoli.html, date accessed 1 June 2010.

Bagnoli, A. (2007) 'Between Outcast and Outsider: Constructing the Identity of the Foreigner', *European Societies*, 9 (1), 23–44.

Bagnoli, A. (2009a) '"On an Introspective Journey": Identities and Travel in Young People's Lives', *European Societies*, special issue, 11 (3), 325–45.

Bagnoli, A. (2009b) 'Beyond the Standard Interview: The Use of Graphic Elicitation and Arts-based Methods', *Qualitative Research*, 9 (5), 547–70.

Banks, M. (2001) *Visual Methods in Social Research* (London: Sage).

Banks, M. (2009) *Using Visual Data in Qualitative Research* (The SAGE Qualitative Research Kit) (London: Sage).

Barry, M. (1996) 'The Empowering Process: Leading from Behind?', *Youth and Policy. The Journal of Critical Analysis*, 54, 1–12.

Barthes, R. (1977) *Image-Music-Text* (Glasgow: Fontana).

Bassett, E. H. and O'Riordan, K. (2002) 'Ethics of Internet Research: Contesting the Human Subjects Research Model', *Ethics and Information Technology*, 4 (3), 233–47.

Batt-Rawden, K. B. (2006) 'Music – a Key to the Kingdom? A Qualitative Study of Music and Health in Relation to Men and Women with Long-term Illnesses', *Electronic Journal of Sociology* http://www.sociology.org/content/2006/tier1/batt-rawden.html.

Bauman, Z. (1995) *Life in Fragments: Essays in Postmodern Morality* (Oxford: Blackwell).

Beazley, H., Bessell, S., Ennew, J. and Waterson, R. (2009) 'The Right to be Properly Researched: Research with Children in a Messy, Real World', *Children's Geographies*, 7 (4), 365–78.

Beck, U. (1992) *Risk Society: Towards a New Modernity* (London: Sage.)

Becker, H. S. (1951) 'The Professional Dance Musician and his Audience', *American Journal of Sociology*, 57 (2) 136–44.

Becker, H. S. (1998) *Tricks of the Trade* (Chicago: Chicago University Press).

Beer, D. and Burrows, R. (2007) 'Sociology of and in Web 2.0: Some Initial Considerations', *Sociological Research Online*, 12 (5) http://www.socresonline.org.uk/12/5/17.html, date accessed 1 July 2010.

Benford, R. D. and Snow, D. A. (2000) 'Framing Processes and Social Movements: An Overview and Assessment', *Annual Review of Sociology*, 26, 611–39.

Bennett, A. (1999) 'Subcultures or Neo-tribes? Re-thinking the Relationship between Youth, Style and Musical Taste', *Sociology*, 33 (3), 599–617.

Binnie, J., Edensor, T., Holloway, J. Millington, S. and Young, C. (2007) 'Mundane Mobilities, Banal Travels', *Social and Cultural Geography*, 8 (2), 165–74.

Blackman, S. J. (1995) *Youth: Positions and Oppositions – Style, Sexuality and Schooling* (Aldershot: Avebury Press).

Blackman, S. J. (1998) 'Poxy Cupid: An Ethnographic and Feminist Account of a Resistant Female Youth Culture – the New Wave Girls', in T. Skelton and G. Valentine (eds) *Cool Places* (London: Routledge), 207–28.

Blackman, S. J. (2007) 'Hidden Ethnography: Crossing Emotional Borders in Qualitative Accounts of Young People's Lives', *Sociology*, 41 (4), 699–716.

Blackman, S. J. (2010) '"The Ethnographic Mosaic" of the Chicago School: Critically Locating Vivien Palmer, Clifford Shaw and Frederic Thrasher's Research Methods in Contemporary Reflexive Sociological Interpretation', in C. Hart (ed.) *The Legacy of the Chicago School of Sociology* (Kingswinsford: Midrash), 195–215.

Blades, M., Blaut, J. M., Darvizeh, Z., Elguea, S., Sowden, S., Soni, D., Spencer, C., Stea, D., Surajpaul, R. and Uttal, D. (1998) 'A Cross-Cultural Study of Young Children's Mapping Abilities', *Transactions of the Institute of British Geographers*, 23 (2), 269–77.

Blank, G. (2008) 'Online Research Methods and Social Theory', in N. Fielding, R. M. Lee and G. Blank (eds) *The SAGE Handbook of Online Research Methods* (London: SAGE), 537–49.

Blood, R. (2004) 'How Blogging Software Reshaped the Online Community', *Communications of the ACM*, December 2004, http://www.rebeccablood.net/essays/blog_software.html, date accessed 20 December 2007.

Bober, M. (2004) 'Virtual Youth Research: An Exploration of Methodologies and Ethical Dilemmas from a British Perspective', in E. A. Buchanan (ed.) *Readings in Virtual Research Ethics: Issues and Controversies* (London: Information Science Publishing).

Booth, T. and Booth, W. (2003) 'In the Frame: Photovoice and Mothers with Learning Difficulties', *Disability and Society*, 18 (4), 431–42.

Borland, M., Hill, M., Laybourn, A., and Stafford, A. (2001) *Improving Consultation with Children and Young People in Relevant Aspects of Policy-making and Legislation in Scotland* (Edinburgh: Scottish Parliament).

Bortree, D. (2005) 'Presentation of Self on the Web: An Ethnographic Study of Teenage Girls' Weblogs', *Education, Communication and Information*, 5 (1), 25–39.

Bourdieu, P. (1986) 'The Forms of Capital', in J. Richardson (ed.) *Handbook of Theory and Research for the Sociology of Education* (New York: Greenwood), 241–58.

Bourdieu, P. (1992) 'The Practice of Reflexive Sociology (The Paris Workshop)', in P. Bourdieu and L. Wacquant, *An Invitation to Reflexive Sociology* (Cambridge: Polity Press), 217–60.

boyd, d. m. (2009) 'Social Media is Here to Stay ... Now What?', Microsoft Research Tech Fest, Redmond, 26 February, http://www.danah.org/papers/talks/MSRTechFest2009.html, date accessed 1 May 2010.

Boyden, J., and Ennew, J. (eds) (1997) *Children in Focus: A Manual for Participatory Research with Children* (Stockholm: Radda Barnen), date accessed 1 April 2010.

BPS (2007) 'Conducting Research on the Internet: Guidelines for Ethical Practice in Psychological Research Online', The British Psychological Society, available from www.bps.org.uk (home page), date accessed 1 March 2010.

Brake, A. and Büchner, P. (1996) 'Kindsein in Ost- und Westdeutschland. Allgemeine Rahmenbedingungen des Lebens von Kindern und jungen Jugendlichen', in P. Büchner, B. Fuhs and H.-H. Krüger, (eds) *Vom Teddybär zum ersten Kuss. Wege aus der Kindheit in Ost- und Westdeutschland* (Opladen: Leske and Budrich), 43–66.

Brannen, J. (2005) 'Mixed Methods Research: A Discussion Paper', ESRC National Centre for Research Methods, NCRM Methods Review Paper, NCRM/005.

Brannen, J., Lewis, S., Nilsen, A. and Smithson, J. (eds) (2002) *Young Europeans, Work and Family: Futures in Transition* (London: Routledge).

Brannen, J., and Nilsen, A. (2002) 'Young People's Time Perspectives: From Youth to Adulthood', *Sociology*, 36 (3), 513–36.

Brannen, J., and Nilsen, A. (2005) 'Individualisation, Choice and Structure: A Discussion of Current Trends in Sociological Analysis', *The Sociological Review*, 53 (3), 412–28.

Brewer, J. (2000) *Ethnography* (London: Sage).

Brownlie, J. (2009) 'Researching, not Playing, in the Public Sphere', *Sociology* 43 (4), 699–716.

Bruckman, A. (2002) 'Studying the Amateur Artist: A Perspective on Disguising Data Collected in Human Subjects Research on the Internet', *Ethics and Information Technology*, 4 (3), 217–31.

Bruckman, A. (2004) 'Opportunities and Challenges in Methodology and Ethics', in M. D. Johns, S. -L. Chen, and G. J. Hall (eds) *Online Social Research: Methods, Issues and Ethics* (New York: Peter Lang), 101–04.

Bryman, A. (ed.) (2006) *Qualitative Research*, special issue, 6 (1).

BSA (2002) *Statement of Ethical Practice for the British Sociological Association*, http://www.britsoc.co.uk/equality/Statement+Ethical+Practice.htm, date accessed 27 May 2010.

Büscher, M. and Urry, J. (2009) 'Mobile Methods and the Empirical', *European Journal of Social Theory*, 12 (1), 99–116.

Bull, M. (2001) 'The World According to Sound: Investigating the World of Walkman Users', *New Media Society* 3 (2), 179–97.

Bull, M. (2003) 'Soundscapes of the Car: A Critical Study of Automobile Habitation', in M. Bull and L. Back (eds) *The Auditory Culture Reader* (Oxford: Berg), 357–74.

Bull, M. and Back, L. (eds) (2008) *The Auditory Culture Reader* (Oxford: Berg).

Bundesamt für Bauwesen und Raumordnung (2000) *Raumordnungsbericht 2000*, Band 7, Bonn: Selbstverlag des Bundesamtes für Bauwesen und Raumordnung.

Burns, S. and Schubotz, D. (2009) 'Demonstarting the Merit of the Peer Research Process: A Northern Ireland Case Study', *Field Methods*, 21 (3), 309–26.

Carins, R. (1994) *Lifetimes and Risk: Pathways of Youth in our Time* (London: Harvester Wheatsheaf).

Carter, J. (2004) 'Research Note: Reflections on Researching across the Ethnic Divide', *International Journal of Social Research Methodology*, 7 (4) 345–53.

Castleden, H. and Garvin, T. and Huu-ay-aht First Nation (sic) (2008) 'Modifying Photovoice for Community-based Participatory Indigenous Research', *Social Science and Medicine*, 66 (6), 1393–405.

Cavicchi, D. (1998) *Tramps Like Us: Music and Meaning among Springsteen Fans* (Oxford: Oxford University Press).

Chase, E., Simon, A. and Jackson, S. (eds) (2006) *In Care and After: A Positive Perspective* (London: Routledge).

Christensen, P. (2004) 'Children's Participation in Ethnographic Research: Issues of Power and Representation', *Children and Society*, 18 (2), 165–76.

Christensen, P. and James, A. (2000) *Research with Children: Perspectives and Practices* (London: Routledge Falmer).

Cieslik, M. (2003) 'Introduction: Contemporary Youth Research Issues', in A. Bennett, M. Cieslik, and S. Miles (eds) *Researching Youth* (Basingstoke: Palgrave Macmillan).

Cinderby, S. (2010) 'How to Reach the 'Hard-to-reach': The Development of Participatory Geographic Information Systems (P-GIS) for Inclusive Urban Design in UK Cities', *Area*, 42 (2), 239–51.

Clarke, J. (1976) 'The Skinheads and the Magical Recovery of Community' in S. Hall and T. Jefferson (eds) *Resistance through Rituals*, 2nd edn (London: Routledge), 80–83.

Clifford, J. and Marcus, G. (1986) (eds) *Writing Cultures* (Berkeley: University of California Press).

Coffey, A. (1999) *The Ethnographic Self* (London: Sage).

Coffey, S. (2011) 'Revisiting Innovation in Qualitative Research', *Qualitative Researcher*, 13, Spring 2011, 1–2.

Cohen, P. (1997) *Rethinking the Youth Question* (Basingstoke: Palgrave Macmillan).

Cohen. P. and Ainley, P. (2000) 'In the Country of the Blind? Youth Studies and Cultural Studies in Britain', *Journal of Youth Studies*, 3 (1), 79–95.

Coles, B. (1995) *Youth and Social Policy* (London: UCL Press).

Coles, R. (1997) *Doing Documentary Work* (Oxford: Oxford University Press).

Collier, J. and Collier, M. (1986) 'Visual Anthropology: Photography as a Research Method', in J. P. Joanou (2009) 'The Bad and the Ugly: Ethical Concerns in Participatory Photographic Methods with Children Living and Working on the Streets of Lima, Peru', *Visual Studies*, 24 (3), 214–23.

Colosi, R. (2010) 'A Return to the Chicago School? From the Subculture of Taxi-dancers to the Contemporary Lap-dancer', in *Journal of Youth Studies*, 13 (1), 1–16.

Colosi, R. (2010) *Dirty Dancing? An Ethnography of Lap-Dancing* (Devon: Willan).

Conrad, F and Scober, M (2007) *Envisioning the Survey Interview of the Future* (Hoboken: Wiley-Blackwell).

Cooke, B. and Kothari, U. (eds) (2001) *Participation: The New Tyranny?* (London, New York: Zed Books).

Cope, M. S. and Elwood, S. (2009) *Qualitative GIS: A mixed methods approach* (London: Sage).

Cotterill, P. (1992) 'Interviewing Women', *Women's Studies International Forum*, 15 (5/6), 593–606.

Crang, M. and Cook, I. (2007) *Doing Ethnographies* (London: Sage).

Creative Commons (CC) (2011) *Attribution-NonCommercial 2.0 Generic (CC BY-NC 2.0)*, http://creativecommons.org/licenses/by-nc/2.0/deed.en, date accessed 10 January 2011.

Cresswell T. (2006) *On the Move* (London: Routledge).

Criminal Justice and Public Order Act (1994) http://www.legislation.gov.uk/ukpga/1994/33/contents, date accessed 1 March 2009.

Curtis, K., Liabo, K., Roberts, H. and Barker, M. (2004) 'Consulted but not Heard: A Qualitative Study of Young People's Views of their Local Health Service', *Health Expectations*, 7 (2), 149–56.

Darkthrone, 'En As I Dype Skogen', *Transylvanian Hunger*, Peacevile Records, 1994.

Davis, C. (1999) *Reflexive Ethnography* (Routledge: London).

Daykin, N. (2008) 'The Role of Music in Arts-based Qualitative Inquiry', in P. Leavy (ed.) *Method Meets Art: Arts-Based Research Practice* (New York: Guildford Publishers), 123–34.

Delgado, M. (2006) *Designs and Methods for Youth-Led Research* (London: Sage).

Dennis Jr S. F., Gaulocher, S., Carpiano, R. M. and Brown, D. (2009) 'Participatory Photo Mapping (PPM): Exploring an Integrated Method for Health and Place Research with Young People', *Health and Place*, 15 (2), 466–73.

Dennis, S. F. (2006) 'Prospects for Qualitative GIS at the Intersection of Youth Development and Participatory Urban Planning', *Environment and Planning*, 38 (11), 2039–54.

DeNora, T. (2000) *Music in Everyday Life* (Cambridge: Cambridge University Press).

DeNora, T. (2006) 'Music and Self Identity' in A. Bennett, B. Shank and J. Toynbee (eds) *Popular Music Studies Reader* (New York: Routledge), 141–47.

Department for Children, Schools and Families (2007) *Aiming High for Young People: A Ten Year Strategy for Positive Activities* (London: HM Treasury/DCSF).

Department for Education and Skills (2005) *Youth Matters*, Cm6629 (Norwich: The Stationery Office).

Devadoss, M. (2007) *Multiple Facets of My Madurai* (Madras: East West Books).

Dicks, B. and Hurdley, R. (2009) 'Using Unconventional Media to Disseminate Qualitative Research', *Qualitative Researcher*, 10, 2–5.

Dicks, B., Mason, B., Coffey, A. and Atkinson, P. (2005) *Qualitative Research and Hypermedia: Ethnography for the Digital Age* (London: Sage).

Dicks, B., Soyinka, B. and Coffey, A. (2006) 'Multimodal Ethnography', *Qualitative Research*, 6 (1), 77–96.

Dienel, C. and Gerloff, A. (2003) 'Geschlechtsspezifische Besonderheiten der innerdeutschen Migration für Sachsen-Anhalt', in T. Claus (ed.) *Gender- Report Sachsen-Anhalt 2003. Daten, Fakten und Erkenntnisse zur Lebenssituation von Frauen und Männern*, Magdeburg: Gender-Institut Sachsen-Anhalt (G/I/S/A), 47–64.

Dingwall, R. (2008) 'The Ethical Case against Ethical Regulation in Humanities and Social Science Research', *Contemporary Social Science: Journal of the Academy of Social Sciences*, 3 (1), 1–12.

Downs, R. M. and Stea, D. (1973) *Image and Environment* (Chicago: Aldine Publishing Company).

Downs, R. M. and Stea, D. (1977) *Maps in Minds: Reflections on Cognitive Mapping* (New York: Harper and Row).

Duffy, M., and Waitt, G. (2011) 'Sound Diaries: A Method for Listening to Place', in *Aether: The Journal of Media Geography*, 7 January, 119–36.

Dutton, W. H., Helsper, E. J., and Gerber, M. M. (2009) *The Internet in Britain: 2009* (Oxford Internet Institute, University of Oxford).

Educable (2000) *No Choice: No Chance: The Educational Experiences of Young People with Disabilities* (Belfast: Save the Children).

Elliot, J. (2005) *Using Narrative in Social Research: Qualitative and Quantitative Approaches* (London: SAGE).

Emond, R. (2003) 'Ethnography in Practice: A Case Study Illustration', in A. Bennett, M. Cieslik and S. Miles (eds) *Researching Youth* (Basingstoke: Palgrave Macmillan), 103–19.

Ensiferum, 'LAI, LAI, HEI', *Iron*, Spinefarm, 2004.

Erikson, E. H. (1980) *Identity and the Life Cycle* (New York: W.W. Norton and Company).

ESRC (2010) 'ESRC Framework for Research Ethics', http://www.esrcsocietytoday. ac.uk/ESRCInfoCentre/Images/Framework for Research Ethics 2010_tcm6-35811.pdf, date accessed 27 May 2010.

Ess, C. and the AoIR Ethics Working Committee (2002) *Ethical Decision-making and Internet Research: Recommendations from the AoIR Ethics Working Committee*, http://aoir.org/reports/ethics.pdf, date accessed 27 May 2010.

Eyehategod, 'Take as Needed for Pain', *Take as Needed for Pain*, Century Media, 1993.

Eynon, R., Fry, J. and Schroeder, R. (2008) 'The Ethics of Internet Research', in N. Fielding, R. M. Lee and G. Blank (eds) *The SAGE Handbook of Online Research Methods* (London: SAGE), 23–41.

Facebook (2010) *Statistics*, http://www.facebook.com/press/info.php?statistics, date accessed 27 May 2010.

Faust, D. and Nagar, R. (2001) 'Politics of Development in Postcolonial India: English-Medium Education and Social Fracturing', *Economic and Political Weekly*, 36 (30), 2878–83.

Fay, B. (1996) *Contemporary Philosophy of Social Sciences: A Multicultural Approach* (Oxford: Wiley-Blackwell).

Ferguson, H. (2008) 'Liquid Social Work: Welfare Interventions as Mobile Practices', *British Journal of Social Work*, 38 (3), 561–79.

Fernandez-Kelly, P. (1994) 'Towanda's Triumph: Social and Cultural Capital in the Transition to Adulthood in the Urban Ghetto', *International Journal of Urban and Regional Research* 18 (1), 88–111.

Fielding, M., and Bragg S. (2003) *Students as Researchers: Making a Difference* (Cambridge: Pearson Publishing).

Finch, J. (1984) '"It's Great to Have Someone to Talk to": The Ethics and Politics of Interviewing Women', in C. Bell and H. Roberts (eds) *Social Researching: Politics, Problems Practice* (London: Routledge and Kegan Paul).

Fincham, B., McGuinness, M. and Murray, L. (eds) (2010) *Mobile Methodologies* (Basingstoke: Palgrave Macmillan).

Fischer, H. and Kück, U. (2004) 'Bevölkerungsentwicklung und Migration von 1990 bis 2002: Berlin und die neuen Bundesländer im Vergleich', *Statistische Monatszeitschrift*, Statistisches Landesamt Berlin.

Fiske, J. (1989) *Reading the Popular* (Boston: Unwin Hyman).

Flew, T. (2002) *New Media: An Introduction* (Auckland: Oxford University Press).

Foote Whyte, W. (1943/55) *Street Corner Society* (Chicago: Chicago University Press).

France, A. (2000) *Youth Researching Youth: The Triumph and Success Peer-Research Project* (Leicester: Youth Work Press).

France, A (2004) 'Young people', in S. Fraser, V. Lewis, S. Ding, M. Kellett and C. Robinson (eds) *Doing Research with Children and Young People* (London: Sage).

Frankel, M. and Siang, S. (1999) 'Ethical and Legal Aspects of Human Subjects Research on the Internet', *American Association for the Advancement of Science Workshop Report*, http://www.aaas.org/spp/sfrl/projects/intres/main.htm, date accessed 27 May 2010.

Fraser, S., Lewis V., Ding, S., Kellett, M. and Robinson C. (eds) (2004) *Doing Research with Children and Young People* (London: Sage).

Frost, L. (2003) 'Researching Young Women's Bodies: Values, Dilemmas and Contradictions', in A. Bennett, M. Cieslik, and S. Miles, (eds) *Researching Youth* (Basingstoke: Palgrave Macmillan), 120–37.

Furlong, A. and Cartmel, F. (1994) 'Aspirations and Opportunity Structures: Thirteen-year-olds in Areas with Restricted Opportunities', Strathclyde Papers on Sociology and Social Policy, No.1 (Glasgow: University of Strathclyde).

Gallagher, L. and Gallagher, M. (2008) 'Methodological Immaturity in Childhood Research? Thinking Through "Participatory Methods"', *Childhood*, 15 (4), 499–516.

Geertz, C. (1973) *The Interpretation of Culture* (London: Hutchinson).

Gergen, K. J., and Gergen, M. M. (1988) 'Narrative and the Self as Relationship', *Advances in Experimental Social Psychology*, 21, 17–56.

Giddens, A. (1991) *Modernity and Self-Identity: Self and Society in the Late Modern Age* (Cambridge: Polity Press).

Gillespie, C. A. (2010) 'How Culture Constructs our Sense of Neighborhood: Mental Maps and Children's Perceptions of Place', *Journal of Geography*, 109 (1), 18–29.

Gillies, V., Holland, J., and Ribbens McCarthy, J. (2000) *Past/Present/Future: Time and the Meaning of Change in the 'Family'*, Paper presented at the BSA Annual Conference 'Making Time/Marking Time', 17–20 April, University of York.

Glaser, B. G. and Strauss, A. L. (1967) *The Discovery of Grounded Theory: Strategies for Qualitative Research* (Chicago: Aldine).

Glendinning, A., Pak, O. and Popkov, Iu V. (2004) 'Youth, Community Life and Well-being in Rural Areas of Siberia', *Siberica*, 4 (1), 31–48.

Goffman, E. (1974) *Frame Analysis: An Essay on the Organization of Experience* (Boston: Northeastern University Press).

Goodchild, B. (1974) 'Class Differences in Environmental Perception: An Exploratory Study', *Urban Studies*, 11 (1), 157–69.

Gould, P. R. and White, R. R. (1968) 'The Mental Maps of British School Leavers', *Regional Studies*, 2 (2), 161–82.

Gould, P. R. and White, R. R. (1974) *Mental Maps* (Harmondsworth: Penguin).

Gould, P. R. and White, R. R. (1986) *Mental Maps* (2nd edition) (London: Allen and Unwin).

Gray, A. (2003) *Research Practice for Cultural Studies: Ethnographic Methods and Lived Cultures* (London: Sage).

Graziano, K. J. (2004) 'Oppression and Resiliency in Post-apartheid South Africa: Unheard Voices of Black Gay Men and Lesbians', *Cultural Diversity and Ethnic Minority Psychology*, 10 (3), 302–16.

Green, A. E. and White, R. J. (2007) *Attachment to Place: Social Networks, Mobility and Prospects of Young People* (York: Joseph Rowntree Foundation).

Green, A. E., Shuttleworth, I. and Lavery, S. (2005) 'Young People, Job Search and Labour Markets: The Example of Belfast', *Urban Studies*, 42 (2), 301–24.

Green, E. and Kloos, B. (2009) 'Facilitating Youth Participation in a Context of Forced Migration: A Photovoice Project in Northern Uganda', *Journal of Refugee Studies*, 22 (4) 460–82.

Greene, S., and Hill, M. (2005) 'Researching Children's Experience: Methods and Methodological Issues', in S. Greene, and D. Hogan (eds) *Researching Children's Experience: Methods and Approaches* (London: Sage), 1–21.

Griffin, C. (1993) *Representations of Youth: The Study of Youth and Adolescence in Britain and America* (Cambridge: Polity Press).

Grinyer, A. (2007) 'The Ethics of Internet Usage in Health and Personal Narratives Research', *Social Research Update 49*, University of Surrey.

Gunter, A. (2010) *Growing Up Bad* (London: Tufnell Press).

Halkier, B. (2010) 'Focus Groups as Social Enactments: Integrating Interaction and Content in the Analysis of Focus Group Data', *Qualitative Research*, 10 (1), 71–89.

Hall, T., Lashua, B. and Coffey, A. (2008) 'Sound and the Everyday in Qualitative Research', *Qualitative Inquiry*, 14 (6), 1019–40.

Hammersley, M. and Atkinson, P. (1995) *Ethnography: Principles in Practice* (London: Routledge).

Harden, J., Scott, S., Backett-Milburn, K. and Jackson, S. (2000) 'Can't Talk, Won't Talk?: Methodological Issues in Researching Children', *Sociological Research Online*, 5 (2), 1–16.

Hart, R. (1979) *Children's Experience of Place* (London: John Wiley and Sons).

Hart, R. (1997) *Children's Participation: The Theory and Practice of Involving Young Citizens in Community Development and Environmental Care* (New York and London: Unicef and Earthscan Publications Limited).

Hart, R. A., and U. I. C. D. Centre (1992) *Children's Participation: From Tokenism to Citizenship* (Florence: UNICEF International Child Development Centre).

Heath, S. (2007) 'Widening the Gap: Pre-university Gap Years and the "Economy of Experience"', *British Journal of Sociology of Education*, 28 (1), 89–103.

Heath, S. and Cleaver, E. (2003) *Young, Free and Single? Twenty-somethings and Household Change* (Basingstoke: Palgrave Macmillan).

Heath, S., Brooks, R., Cleaver, E. and Ireland, E. (2009) *Researching Young People's Lives* (London: Sage).

Heath, S., Charles, V., Crow, G., and Wiles, R (2007) 'Informed Consent, Gatekeepers and Go-betweens: Negotiating Consent in Child- and Youth-orientated Institutions', *British Educational Research Journal*, 33 (3), 403–417.

Heath, S., R. Brooks, E. Cleaver and E. Ireland (2009) 'Using the Internet for Youth Research', in *Researching Young People's Lives* (London: SAGE).

Hebdige, D. (1976) 'The Meaning of Mod', in S. Hall and T. Jefferson (eds) *Resistance through Rituals: Youth Subcultures in Post-War Britain*, 2nd edn (London: Routledge), 71–9.

Henderson, S., Holland, J., McGrellis, S., Sharpe, S. and Thomson, R. (2007) *Inventing Adulthoods: A Biographical Approach to Youth Transitions* (London: Sage).

Hergenrather, K. C., Rhodes, S. D. and Bardhoshi, G. (2009) 'Photovoice as Community-based Participatory Research: A Qualitative Review', *American Journal of Health Behaviour*, 33 (6), 686–98.

Hergenrather, K. C., Rhodes, S. D. and Clarke G. (2006) 'Windows to Work: Exploring Employment Seeking Behaviours of Persons with HIV/AIDS through Photovoice', *AIDS Education Prevention*, 18 (3), 243–58.

Hermans, H. J. M. and Kempen, H. J. G. (1993) *The Dialogical Self* (London: Academic Press).

Herring, S. C., Scheidt, L. A., Bonus, S., and Wright, E. (2004) 'Bridging the Gap: A Genre Analysis of Weblogs', *Proceedings of the 37th Hawai'i International Conference on System Sciences (HICSS-37)* (Los Alamitos: IEEE Computer Society Press), http://www.blogninja.com/DDGDD04.doc, accessed 27 May 2010.

Hesmondhalgh, D. (2007) 'Audiences and Everyday Aesthetics: Talking about Good and Bad Music', *European Journal of Cultural Studies*, 10 (4), 507–27.

Hesse-Biber, S. (ed.) (2010) *Qualitative Inquiry*, special issue, 16 (6).

Hewson C., Yule, P., Laurent, D., and Vogel, C. (2003) *Internet Research Methods: A Practical Guide for the Social and Behavioural Sciences* (London: SAGE).

Hill, M. (2006) 'Children's voices on ways of having a voice: children's and young people's perspectives on methods used in research and consultation', *Childhood*, 13 (1), 69–89.

Hillman, A., Holland, S., Renold, E. and Ross, N.J. (2008) 'Negotiating Me, Myself and I: Creating a Participatory Research Environment for Exploring the

Everyday Lives of Children and Young People "in Care"', *Qualitative Researcher*, 7, 4–7.

Hinchman, L. P. and Hinchman, S. K. (eds), (1997), *Memory, Identity, Community. The Idea of narrative in the Human Sciences* (New York: SUNY Press).

Hine, C. (2000) *Virtual Ethnography*, http://socantcafe.org/uploads//2009/10/hine-2000-virtual-ethno.pdf, date accessed 1 January 2010.

HM Government (2004) *Every Child Matters: Change for Children*, www.everychildmatters.gov.uk/_files/F9E3F941DC8D4580539EE4C743E9371 D.pdf, date accessed 5 March 2010.

Hodkinson, H. (2005) 'Combining Life History and Longitudinal Qualitative Research to Explore Transitions and Learning in the Life Course', paper presented at the 13th Annual International Conference on Post-compulsory Education and Training, *Vocational Learning: Transitions, Inter-relationships, Partnerships and Sustainable Futures*, 5–7 December, Queensland, Australia.

Hodkinson, P. (2002) *Goth: Identity, Style and Subculture* (Oxford: Berg).

Hodkinson, P. (2005) 'Insider Research in the Study of Youth Culture', *Journal of Youth Studies*, 8 (2), 131–50.

Hodkinson, P. (2007) 'Interactive Online Journals and Individualisation', *New Media and Society*, 9 (4), 625–50.

Hodkinson, P. and Lincoln, S. (2008) 'Online Journal as Virtual Bedrooms? Young People, Identity and Personal Space', *Young*, 16 (1), 27–46.

Holland, S., Renold, E., Ross, N. and Hillman, A. (2008) 'Rights, "Right on" or the Right Thing to do? A Critical Exploration of Young People's Engagement in Participative Social Work Research', *Working Paper – Qualiti/* WPS/006, 1–28.

Holland, S., Renold, E., Ross, N. J., and Hillman, A. (2010) 'Power, Agency and Participatory Agendas: A Critical Exploration of Young People's Engagement in Participative Qualitative Research', *Childhood*, 17 (3), 360–75.

Holland, S., Renold, E., Ross, N. J., and Hillman, A. (2008) 'The Everyday Lives of Children in Care: Using a Sociological Perspective to Inform Social Work Practice', in B. Luckock and M. Lefevre (eds) *Direct Work: Social Work with Children and Young People in Care* (London: British Association for Adoption and Fostering (BAAF)).

Hollands, R. (2003) 'Double Exposure: Exploring the Social and Political Relations of Ethnographic Youth Research', in A. Bennett, M. Cieslik and S. Miles (eds) *Researching Youth* (Basingstoke: Palgrave Macmillan), pp.157–69.

Holliday, R. (2007) 'Performances, Confessions, and Identities: Using Video Diaries to Research Sexualities', in G. C. Stanczak (ed.) *Visual Research Methods: Image, Society and Representation* (London: Sage), 255–79.

Holloway, S. and Valentine, G. (2000) 'Spatiality and the New Social Studies of Childhood', *Sociology*, 34 (4), 763–83.

Holloway, S. L., and Valentine, G. (eds) (2000) *Children's Geographies: Playing, Living, Learning* (London: Routledge).

Hookway, N. (2008) '"Entering the Blogosphere": Some Strategies for Using Blogs in Social Research', *Qualitative Research*, 8 (1), 91–113.

Hörschelmann, K. and Schäfer, N. (2005) 'Performing the Global through the Local-globalisation and Individualisation in the Spatial Practices of Young East Germans', *Children's Geographies*, 3 (2), 219–42.

Hörschelmann, K. and Schäfer, N. (2007) '"Berlin is not a Foreign Country, Stupid!" – Growing up "Global" in Eastern Germany', *Environment and Planning A*, 39 (8), 1855–72.

Huffaker, D. (2006) 'Teen Blogs Exposed: The Private Lives of Teens made Public', *Presented to the American Association for the Advancement of Science in St Louis, MO*, February 16–19, 2006.

Huffaker, D. and Calvert, S. (2005) 'Gender, Identity and Language use in Teenage Blogs', *Journal of computer-mediated communication*, 10 (2), available from: http://jcmc.indiana.edu/vol10/issue2/huffaker.html, date accessed 1 February 2010.

Hurdley, R. (2006) 'Dismantling Mantelpieces: Narrating Identities and Materializing Culture in the Home', *Sociology*, 40 (4), 717–33.

Hurworth, R. (2003) 'Photo-interviewing for Research', *Social Research Update*, 40 (1), 1–4.

Ingold, T. and Lee Vergunst, J. (eds) (2008) *Ways of Walking: Ethnography and Practice on Foot* (Aldershot: Ashgate).

Ito, M., Horst, H., Bittanti, M., boyd, d., Herr-Stephenson, B., Lange, P., Pascoe, C. J. and Robinson, L. (2009) *Living and Learning with New Media Summary of Findings from the Digital Youth Project* (Massachusetts: MIT Press).

Jackson, P. (2004) *Inside Clubbing* (London: Berg).

James, A. and Prout, A. (1998) *Constructing and Reconstructing Childhood* (London: Falmer Press).

James, A., Jenks, C., and Prout, A. (1998) *Theorizing Childhood* (Cambridge: Polity Press).

James, S. (1990) 'Is There a "Place" for Children in Geography?', *Area*, 22 (3), 278–83.

Joanou, J. P. (2009) 'The Bad and the Ugly: Ethical Concerns in Participatory Photographic Methods with Children Living and Working on the Streets of Lima, Peru', *Visual Studies*, 24 (3), 214–23.

Jones, A. (2004) 'Children and Young People as Researchers', in S. Fraser, V. Lewis, S. Ding, M. Kellett and C. Robinson (eds) *Doing Research with Children and Young People* (London: Sage), 113–30.

Jung, C. G. (1967) 'The Philosophical Tree', in *Alchemical Studies* (Hull, R. F. C. Trans.) vol 13, 251–349 (London: Routledge & Kegan Paul).

Kaplan, A. E. (1987) *Rocking Around the Clock: Music Television, Postmodernism and Consumer Culture* (New York: Methuen).

Karlsson, L. (2006) 'The Diary Weblog and the Travelling Tales of Diasporic Tourists', *Journal of Intercultural Studies*, 27 (3), 299–312.

Kassof, A. (1965) *The Soviet Youth Program: Regimentation and Rebellion* (Cambridge, MA: Harvard University Press).

Katz, C. (2004) *Growing Up Global. Economic Restructuring and Children's Everyday Lives* (Minneapolis: University of Minnesota Press).

Kearney, M.C. (1998) '"Don't Need You" Rethinking Identity Politics and Separatism from a Grrrl Perspective' in J. S. Epstein (ed.) *Youth Culture: Identity in a Postmodern World* (Oxford: Blackwell), 148–88.

Keightley, E. (2010) 'Remembering Research: Memory and Methodology in the Social Sciences', in *International Journal of Social Research Methodology*, 13 (1), 55–70.

Keightley, E., and Pickering, M. (2006) 'For the Record: Popular Music and Phonography as Technologies of Memory', *European Journal of Cultural Studies*, 9 (2), 149–65.

Kellett, M. (2005a) *How to Develop Children as Researchers: A Step-by-Step Guide to Teaching the Research Process* (London: Paul Chapman Publishing).

Kellett, M. (2005b) 'Children as Active Researchers: A New Research Paradigm for the 21st century?', *NCRM Methods Review Papers*, ESRC National Centre for Research Methods, NCRM/003, 1–33.

Kellett, M. (2010) *Rethinking Children and Research, Attitudes in Contemporary Society* (London, Continuum International).

Kenney, K. (2009) *Visual Communication Research Designs* (London: Routledge).

Kesby, M. (2000) 'Participatory Diagramming: Deploying Qualitative Methods through an Action Research Epistemology', *Area*, 32 (4), 423–35.

Kesby, M. (2005) 'Re-theorising Empowerment-through-participation as a Performance in Space: Beyond Tyranny to Transformation', *Signs: Journal of Women in Culture and Society*, 30 (4), 2037–65.

Kintrea, K., Bannister, J., Pickering, J, Reid, M. and Suzuki, N. (2008) *Young People and Territoriality in British Cities* (York: Joseph Rowntree Foundation).

Kirby, P. (1999) *Involving Young Researchers: How to Enable Young People to Design and Conduct Research* (York: Joseph Rowntree Foundation).

Kirby, P., Laws, S., and Pettitt, B. (2004) 'Assessing the Impact of Children's Participation: A Discussion Paper towards a New Study', unpublished discussion paper, International Save the Children Alliance Child Participation Working Group, April.

Kitchen, R. M. (1994) 'Cognitive Maps: What are They and Why Study Them?' *Environmental Psychology*, 14 (1), 1–19.

Kollmorgen, R. (2003) 'Das Ende Ostdeutschlands? Zeiten und Perspektiven eines Forschungsgegenstandes', *Berliner Debatte Initial*, 14 (2), 2–4.

Kozinets, R. V. (2002b) 'The Field behind the Screen: Using Netnography for Marketing Research in Online Communities', *Journal of Marketing Research*, 39 (1), 61–72.

Kozinets, R.V. (2002a) 'Can Consumers Escape the Market? Emancipatory Illuminations from Burning Man', *Journal of Consumer Research*, 29 (1), 20–38.

Kröhnert, S., van Olst, N. and Klingholz, R. (2004) 'Mecklenburg-Vorpommern. Das wichtigste Kapital sind die Leere und die Landschaft', in S. Kröhnert, N. van Olst and R. Klingholz (eds) *Deutschland 2020. Die demographische Zukunft der Nation*, Berlin: Berliner Institut für Bevölkerung und Entwicklung, 36–40.

Kulick, D. and Willson, M. (eds) *Taboo: Sex, Identity and Erotic Subjectivity in Anthropological Fieldwork* (London: Routledge).

MacDonald, R., Shildrick, T. and Blackman, S. (eds) (2010) *Young People, Class and Place* (London: Routledge).

Kusenbach, M. (2003) 'Street Phenomenology: The go-along as Ethnographic Research Tool', *Ethnography*, 4 (3), 455–85.

Lampe, C., Ellison, N., and Steinfield, C., (2006) 'A Face(book) in the Crowd: Social Searching vs. Social Browsing', *Proceedings of the 2006 20th Anniversary Conference on Computer Supported Cooperative Work* (New York: ACM Press), 167–70.

Lange, P. (2008) 'Publicly Private and Privately Public: Social Networking on YouTube', *Journal of Computer-Mediated Communication*, 13 (1), 361–80.

Latham, A. (2003) 'Research, Performance, and Doing Human Geography: Some Reflections on the Diary-photograph, Diary-interview method', *Environment and Planning A*, 35 (11), 1993–2017.

Laughey, D. (2006) *Music and Youth Culture* (Edinburgh: Edinburgh University Press).

Laurier E, (2002) 'The Region as a Socio-technical Accomplishment of Mobile Workers', in B. Brown, N. Green and R. Harper (eds) *Wireless World* (London: Springer), 46–60.

Laurier, E., Lorimer, H, Brown, B., Jones, O., Juhlin, O., Noble, A., Perry, M., Pica, D., Sormani, P., Strebel, I., Swan, L., Taylor, A. S., Watts, L. and Weilenmann, A. (2008) 'Driving and Passengering: Notes on the Ordinary Organisation of Car Travel', *Mobilities*, 3 (1), 1–23.

Law, J. (2004) *After Method: Mess in Social Science Research* (London: Routledge).

Lea, J. (2006) 'Experiencing Festival Bodies: Connecting Massage and Wellness', *Tourism Recreation Research*, 31 (1), 57–66.

Leavy, P. (2008) *Method Meets Art: Arts-Based Research Practice* (New York: Guildford Publishers).

Lee, T. (1970) 'Perceived distance as   function of direction in the city', Environment and Behavior, 2, 1, 40–51.

Lee, J. and Ingold, T. (2006) 'Fieldwork on Foot: Perceiving, Routing, Socializing', in S. Coleman and P. Collins (eds) *Locating the Field: Space, Place and Context in Anthropology* (Oxford: Berg), 67–85.

Leonard, M. (1997) '"Rebel Girl, You are the Queen of my World": Feminism, "Subculture" and Grrrl Power', in S. Whiteley (ed.) *Sexing the Groove: Popular Music and Gender* (London: Routledge), 230–56.

Leonard, M. (2006) 'Teenagers Telling Sectarian Stories', *Sociology*, 40 (6), 1117–33.

Levi-Strauss, C. (1989) *Tristes Tropiques* (London: Pan Books).

Lewis, P. (2006) '200 Riot Police Break up Illegal Rave', *The Guardian*, August 28.

Lewis, V., Kellet, M., Robinson, C., Fraser, S., and Ding, S. (eds) (2004) *The Reality of Research with Children and Young People* (London: Sage).

Ley, D (2009) 'Mental Maps/Cognitive Maps', in D. Gregory, R. Johnston, G. Pratt, M. J. Watts and S. Whatmore (eds) *The Dictionary of Human Geography 5th Edition* (Oxford: Wiley-Blackwell), 455.

Li, D., and Walejko, G. (2008) 'Splogs and Abandoned Blogs: The Perils of Sampling Bloggers and Their Blogs', *Information, Communication and Society* 11 (2), 279–96.

Lieblich, A., Tuval-Masiach, R., and Zilber, T. (1998) *Narrative Research: Reading, Analysis and Interpretation*, vol. 47 (London: Sage).

Lightfoot, J. and Sloper, P. (2002) *Involving Young People in Health Service Development, Research Work, 2002* (Social Policy Research Unit: University of York).

Luckock, B. and Lefevre M. (eds) (2008) *Direct Work: Social Work with Children and Young People in Care,* (London: BAAF).

Lunch, N. and Lunch, C. (2006) *Insights into Participatory Video: A Handbook from the Field Insight*, http://insightshare.org/resources/pv-handbook.

Luttrell, W. and Chalfen, R. (eds) (2010) 'Lifting up Voices of Participatory Visual Research', *Visual Studies*, special issue, 25 (3).

Lynch, K. (1960) *The Image of the City* (Cambridge, MA: MIT Press).

MacDonald, R. and Marsh, J. (2005) *Disconnected Youth?: Growing up in Britain's Poor Neighbourhoods* (Basingstoke: Palgrave Macmillan).

MacDonald, R., Mason, P., Shildrick, T., Webster, C., Johnston, L. and Ridley, L. (2001) 'Snakes and Ladders: In Defence of Studies of Youth Transition', *Sociological Research Online*, 5 (4), http://www.socresonline.org.uk/5/4/macdonald.html, date accessed 1 January 2010.

MacDonald, R., Shildrick, T. and Blackman, S. (eds) (2010) *Young People, Class and Place* (London: Routledge).

Madge, C. (2006) *Online Research Ethics*, http://www.geog.le.ac.uk/orm/ethics/ethcontents.htm, date accessed 29 January 2007.

Madge, C. O'Connor, H. and Shaw, R. (2006) *Exploring Online Research Methods in a Virtual Training Environment*, http://www.restore.ac.uk/orm/site/home.htm

Malbon, B. (1999) *Clubbing: Dancing, Ecstasy and Vitality* (London: Routledge).

Mann, C. and F. Stewart (2000) *Internet Communication and Qualitative Research*, (London: SAGE).

Marcus, G. (1998) *Ethnography Through Thick and Thin* (Princeton, NJ: Princeton University Press).

Markham, A. N. (2005) 'The Methods, Politics and Ethics of Representation in Online Ethnography', in N. K. Denzin and Y. S. Lincoln (eds) *The SAGE Handbook of Qualitative Research* (Thousand Oaks: SAGE), 793–820.

Markus, H. R., and Nurius, P. (1986) 'Possible Selves', *American Psychologist*, 41 (9), 954–69.

Mason, B. and Dicks, B. (2001) 'Going beyond the Code: The Production of Hypermedia Ethnography', *Social Science Computer Review*, 19 (4), 445–57.

Mason, J. (2006) 'Six Strategies for Mixing Methods and Linking Data in Social Science Research', Real Life Methods Working Papers, University of Manchester http://www.socialsciences.manchester.ac.uk/realities/publications/workingpapers/4-2006-07-rlm-mason.pdf

Mason, J. (2008) 'Tangible Affinities and the Real Life Fascination of Kinship', *Sociology*, 42 (1), 29–46.

Mason, J. and Davies, K. (2009) 'Coming to Our Senses? A Critical Approach to Sensory Methodology', *Qualitative Research*, 9 (5), 587–603.

Massey, D. (1993) 'Power Geometry and a Progressive Sense of Place', in Burt, J., Curtis, B., Putnam, F., Robertson, G. and Tickner L. (eds) *Mapping the Futures: Local Cultures, Global Change* (London: Routledge), 59–69.

Matthews, H. and Limb, M (1999) 'Defining an Agenda for the Geography of Children: Review and Prospect', *Progress in Human Geography*, 23 (1), 61–90.

May, V. (2010) 'What to do with Contradictory Data?', Realities Toolkit 12, http://www.socialsciences.manchester.ac.uk/realities/resources/toolkits/contradictory-data/index.html, date accessed 1 February 2011.

Mazur, E. and Kozarian, L. (2010) 'Self-presentation and Interaction in Blogs of Adolescents and Young Emerging Adults', *Journal of Adolescent Research*, 25 (1), 124–44.

McAdams, D. (1993) *The Stories We Live By* (New York and London: The Guilford Press).

McAuley, A. (1995) 'Inequality and Poverty', in D. Lane (ed.) *Russia in Transition: Politics, Privatisation and Inequality* (London and New York: Longman), 177–189.

McAuley, C. (1998) 'Child Participatory Research: Ethical and Methodological Considerations', in D. Iwaniec, and J. Pinkerton (eds) *Making Research*

Work: Promoting Child Care Policy and Practice (Chichester: John Wiley & Sons), 163–77.

McCartan, C., Kilpatrick, R., and McKeown, P. (2004) 'Disaffected Young People and their Experience of Alternative Education: Involving Peer Researchers in the Research Process', Discussion paper, European Conference on Educational Research, Council of Europe, Strasbourg.

McDowell, L. (2003) *Redundant Masculinities? Employment Change and White Working-Class Youth* (Oxford: Blackwell).

McIntyre, A. (2003) 'Through the Eyes of Women: Photovoice and Participatory Research as Tools for Reimagining Place', *Gender, Place and Culture*, 10 (1), 47– 66.

McLaughlin, H. (2005) 'Young Service Users as Co-researchers: Methodological Problems and Possibilities', *Qualitative Social Work*, 4 (2), 211–28.

McLeod, A. (2007) 'Whose Agenda? Issues of Power and Relationship when Listening to Looked-after Young People', *Child and Family Social Work*, 12 (3), 278–86.

McLeod, J. and Thomson, R. (2009) *Researching Social Change* (London: Sage).

Mead, M. (1973) *Coming of Age in Samoa: A Psychological Study of Primitive Youth for Western Civilization* (New York: HarperCollins).

Merrill, B. and West, L. (2009) *Using Biographical Methods in Social Research* (London: Sage).

Mitra, A., and Cohen, E. (1999) 'Analyzing the Web: Directions and Challenges', in S. Jones (ed.) *Doing Internet Research: Critical Issues and Methods for Examining the Net*, (Thousand Oaks: SAGE), 179–202.

Moles, K. (2008) 'A Walk in Thirdspace: Place, Methods and Walking', *Sociological Research Online*, 13 (4) (http://www.socresonline.org.uk/13/4/2.html).

Moodysson, L. (2002) *Lilja 4-ever* [Film], (Sweden: Memfis Film).

Moore, K. (2003) 'E-heads versus Beer Monsters: Researching Young People's Music and Drug Consumption in Dance Club Settings', in A. Bennett, M. Cieslik, and S. Miles (eds) *Researching Youth* (Basingstoke: Palgrave Macmillan), 138–56.

Moran-Ellis, J. and Venn, S. (2007) 'The Sleeping Lives of Children and Teenagers: Night-worlds and Arenas of Action', *Sociological Research Online*, 12 (5), http://www.socresonline.org.uk/12/5/9.html, date accessed 1 December 2009.

Moreno, E. (1995) 'Rape in the Field: Reflections from a Survivor', in D. Kulick and M. Willson (eds) *Taboo: Sex, Identity and Erotic Subjectivity in Anthropological Fieldwork* (London and New York: Routledge), 219–50.

Morris, S. (2006) 'Police Hunt for "Mega" Outdoor Party as Dance Fans Tire of Legal Venues', *The Guardian*, July 24.

Morrow, V. (2001) 'Using Qualitative Methods to Elicit Young People's Perspectives on their Environments: Some Ideas for Community Health Initiatives', *Health Education Research*, 16 (3), 255–68.

Moscovici, S. (2000) 'The Phenomenon of Social Representations', in G. Duveen (ed) *Social Representations: Explorations in Social Psychology* (Cambridge: Polity), 18–77.

Muggleton, D. (2000) *Inside Subculture: The Postmodern Meaning of Style* (Oxford: Berg).

Muhr, T. (2007) *Atlas.ti (Version 5.7)* (Berlin: Scientific Software Development).

Murad, N. (2002) 'The Shortest Way Out of Work', in P. Chamberlayne, M. Rustin and T. Wengraf (eds) *Biography and Social Exclusion in Europe* (Bristol: Policy Press), 97–114.

Murray, D. and Spencer, C. (1979) 'Individual Differences in the Drawing of Cognitive Maps: The Effects of Geographical Mobility, Strength of Mental Imagery and Basic Graphic Ability', *Transactions of the Institute of British Geographers, New Series*, 4 (3), 385–91.

Murray, L. (2009) 'Looking at and Looking back: visualization in Mobile Research', *Qualitative Research*, 9 (4), 469–88.

Murthy, D. (2008) 'Digital Ethnography: An Examination of the Use of New Technologies for Social Research, *Sociology*, 42 (5), 837–55.

Nachtfalke, 'Valhalla', *Doomed to Die*, CHP, 2002.

Nairn, K., Panelli, R., and McCormack, J. (2003) 'Destabilizing Dualisms: Young People's Experiences of Rural and Urban Environments', *Childhood*, 10 (1), 9–42.

National Youth Agency (2010) The Young Researcher Network Research Training Toolkit, available at: http://nya.org.uk/dynamic_files/yrn/YRN Toolkit Dec 2010.pdf.

Naughton, J. (2000) *A Brief History of the Future: The Origins of the Internet* (London: Orion).

Nayak, A. (2003) *Race, Place and Globalization: Youth Cultures in a Changing World* (Oxford: Berg).

Nayak, A. (2006) 'Displaced Masculinities: Chavs, Youth and Class in the Post-industrial City', *Sociology*, 40 (5), 813–31.

Nayak, A. and Kehily, M. J. (2008) *Gender, Youth and Culture* (Basingstoke: Palgrave Macmillan).

Nayak, A. and Kehily, M. J. (2008) *Gender, Youth and Culture* (London: Palgrave Macmillan).

NCB NI and ARK/YLT (2010) *Attitudes to Difference: Young People's Attitudes to and Experiences of Contact with People from Different Minority Ethnic and Migrant Communities in Northern Ireland* (London: National Children's Bureau).

Negus, K. (1996) *Popular Music in Theory: An Introduction* (Cambridge: Polity Press).

Northern Ireland Youth Forum, Save the Children Northern Ireland, Youth Council for Northern Ireland and Youthnet (2005) *Turning Up the Sound* (Belfast: Northern Ireland Youth Forum) www.ycni.org/downloads/publications/TurningUpTheSound.pdf, date accessed 1 June 2010.

O'Brien, K. (2009) 'Inside Doorwork: Gendering the Security Gaze', in R. Ryan-Flood and R. Gill (eds) *Silence and Secrecy in the Research Process: feminist reflections* (London: Routledge).

O'Connor, H. (2006) 'Online Interviews', http://www.geog.le.ac.uk/orm/ethics/ethcontents.htm, date accessed 29 January 2007.

Office of Public Management (2010) *Creative Influence: Research Led by Young People*, (London: OPM), http://www.opm.co.uk/ (home page).

OFMDFM (2006) *Our Children – Our Pledge: A Ten-year Strategy for Children and Young People in Northern Ireland 2006–2016* (Belfast: Office of the First Minister and Deputy First Minister).

Padfield, M. and Proctor, I. (1996) 'The Effect of Interviewer's Gender on the Interviewing Process: A Comparative Enquiry', *Sociology*, 30 (2) 355–66.

Pain, R. and Francis, P. (2003) 'Reflections on Participatory Research', *Area*, 35 (1), 46–54.

Piano, D. (2003) 'Resisting Subjects: DIY Feminism and the Politics of Style in Subcultural Production', in D. Muggleton and R. Weinzierl (eds) *The Post-Subcultures Reader* (Oxford: Berg), 253–68.

Pilkington, H. (1994) *Russia's Youth and its Culture: A Nation's Constructors and Constructed* (London: Routledge).

Pilkington, H. (1994) *Russia's Youth and its Culture: A Nation's Constructors and Constructed* (London: Routledge), pp. 144–55.

Pilkington, H., Omel'chenko, E., Flynn, M., Bliudina, U. and Starkova, E. (2002) *Looking West? Cultural Globalization and Russian Youth Cultures* (Philadelphia: Pennsylvania State University Press).

Pink, S. (2001) *Doing Visual Ethnography* (London: Sage Publications).

Pink, S. (2006) *The Future of Visual Anthropology: Engaging the Senses* (London: Routledge).

Pink, S. (2007a) 'Walking with Video', *Visual Studies*, 22 (3), 240–52.

Pink, S. (2007b) *Doing Visual Ethnography* (London: Sage).

Pink, S. (2008) 'An Urban Tour: The Sensory Sociality of Ethnographic Place-making', *Ethnography*, 9 (2), 175–96.

Pink, S. (2009) *Doing Sensory Ethnography* (London: Sage).

Pitts, V. (2003) *In the Flesh: The Cultural Politics of Body Modification* (New York: Palgrave Macmillan).

Pocock, D. C. D. (1976) 'Some Characteristics of Mental Maps: An Empirical Study', *Transactions of the Institute of British Geographers*, New Series, 1 (4), 493–512.

Polkinghorne, D. E. (1995) 'Narrative Configuration in Qualitative Analysis', *International Journal of Qualitative Studies in Education*, 8 (1), 5–23.

Porter, H. (2006) 'Bands and Brands', *Time Magazine*, June 18.

Pringle, R. (1988) *Secretaries Talk: Sexuality, Power and Work* (Verso: London).

Prosser, J. (ed.) (1998) *Image-based Research: A Sourcebook for Qualitative Researchers* (London: RoutledgeFalmer).

Prosser, J. and Loxley, A. (2007) 'Enhancing the Contribution of Visual Methods to Inclusive Education', *Journal of Research in Special Educational Needs* 7 (1), 55–68.

Prosser, J. and Loxley, A. (2008) 'Introducing Visual Methods', ESRC National Centre for Research Methods, NCRM Methods Review Paper, NCRM/010 October, http://eprints.ncrm.ac.uk/420/1/MethodsReviewPaperNCRM-010.pdf.

Public Order Act (1986) http://www.legislation.gov.uk/ukpga/1986/64, date accessed 21 September 2011.

Punch, S. (2001) 'Multiple Methods and Research Relations with Children in Rural Bolivia', in M. Limb and C. Dwyer (eds) *Qualitative Methodologies for Geographers: Issues and Debates* (London: Arnold), 165–80.

Purdue, D., Durrschmidt, J., Jowers, P. and O'Doherty, R. (1997) 'DIY Culture and Extended Milieux: LETS, Veggie Boxes and Festivals', *The Sociological Review*, 45 (4), 645–67.

Puri, A. (2007) 'The Web of Insights: The Art and Practice of Webnography', *International Journal of Market Research*, 49 (3), http://lk.nielsen.com/documents/WebofInsightsPaperMay07.pdf, date accessed 1 July 2010.

Pyšňáková, M. and Miles. S. (2010) 'The Post-revolutionary Consumer Generation: 'Mainstream' Youth and the Paradox of Choice in the Czech Republic', *Journal of Youth Studies*, 13 (5), 533–47.

Quinn, D. J. (1986) 'Accessibility and Job Search: A Study of Unemployed School Leavers', *Regional Studies*, 20 (2), 163–73.

Rabinow, P (2003) *Anthropos Today: Reflections on Modern Equipment* (Princeton, NJ: Princeton University Press).

Read, R. (2010) 'Creating Reflexive Volunteers? Young People's Participation in Czech Hospital Volunteer Programmes', *Journal of Youth Studies*, 13 (5), 549–63.

Reay, D. and Lucey, H. (2000) '"I Don't Really Like it Here but I Don't Want to be Anywhere Else": Children and Inner City Council Estates', *Antipode*, 32 (4), 410–28.

Reed, A. (2005) '"My Blog is Me": Texts and Persons in UK Online Journal Culture (and Anthropology)', *Ethnos*, 70 (2), 220–42.

Renold, E., Holland, S., Ross, N.J., and Hillman, A. (2008) '"Becoming Participant": Problematising "Informed Consent" in Participatory Research with Children and Young People in Care', *Qualitative Social Work*, 7 (4), 431–51.

Rettberg, J. W. (2008) *Blogging* (Cambridge: Polity).

Ribbens, J. and Edwards, R. (1998) (eds) *Feminist Dilemmas in Qualitative Research* (London: Sage).

Richards, G. and Wilson, J. (eds) (2004) *The Global Nomad: Backpacker Travel in Theory and Practice* (Clevedon: Channel View Publications).

Ricketts Hein, J., Evans, J. and Jones, P. (2008) 'Mobile Methodologies: Theory, Technology and Practice', *Geography Compass*, 2 (5), 1266–85.

Riessman, C. K. (2008) *Narrative Methods for the Human Sciences* (London: Sage).

Riley, S., Griffin, C., and Morey, Y. (2010) 'The Case for "Everyday Politics": Evaluating Neo-tribal Theory as a Way to Understand Alternative Forms of Political Participation, Using Electronic Dance Music Culture as an Example', *Sociology*, 44 (2), 345–63.

Riley, S.; Morey, Y.; and Griffin, C. (2008) 'Ketamine: The Divisive Dissociative: A Discourse Analysis of the Constructions of Ketamine by Participants of a Free Party (Rave) Scene, *Addiction Research and Theory*, 16 (3), 217–30.

Riordan, J., Williams, C. and Ilynsky, I. (1996) *Young People in Post-Communist Russia and Eastern Europe* (Aldershot: Dartmouth).

Roberts, H. (2000) 'Listening to Children: and Hearing Them', in P. Christensen and A. James (eds) *Research with Children: Perspectives and Practices* (London: Falmer Press), 225–40.

Roberts, K. (1997) 'Structure and Agency: The New Youth Research Agenda', in J. Bynner, L. Chisholm and A. Furlong (eds) *Youth, Citizenship and Social Change in a European Context* (Aldershot: Ashgate), 56–65.

Roberts, K. (2009) *Youth in Transition: Eastern Europe and the West* (Basingstoke: Palgrave Macmillan).

Roberts, K. and Pollock, G. (2009) 'New Class Divisions in the New Market Economies: Evidence from the Careers of Young Adults in Post-Soviet Armenia, Azerbaijan and Georgia', *Journal of Youth Studies*, 12 (5), 579–96.

Robinson, C. (2010) Nightscapes and Leisure Spaces: An Ethnographic Study of Young People's Use of Free Space, in R. MacDonald, T. Shildrick and S. Blackman (eds) *Young People, Class and Place* (London: Routledge), 44–57.

Rose, G. (2007) *Visual Methodologies: An Introduction to the Interpretation of Visual Materials* (2nd Edition) (London: Sage).

Ross, N. (2007) '"My Journey to School ...": Foregrounding the Meaning of School Journeys and Children's Engagements and Interactions in their Everyday Localities', *Children's Geographies*, 5 (4), 373–91.

Ross, N.J., Renold, E., Holland, S. and Hillman, A. (2009) 'Moving Stories: Using Mobile Methods to Explore the Everyday Lives of Young People in Public Care', *Qualitative Research*, 9 (5), 605–23.

Rowe, G. and Frewer, L. J. (2004) 'Evaluating Public Participation Exercises', *Science Technology and Human Values*, 29 (4), 512–57.

Russell, L. (2007) 'Visual Methods in Researching the Arts and Inclusion: Possibilities and Dilemmas', *Ethnography and Education*, 2 (1), 39–55.

Savage, M. (2010) *Identities and Social Change in Britain since 1940* (Oxford: Oxford University Press).

Savage, M. and Burrows, R. (2007) 'The Coming Crisis of Empirical Sociology' *Sociology*, 41 (5), 885–99.

Schäfer, N. (2007) '"I Mean, it Depends on Me in the End, Doesn't it?" Young People's Perspectives on their Daily Life and Future Prospects in Rural East-Germany', in R. Panelli, S. Punch and E. Robson (eds) *Global Perspectives on Rural Childhood and Youth* (New York: Routledge), 121–34.

Schäfer, N. (2008). *Young People's Geographies in Rural Post-socialist Germany: A Case Study in Mecklenburg-Vorpommern*, unpublished Ph.D. Thesis, University of Plymouth.

Schäfer, N. (2010) 'The Spatial Dimension of Risk: Young People's Perceptions of the Risks and Uncertainties of Growing up in Rural East Germany', *Forum Qualitative Social Research* 11 (1).

Schäfer, N. and Yarwood, R. (2008) 'Involving Young People as Researchers: Uncovering Multiple Power Relations among Youths', *Children's Geographies*, 6 (2), 121–35.

Scheidt, L. and Wright, E. (2004) 'Common Visual Design Elements of Weblos', in L. J. Gurak, S. Antonijevic, L. Johnson, C. Ratliff, and J. Reyman (eds), *Into the Blogosphere: Rhetoric, Community, and Culture of Weblogs*, http://blog.lib.umn.edu/blogosphere/common_visual.html, date accessed 27 May 2010.

Schubotz, D., and Devine, P. (2008) 'Giving Young People a Voice Via Social Research Projects: Methodological Challenges', in D. Schubotz and P. Devine (eds) *Young People in post-conflict Northern Ireland: The Past Cannot be Changed, but the Future can be Developed* (Lime Regis: Russell House Publishing), 111–23.

Schubotz, D., and Sinclair, R. (2006) *Being Part and Parcel of the School: The Views and Experiences of Children and Young People in Relation to the Development of Bullying Policies in Schools* (Belfast: Northern Ireland Commissioner for Children and Young People).

Schubotz, D., McCartan, C., McDaid, A., McIntyre, B., McKee, F., McManus, M., O'Kelly, S., Roberts, A., and Whinnery. L. (2008) *Cross-community Schemes: Participation, Motivation, Mandate*, ARK Research Update Nr. 55, Belfast: ARK, http://www.ark.ac.uk/publications/occasional/crosscommunityschemesfinal.pdf.

Scott, J. (1990) *A Matter of Record: Documentary Sources in Social Research* (Cambridge: Polity Press).

Seale, C. (2000) 'Using Computers to Analyse Qualitative Data', in D. Silverman (ed.) *Doing Qualitative Research: A Practical Handbook* (London: SAGE), 154–74.

Sennett, R. (1996) *The Uses of Disorder: Personal Identity and City Life* (London: Faber and Faber).

Sharpe, D. (2009) 'The Value of Young People doing Research: Where do Young People's Voices Count?', *Research, Policy and Planning: The Journal of the Social Services Research Group* 27 (2), 97–106.

Sharpe, D. and Boeck, T. (2009) 'An Exploration of Participatory Research with Young People', *Coyote*, 14, 14–17.

Shaw, J. and Robertson, C. (1997) *Participatory Video: A Practical Guide to Using Video Creatively in Group Development Work* (London, Routledge).

Sheller, M. (2004) 'Automotive Emotions: Feeling the Car', *Theory, Culture & Society*, 21 (4/5), 221–42.

Sheller, M. and Urry, J. (2006) 'The New Mobilities Paradigm', *Environment and Planning A*, 38 (2), 207–26.

Sidaway, J. D. (1992) 'In Other Worlds: On the Politics of Research by 'First World' Geographers in the 'Third World', *Area*, vol. 24, No. 4 (Dec. 1992), pp. 403–8.

Sikes, P. (2006) 'On Dodgy Ground? Problematics and Ethics in Educational Research', *International Journal of Research and Methods in Education*, 29 (1), 105–17.

Silverman, D. (2007) *A Very Short, Fairly Interesting and Reasonably Cheap Book About Qualitative Research* (London: SAGE).

Sime, D. (2008) 'Ethical and Methodological Issues in Engaging Young People Living in Poverty with Participatory Research Methods', *Children's Geographies*, 6 (1), 63–78.

Simpson, K. (2004) 'Doing Development: The Gap Year, Volunteer-tourists and a Popular Practice of Development', *Journal of International Development*, 16 (5), 681–92.

Simpson, K. (2005) 'Dropping out or Signing up? The Professionalisation of Youth Travel', *Antipode* 37 (3), 447–69.

Smith, G. C. and Ford, R. G. (1985) 'Urban Mental Maps and Housing Estate Preferences of Council Tenants', *Geoforum*, 16 (1), 25–36.

Snee, H. (2008) 'Web 2.0 as a Social Science Research Tool', ESRC Government Placement Scheme, The British Library, http://www.bl.uk/reshelp/bldept/socsci/socint/web2/report.html, date accessed 1 August 2010.

Snyder, E.E. (1993) 'Responses to Musical Selections and Sport: An Auditory Elicitation Approach', *Sociology of Sport Journal*, 10 (2), 168–82.

Soini, K. (2001) 'Exploring Human Dimensions of Multifunctional Landscapes through Mapping and Map-making', *Landscape and Urban Planning*, 25 (3), 225–39.

Solnit, R. (2001) *Wanderlust: A History of Walking* (London: Verso).

Soyinka, B. (2008) *Place in me* (Cardiff University [DVD]).

SRA (2003) *Social Research Association Ethical Guidelines*, http://www.the-sra.org.uk/ethical.htm, accessed 27 May 2010.

Stanczak, G. C. (ed.) (2007) *Visual Research Methods: Image, Society and Representation* (London: Sage).

Statistisches Landesamt Mecklenburg-Vorpommern (2003) *Statistisches Jahrbuch Mecklenburg-Vorpommern 2003*, Schwerin: Statistisches Landesamt Mecklenburg-Vorpommern.

Statistisches Landesamt Mecklenburg-Vorpommern (2005) *Zahlenspiegel Mecklenburg-Vorpommern. Landesdaten ausgewählte Kreisdaten*, Schwerin: Statistisches Landesamt Mecklenburg-Vorpommern.

Strack, R. W., Magill, C. and McDonagh, K. (2004) 'Engaging Youth through Photovoice', *Health Promotion Practice*, 5 (1), 49–58.

Swartz, S. (2011) 'Going Deep and Giving Back: Strategies for Exceeding Ethical Expectations when Researching Vulnerable Youth', *Qualitative Research*, 11: 1, 47–68.

Symes, C. (1999) 'Chronicles of Labour. A Discourse Analysis of Diaries', *Time & Society*, 8 (2), 357–80.

Tashakorri, A and Teddlie, C. (eds) (2002) *Handbook of Mixed Methods for the Social and Behavioral Sciences* (Thousand Oaks, CA: Sage).

Taylor, C. and Coffey, A. (2008) *Innovation in Qualitative Research Methods: Possibilities and Challenges*, Cardiff: Cardiff University.

Teli, M., Pisanu, F., and Hakken, D. (2007) 'The Internet as a Library-of-people: For a Cyberethnography of Online Groups', *Forum: Qualitative Social Research*, 8 (3), http://www.qualitative-research.net/index.php/fqs/article/viewArticle/283, date accessed 1 January 2010.

Tereshchenko, A. (2010) 'Ukrainian Youth and Civic Engagement: Unconventional Participation in Local Spaces', *Journal of Youth Studies*, 13 (5), 597–613.

Thomas, J. (1996) 'Introduction: A Debate about the Ethics of Fair Practices for Collecting Social Science Data in Cyberspace, *The Information Society*, 12 (2), 107–18.

Thomas, N. (2007) 'Towards a Theory of Children's Participation', *International Journal of Children's Rights*, 15 (2), 199–218.

Thompson, H. S. (1966) *Hell's Angels* (Harmondsworth: Penguin).

Thomson, F. (2007) 'Are Methodologies for Children Keeping Them in Their Place?' *Children's Geographies*, 5 (3), 207–18.

Thomson, P. (ed.) (2008) *Doing Visual Research with Children and Young People* (New York: Routledge).

Thomson, R., Bell, R., Holland, J., Henderson, S., McGrellis, S., and Sharpe, S. (2002) 'Critical Moments: Choice, Chance and Opportunity in Young People's Narratives of Transition', *Sociology*, 36 (2), 335–54.

Thornton, S. (1995) *Club Cultures: Music, Media and Subcultural Capital* (Cambridge: Polity Press).

Thrasher, F. (1927/63) *The Gang: a study of 1313 gangs in Chicago*, Chicago: Chicago University Press.

Thrift, N. (2004a) 'Intensities of Feeling: The Spatial Politics of Affect', *Geografiska Annaler* Series B 86, 57–78.

Thrift, N. (2004b) 'Driving in the City', *Theory, Culture & Society*, 21 (4/5), 41–59.

Todorovsky, P. (1989) *Interdevochka* [Film] (USSR: Mosfilm).

Tomanovic, S. and Ignjatovic, S. (2006) 'The Transition of Young People in a Transitional Society: The Case of Serbia', *Journal of Youth Studies*, 9 (3), 269–85.

Travers, M. (2009) 'New methods, old problems: a sceptical view of innovation in qualitative research', *Qualitative Research*, 9 (2), 161–79.

Tsentr sotsial'nogo prognozirovaniya (eds) (2005) *Rossiiskaya Molodezh': problemy i resheniya* (Liubertsy: VINITI).

Turkle, S. (1995) *Life on the Screen: Identity in the Age of the Internet* (New York: Simon and Schuster).

UKYP (2007) *Sex and Relationships Education – Are You Getting It?* (London: United Kingdom Youth Parliament), http://www.ukyouthparliament.org.uk/campaigns/sre/AreYouGettingIt.pdf, date accessed 10 December 2009.

United Nations (1989) 'Convention on the Rights of the Child', http://www.unicef.org/crc/, date accessed 10 February 2010.

Urry, J (2003) *Global Complexity* (Cambridge: Polity).

Valentine, G. (1999) '"Being Seen and Heard?" The Ethical Complexities of Working with Children and Young People at Home and at School', *Ethics, Place and Environment*, 2 (2), 141–55.

Viegas, F. B. (2005) 'Bloggers' Expectations of Privacy and Accountability: An Initial Survey', *Journal of Computer-Mediated Communication*, 10 (3), article 12.

Wakeford, N. and Cohen, K. (2008) 'Fieldnotes in Public: Using Blogs for Research', in N. Fielding, R. M. Lee and G. Blank (eds) *The SAGE Handbook of Online Research Methods* (London: SAGE), 307–26.

Walker, C. (2005) 'Sistema NPO Ul'ianovskoi oblasti: vneshnie i vnutrennie problemy', *Professional'noe Obrazovanie*, 2, 23.

Walker, C. (2010) 'Space, Kinship Networks and Youth Transition in Provincial Russia: Negotiating Urban–rural and Inter-regional Migration', *Europe-Asia Studies*, 62 (4), 647–69.

Walker, C. (2011) *Learning to Labour in Post-Soviet Russia: Vocational Youth in Transition* (London: Routledge).

Walker, C. and Stephenson, S. (2010) 'Youth and Social Change in Eastern Europe and the Former Soviet Union', *Journal of Youth Studies*, 13 (5), 521–32.

Walkerdine, V., Lucey, H. and Melody, J. (2001) *Growing up Girl: Psycho-Social Explorations of Gender and Class* (Basingstoke: Palgrave Macmillan).

Wallace, C. and Kovatcheva, S. (1998) *Youth in Society: The Construction and Deconstruction of Youth in East and West Europe* (Basingstoke: Palgrave Macmillan).

Wang, C. and Burris, M. (1994) 'Empowerment through Photo Novella: Portraits of Participation', *Health Education Quarterly* 21 (2), 171–86.

Wang, C., Burris, M. and Ping, X. Y. (1996) 'Chinese Village Women as Visual Anthropologists: A Participatory Approach to Reaching Policymakers', *Social Science and Medicine*, 42, 1391–1400.

Wang, C. and Burris, M. A. (1997) 'Photovoice: Concept, Methodology, and Use for Participatory Needs Assessment', *Health Education and Behaviour*, 24 (3), 369–87.

Ward, C. (1978) *The Child in the City* (London: The Architectural Press).

Warner, M. (1989) 'Signs of the Fifth Element', in *The Tree of Life: New Images of an Ancient Symbol* (exhibition catalogue) (London: The South Bank Centre), 7–48.

Warren, C. (1988) 'Gender Issues in Field Research', Qualitative Research Methods Series, No. 9 (London: Sage).

Warren, C. (2002) 'Qualitative Interviewing', in J. Gubrium and J. Holstein (eds) *Handbook of Interview Research: Context and Method* (London: Sage), 83–101.

Weakling (2000) 'Dead as Dreams', *Dead as Dreams*, tUMULt.

Weber, S. (2008) 'Visual Images in Research', in J. G. Knowles and A. L. Cole (eds) *Handbook of the Arts in Qualitative Research: Perspectives, Methodologies, Examples, and Issues* (London: Sage), 41–53.

West, A. (1999) 'Children's Own Research: Street Children and Care in Britain and Bangladesh', *Childhood*, 6 (1), 145–55.

Whiteman, N. (2007) *The Establishment, Maintenance and Destabilisation of Fandom: A Study of Two Online Communities and an Exploration of Issues Pertaining to Internet Research*, unpublished Ph.D. thesis, Institute of Education, University of London.

Wiles, R., Coffey, A., Robinson, J. and Prosser, J. (2010a) *Ethical Regulation and Visual Methods: Making Visual Research Impossible or Developing Good Practice?*

ESRC National Centre for Research Methods Working Paper, NCRM Series 01/10.

Wiles, R., Pain, H. and Crow, G. (2010b) 'Innovation in Qualitative Research Methods: A Narrative Review', NCRM Working Paper 03/10, http://eprints.ncrm.ac.uk/919/1/innovation_in_qualitative_research_methods.pdf.

Wiles, R., Prosser, J., Bagnoli, A., Clark, A., Davies, K., Holland, S. and Renold, E. (2008) 'Visual Ethics: Ethical Issues in Visual Research', National Centre for Research Methods Working Paper (http://eprints.ncrm.ac.uk/421/), date accessed 15 March 2010.

Wiles, R., Prosser, J., Bagnoli, A., Clark, A., Davies, K., Holland, S., Renold, E. (2008) 'Visual Ethics: Ethical Issues in Visual Research', ESRC National Centre for Research Methods Review Paper, NCRM/011.

Williams, C., Chuprov, V. and Zubok, J. (2003) *Youth, Risk and Russian Modernity* (Aldershot: Ashgate).

Williams, R. (1984) *The Long Revolution* (Hardmondsworth: Penguin).

Willis, P. (1978) *Profane Culture* (London: Routledge).

Willis, P. (1997) 'Theoretical Confessions and Reflexive Method', in K. Gelder and S. Thornton (eds) *The Subcultures Reader* (London: Routledge), 246–53.

Wilson, B. (2006) *Fight, Flight or Chill: Subcultures, Youth and Rave into the 21st Century* (Montreal: McGill-Queen's University Press).

Winlow, S. Hobbs, D. Lister, S. and Hadfield, P. (2001) 'Get Ready to Duck: Bouncers and the Realities of Ethnographic Research on Violent Groups', *British Journal of Criminology*, 41 (3), 536–48.

Worrall, S. (2000) *Young People as Researchers: A Learning Resource Pack* (London: Save the Children).

Wright, C. V., Darko N., Standen P. J. and Patel T. G. (2010) 'Visual Research Methods: Using Cameras to Empower Socially Excluded Black Youth', *Sociology*, 44 (3), 541–58.

www.everychildmatters.gov.uk/_files/F9E3F941DC8D4580539EE4C743E9371D.pdf, date accessed 30 April 2010.

Xenitidou, M., and Gilbert, N. (2009) *Innovations in Social Science Research Methods* (Guildford: University of Surrey).

Young, L. and Barrett, H. (2001) 'Adapting Visual Methods: Action Research with Kampala Street Children', *Area*, 33 (2), 141–52.

Index